Vowel Sounds

a	had, sat	(HAD) (SAT)
ah	far, calm	(FAHR) (KAHM)
air	pear, scare	(PAIR) (SKAIR)
aw	law, cause	(LAW) (KAWZ)
ay	bay, rate	(BAY) (RAYT)
e	met, bet	(MET) (BET)
ee	me, fairy	(MEE) (FAIR-ee)
er	fur, after	(FER) (AF-ter)
i	sit, bid	(SIT) (BID)
oh	go, rowboat	(GOH) (ROH-boht)
oi	oil, boy	(OIL) (BOI)
oo	root, soup	(ROOT) (SOOP)
or	for, border	(FOR) (BOR-der)
ow	how, sound	(HOW) (SOWND)
u	fun, cup	(FUN) (KUP)
uh	could, pull	(KUHD) (PUHL)
y	fly, sight	(FLY) (SYT)
yoo	fuse, view	(FYOOZ) (VYOO)
ə	soda	(SOH-də)
ə	silent	(SY-lənt)
ə	pencil	(PEN-səl)
ə	bacon	(BAY-kən)
ə	circus	(SER-kəss)

Consonant Sounds

ch	church, nature	(CHERCH) (NAY-cher)
g	get, great	(GET) (GRAYT)
j	just, age	(JUST) (AYJ)
ks	mix, six	(MIKS) (SIKS)
ng	king, finger	(KING) (FING-ger)
th	three, thin	(THREE) (THIN)
th	then, further	(THEN) (FER-ther)
zh	vision	(VIZH-ən)

Say the other consonants just as you always do when you find them in a word.

Every time you see a "y" with a vowel following it, sound it like the "y" in "yoo," just as you do in "yet."

5

Volume Five · Polio through Stack

The
GOLDEN BOOK
ILLUSTRATED
DICTIONARY
IN SIX VOLUMES

by

Stuart A. Courtis

Professor of Education, Emeritus, University of Michigan

and

Garnette Watters

Formerly Director of the Language Department, Public Schools, Hamtramck, Michigan

Allen Walker Read Consultant on Pronunciation

Associate Professor, Columbia University

GOLDEN PRESS  NEW YORK

Library of Congress Catalog Card Number: 61-7080

po·li·o (POH-lee-oh) *n. Polio* is the short word for *polio*myelitis, a disease which often paralyzes its victims, who are mostly children. It is also known as infantile paralysis. Doctors now give people shots and pills to keep them from getting *polio.*

pol·ish (PAHL-ish) *n.* polishes. A substance that is rubbed or painted onto something to make it bright and smooth.
—v. polishes, polished, polishing. 1. Make shiny or smooth by rubbing.—We *polish* the furniture by rubbing it with furniture polish. 2. Improve by working over.—If you *polish* your story a little, it will be a good one.

po·lite (pə-LYT) *adj.; politely, adv.* Having good manners.—It is *polite* to thank a person who does something for you.

po·lite·ness (pə-LYT-nəss) *n.* Courtesy; a showing of good manners.—Mary is well liked for her *politeness.* She is always pleasant and thoughtful of others.

po·lit·i·cal (pə-LIT-ə-kəl) *adj.; politically, adv.* Having to do with politics or government.—A *political* party is a group of people organized to elect certain people to public office and get certain laws passed.

pol·i·ti·cian (pahl-ə-TISH-ən) *n. politicians.* A person who spends much time in working for the success of a political party in elections.

pol·i·tics (PAHL-ə-tiks) *n.* The business of governing a community, city, state, or nation. The business of getting people elected and appointed to public office is also *politics.*

pol·len (PAHL-ən) *n.* The dusty yellow material that is found in flowers. The flowers use it in making the seeds that will grow into new plants.

pol·li·wog or **pol·ly·wog** (PAHL-ee-wahg) *n.* polliwogs or *pollywogs.* An undeveloped frog or toad; a tadpole. *Polliwogs* begin life in the water, as swimming animals. Later they grow legs, lose their tails and gills, and venture out on land. Then they are *polliwogs* no longer.

polls (POHLZ) *n. pl.* A voting place.—At election time, Father and Mother go to the *polls* to vote.

pol·lute (pə-LOOT *or* -LYOOT) *v.* pollutes, polluted, polluting. Make unclean; foul.—The waste from the factory was dumped in the river and *polluted* the water.

po·lo (POH-loh) *n.* A game played by players on horseback. The players, using long mallets, try to hit a small wooden ball through the opposing team's goal.

pol·y·gon (PAHL-i-gahn) *n. polygons.* A geometric shape with more than four sides and four angles. Some *polygons* are the five-sided pentagon, the six-sided hexagon, and the eight-sided octagon.

pomp (PAHMP) *n.; pompous, adj.* Great splendor; a display of wealth and magnificence.—The princess was married with *pomp.*

pond (PAHND) *n. ponds.* A pool; a little lake.—Children like to sail their boats on the *pond.*

pon·toon (pahn-TOON) *n. pontoons.* 1. A float placed under the wing of a seaplane. Seaplanes have *pontoons* so that they can land on the water.
2. A kind of float that looks like a flat-bottomed boat. *Pontoons* are used to hold up rafts or temporary docks, bridges, and other such structures.
3. A floating raft or dock.

po·ny (POH-nee) *n. ponies.* A small horse.—Children like to ride the *ponies* at the park.

poo·dle (POO-dl) *n. poodles.* A kind of curly-haired dog, intelligent, and easy to train.

pool (POOL) *n. pools.*
1. Any small body of still water.—The boys have gone to the park *pool* to sail their boats.
2. A large tank filled with water.—In summer we often go to the swimming *pool.*

3. A game played on a large table with rubber cushions on all sides. The players try to knock the balls into pockets with long sticks called cues.
—*v. pools, pooled, pooling.* Put together in a common fund.—The children *pooled* their money to buy a gift for Mother.

poor (PUHR) *n. pl.* People who have very little.—Every Christmas we give food to the *poor.*
—*adj.* poorer, poorest; poorly, adv. 1. Having little property and money.—*Poor* people often cannot buy enough to eat.
2. Not good in quality.—*Poor* clothing will not last as long as good clothing.—John is a *poor* ball player. He does not play well.
3. Pitiable.—The *poor* dog was hungry.

pop·corn (PAHP-korn) *n.* A kind of corn that bursts open when the kernels are heated. It is good to eat.

pope (POHP) *n. popes.* The head of the Roman Catholic Church. When you use the word as a title or name, you spell *Pope* with a capital "P."

pop·gun (PAHP-gun) *n. popguns.* A small toy gun that shoots corks.—Boys like to play with *popguns.*

pop·lar (PAHP-ler) *n. poplars.* A tall, slim tree with shiny, heart-shaped leaves that tremble in even the slightest breeze. *Poplars* grow fast.

pop·py (PAHP-ee) *n. poppies.* One of a large group of flowers of different colors, especially the red *poppy. Poppy*-seeds are often sprinkled on bread and rolls.

pop·u·lar (PAHP-yə-ler) *adj.; popularly, adv.; popularity, n.*
1. Well known and liked.—Bob is *popular* in school.
2. Representing the people; of the people.—The United States has a *popular* government.

pop·u·la·tion (pahp-yə-LAY-shən) *n. populations.* The number of people living in a community, town, city, or other area.—The *population* of this city is ten thousand.

por·ce·lain (POR-sə-lin or PORSS-lin) *n. porcelains.* Fine, glossy earthenware; china.—Our new dishes are made of *porcelain.*

porch (PORCH) *n. porches.* A covered entrance to a house or other building.

por·cu·pine (POR-kyə-pyn) *n. porcupines.* A small animal that has sharp quills or spines mixed in with its hair. These quills protect it.

pore (POR) *n. pores.* One of many tiny holes in a surface.—There are *pores* in skin.
—*v. pores, pored, poring.* Study thoroughly.—Bob is *poring* over a book.

pork (PORK) *n.* The meat of a pig.

po·rous (POR-əss) *adj.* 1. Full of very little holes.—The skin of human beings is *porous.*
2. Capable of absorbing fluid or of letting fluid pass through.—Sponges are *porous.*

por·poise (POR-pəss) *n. porpoises.* A cousin of the whale. It looks very much like a dolphin but has a short nose.

port (PORT) *n. ports and adj.* 1. A harbor; a place where ships may load and unload.
2. To or on the left side of a ship.—The cargo shifted to *port* and made the ship tilt.

port·a·ble (PORT-ə-bəl) *adj.* Able to be carried.—Mary has a *portable* typewriter. It is small, and can be easily carried in a case.

por·ter (POR-ter) *n. porters.* 1. A man paid for carrying baggage.—At the depot, the *porter* took our baggage.
2. A man who cleans, moves furniture, and does other such jobs in a building.—The manager called the *porter* to clean up the spilled ink.
3. A man who helps passengers on a train.—The sleeping car *porter* made up the beds.

port·fo·li·o (port-FOH-lee-oh) *n. portfolios.* A light case for carrying papers and pictures. — When Father has had a busy day at the office, he brings work home at night in his *portfolio.*

port·hole (PORT-hohl) *n. portholes.* An opening in the side of a ship to let in light and air. *Portholes* are usually round.

por·tion (POR-shən) *n. portions.* A part or share.—Bob ate a small *portion* of the food.—My *portion* of the money was only fifty cents.
—v. portions, portioned, portioning. Divide and give.—John *portioned* out the candy.

por·trait (POR-trayt *or* -trit) *n. portraits* and *adj.* A picture of a particular person. — The artist painted a *portrait* of Ann.

por·tray (por-TRAY) *v. portrays, portrayed, portraying.* Picture by drawing, painting, acting, or describing in words.—Bob *portrayed* the part of a prince in the play.

po·si·tion (pə-ZISH-ən) *n. positions.* 1. A particular place.—The teams got into *position* for the game. The players took their *positions.*
2. A certain posture or way of holding the body.—The ball player got into *position* to bat.
3. A job.—Uncle Tom has a new *position* in the factory.
4. A rank.—General is the highest *position* in the army.
5. A way of thinking.—Mother's *position* on the question is different from Father's. She disagrees with him.

pos·i·tive (PAHZ-ə-tiv) *adj.; positively, adv.*
1. Very sure; certain.—I am *positive* that I heard the bell ring.
2. Not negative.—She gave us a *positive* answer. She said yes to what we asked of her.—The magnet has a *positive* pole and a negative pole.

pos·se (PAHSS-ee) *n. posses.* A force of men called together by an officer such as a sheriff to help him keep law and order.—A *posse* was formed to capture the outlaw.

pos·sess (pə-ZESS) *v. possesses, possessed, possessing.* 1. Have; own.—This house is all that I *possess.*—John *possesses* great courage.
2. Occupy.—The enemy *possessed* the fort.

pos·ses·sion (pə-ZESH-ən) *n. possessions.*
1. The papers are in my *possession.* I have them.
2. Ownership.—The house passed into Father's *possession* when the papers were signed.
3. Something owned.—Poor people do not have many *possessions.*

pos·ses·sive (pə-ZESS-iv) *adj.; possessively, adv.* 1. Showing ownership.—Words such as "theirs," "yours," "hers," and "mine" are *possessive* pronouns.
2. Showing a desire to hold on to or to own.—Mary is very *possessive* about her favorite doll. She won't let anyone else play with it.

pos·si·bil·i·ty (pahss-ə-BIL-ə-tee) *n. possibilities.* Something that can happen or be done.—Lindbergh proved that flying a plane across the Atlantic, nonstop and alone, was a *possibility.*

pos·si·ble (PAHSS-ə-bəl) *adj.* 1. Able to happen or be done.—It is *possible* to talk by telephone to a person thousands of miles away.
2. That might be usable or suitable for.—Jack found a *possible* new member for the club.—Jim explored for *possible* camping areas.

pos·si·bly (PAHSS-ə-blee) *adv.* 1. Perhaps; maybe.—*Possibly* Father will come on the next train.
2. Within the limits of what can happen or be done.—Bob cannot *possibly* get here in time for lunch.

pos·sum (PAHSS-əm) *n. possums.* An opossum; a small grayish animal with sharp teeth and a long skinny tail. *Possums* live in trees.

post (POHST) *n. posts.* 1. An upright rod or column of wood or metal set in the ground to hold something up.—Telephone *posts* hold up telephone wires.

2. A place where a person is supposed to be when on duty.—The Safety Patrol boys are at their *posts* when school is out.

3. A job.—Mary obtained a *post* as bank clerk.

4. A kind of store in places where few people live, at which people may trade or buy things.—The trappers trade furs for food at the *post*.

5. Mail.—He sent the package by parcel *post*.

—*v. posts, posted, posting.* 1. Mail.—Mary will *post* your letter on the way to school.

2. Put up so that people can see.—The names of the honor students were *posted* on the bulletin board.

post·age (POHSS-tij) *n.* The charge for mailing things.—Mary did not mail the package because she didn't have the *postage*. The *postage* on the package was thirty-seven cents, and Mary only had twenty-five cents with her.

post·al (POHSS-tl) *adj.* Having to do with the mail.—*Postal* service is the delivering and collecting of mail.

post card (POHST kahrd) *post cards.* A small card that may be sent through the mail.—It costs less to send a *post card* than it does to send a letter.

post·er (POHSS-ter) *n. posters.* A sign.—A *poster* about the Red Cross was placed in the window of the store.

post·man (POHST-mən) *n. postmen.* A man who delivers and calls for the mail.—When Father is away, Mother and I always wait impatiently for the *postman*. We know he will be bringing us letters from Father.

post·mark (POHST-mahrk) *n. postmarks.* A mark put on a letter or package to tell the date and place where it was mailed.

post·mas·ter (POHST-mass-ter) *n. postmasters.* A man in charge of a post office or post offices.

post of·fice (POHST awf-əss) *post offices.* A place where letters and packages are mailed, and received to be sorted for delivery, and where postage stamps are sold.

post·pone (pohst-POHN) *v. postpones, postponed, postponing.* Put off; make a later date for.—Do not *postpone* caring for your teeth.—Let's *postpone* the party until next week.

—*postponement, n. postponements.*

post·script (POHSS-skript) *n. postscripts.* A short message written at the end of a letter after the writer's name has been signed. The letters P.S. stand for *postscript*.

pos·ture (PAHSS-cher) *n. postures.* The position of the body; how the body is held.—Children learn good *posture* in health class.

pot (PAHT) *n. pots.* A round vessel used for cooking, serving foods, or other uses.—*Pots* are made of metal, glass, or pottery.

—*v. pots, potted, potting.* Put in a pot.—Mother has *potted* the plants she has in the house.

po·ta·to (pə-TAY-toh) *n. potatoes.* A vegetable whose fleshy root is one of the most important foods in many parts of the world.

potter's wheel

ancient Greek jug

Chinese vase

ancient Roman wine jug

Chinese dish

California Indian jug

ancient Egyptian bottle

New Mexico Indian dish and jar

pot·ter·y (PAHT-ə-ree) *n.* 1. Dishes and other vessels made of clay and hardened by heat or baking.

2. The art or trade of making dishes and other vessels in that way.

3. A place where clay vessels are made.

pouch (POWCH) *n. pouches.* A bag or sack.—The mother kangaroo carries her baby in a *pouch.*—Father keeps his tobacco in a *pouch.*

poul·try (POHL-tree) *n.* Birds, especially chickens, ducks, or turkeys, that are raised for food.

turkey rooster
goose
duck chicken

pounce (POWNSS) *v. pounces, pounced, pouncing.* Jump suddenly.—The cat *pounced* on the dog from above.
—*pounce, n. pounces.*

pound (POWND) *n. pounds.* 1. A measurement of weight. There are sixteen ounces in a *pound.*—Meat is measured in *pounds.*—I weigh sixty-five *pounds.* How heavy are you? How much do you weigh?
2. In Great Britain, a sum of money worth a little less than three dollars.
3. A place where lost or homeless animals are cared for.—Stray dogs are taken to the *pound* by the dogcatcher.
—*v. pounds, pounded, pounding.* 1. Hit; strike; beat.—*Pound* on the door so that the deaf woman will hear you.
2. Beat heavily.—The waves *pounded* against the rocks.—Indian women *pounded* corn into flour.

pour (POR) *v. pours, poured, pouring.* 1. Make a liquid flow in a steady stream.—To *pour* from a pitcher, you tilt the pitcher until the liquid flows out.
2. Flow in a stream. — When you tilt the pitcher, the liquid *pours* out.
3. Let anything flow in great quantity.—Ann *poured* out her troubles to Mrs. Jones.—Mr. Smith *poured* money into his new business.

pout (POWT) *v. pouts, pouted, pouting.* Push out the lips to show anger or disappointment. —Some children *pout* when they cannot get their own ways.
—*pout, n. pouts.*

pov·er·ty (PAHV-er-tee) *n.* 1. Condition of being poor; lack of money, food, clothing, etc.—People in the slums of great cities live in *poverty.*
2. Poor quality.—The *poverty* of the land made it impossible to grow anything on it.

pow·der (POW-der) *n. powders.* Anything that is in fine grains like dust.—Baking *powder* is a white, dustlike substance used in baking.
—*v. powders, powdered, powdering.* 1. Grind or reduce to a powder.—Grain is *powdered* by grinding to make it into flour.
2. Dust or sprinkle with powder.—Mother *powders* Baby's skin after Baby's bath.

pow·er (POW-er) *n. powers.* 1. Strength or ability to do work; force.—It takes *power* to lift heavy things.—The motor of our car has a great deal of *power.*—Our country has *power* in international affairs.—Electric *power* may be created by water *power.*
2. Ability.—The doctor does all that is in his *power* for his patients.
3. The right.—The judge in the contest has the *power* to say who won and who lost.
4. A powerful nation.—America is a great *power* in the world.

pow·er·ful (POW-er-fuhl) *adj.; powerfully, adv.* 1. Having great strength.—A machine which can lift heavy things is *powerful.*
2. Having great authority.—The governor is the most *powerful* official in the state.

pow·er·less (POW-er-ləss) *adj.* Helpless.—The men were *powerless* to prevent the large rock from falling.

prac·ti·cal (PRAK-tə-kəl) *adj.; practicality, n.* 1. Useful.—Mary's new dress is very *practical.* She can wear it for many different occasions.—The man had many *practical* ideas.
2. Able to do many things well; good at making ideas work out.—Mother is a very *practical* person. She can understand and handle most situations.

prac·tice (PRAK-tiss) *n. practices.* 1. Something regularly or commonly done.—It is the *practice* to exchange gifts at Christmas time.
2. Doing something over and over again to perfect it.—Regular *practice* is the only way to learn to play a musical instrument.
3. The business of a professional person.—The doctor has a large *practice.* He has many patients.
4. Use.—The new plan was put into *practice.*
—or *practise, v. practices* or *practises, practiced* or *practised, practicing* or *practising.* 1. Do a thing over and over, until one does it well.—Mary *practices* playing the piano.
2. Work in a profession.—A doctor *practices* medicine.
3. Do or observe regularly.—John *practices* economy. He never spends much money.

prai·rie (PRAIR-ee) *n. prairies.* A plain where grass grows, but trees do not.—Cattle graze on the *prairie.*

prai·rie schoon·er (PRAIR-ee skoo-ner) *prairie schooners.* A canvas-covered wagon with a rounded top. The pioneers crossed the western plains of the United States in *prairie schooners.*

praise (PRAYZ) *n. praises.* A favorable comment; a statement that something is good.— Our work in spelling receives much *praise.* —*v. praises, praised, praising.* 1. Speak well of. —Our teacher *praises* our work in spelling. 2. *Praise* the Lord means worship the Lord.

prance (PRANSS) *v. prances, pranced, prancing.* Move proudly with high steps.— Horses in the circus parade *prance.*

prank (PRANGK) *n. pranks.* A trick.—The children play *pranks* on people at Halloween.

pray (PRAY) *v. prays, prayed, praying.* 1. Ask from God; speak to God.—Children *pray* to God to bless their loved ones. 2. Ask earnestly.—The princess said, "Set me free, I *pray* you."

prayer (PRAIR) *n. prayers.* What one says when speaking to God.—The minister said a *prayer.*

preach (PREECH) *v. preaches, preached, preaching.* 1. Make a speech or sermon about a religious subject.—In church, the minister *preaches.* 2. Speak earnestly about.—Mother *preaches* honesty to us every day.

preach·er (PREECH-er) *n. preachers.* A minister; a person who preaches in church.

pre·am·ble (PREE-am-bəl) *n. preambles.* An introductory statement; a preface which tells the purpose of whatever follows it. The *preamble* to the United States Constitution tells what areas of government the Constitution will cover.

pre·cau·tion (pri-KAW-shən) *n. precautions.* 1. Caution or care exercised beforehand.—Observing the rules of good health is a *precaution* against illness. 2. Anything done beforehand to prevent misfortune or to insure success.—Father had his car brakes checked at the garage as a safety *precaution.*

pre·cede (pree-SEED) *v. precedes, preceded, preceding.* Come before.—Monday *precedes* Tuesday.

pre·ced·ing (pree-SEE-ding) *adj.* Coming before; previous.—On the *preceding* day, we had packed to go.

pre·cept (PREE-sept) *n. precepts.* A rule of conduct.—Father says that everyone should base his actions on a well-reasoned set of *precepts.* He feels that one's life should be guided by rules of conduct.

pre·cinct (PREE-singkt) *n. precincts.* 1. An area or district of a city, especially a police or election district. 2. An area within certain fixed boundaries.— Visitors are not permitted within the hospital *precincts* after nine o'clock at night.

pre·cious (PRESH-əss) *adj.* 1. Valuable.— *Precious* stones or jewels are very expensive. 2. Loved; dear.—Children are very *precious* to their parents.

prec·i·pice (PRESS-ə-piss) *n. precipices.* A high, steep cliff.

pre·cip·i·tate (pri-SIP-ə-tayt) *v. precipitates, precipitated, precipitating.* 1. Bring about suddenly or unexpectedly. — A small quarrel sometimes *precipitates* a big fight. 2. Change from vapor into moisture, or into rain, snow, or sleet.—Rain is water vapor (from a cloud) which has *precipitated.*—The wetness on the outside of a cold glass of lemonade has *precipitated* from the air around it.

pre·cip·i·ta·tion (pri-sip-ə-TAY-shən) *n. precipitations.* 1. Act of bringing about.—The *precipitation* of the fight was an angry word. 2. Rain, snow, hail, or sleet.—In July a *precipitation* of one and a quarter inches was recorded.

pre·cise (pri-SYSS) *adj.; precisely, adv.* 1. Accurate and careful.—Mother is very *precise* about her work.
2. Exact.—Father speaks very *precise* English. He wants to make his meaning clear.

pred·i·cate (PRED-ə-kit) *n. predicates.* The part of a sentence that tells what the subject does or is.—The boys play ball. The words "play ball" form the *predicate* of the sentence. They tell what the boys do.

pre·dict (pri-DIKT) *v. predicts, predicted, predicting.* Tell beforehand.—The farmer *predicted* that the grain would be ripe next month.
—*prediction, n. predictions.*

pref·ace (PREF-iss) *n. prefaces.* An introduction to something spoken or written.—As a *preface* to his talk, the lecturer told an amusing story.—Something about the author's life is in the *preface* of the book.
—*v. prefaces, prefaced, prefacing.*—Introduce something spoken or written.—He *prefaced* his talk with an amusing story.

pre·fer (pri-FER) *v. prefers, preferred, preferring.* Like better.—I *prefer* swimming to hockey.

pre·fix (PREE-fiks) *n. prefixes.* Letters or syllables put before a word to make a new word.—In the word "unfasten," "un-" is a *prefix.*

pre·his·tor·ic (pree-hiss-TOR-ik *or* pree-hiss-TAHR-ik) *adj.* Having to do with, or belonging to, a period before history was written or recorded.—The dinosaur was a *prehistoric* animal.

prej·u·dice (PREJ-ə-diss) *n. prejudices; prejudiced, adj.* 1. An opinion, favorable or unfavorable, formed in advance without good reason.—My aunt had a *prejudice* against Canadians, because she had once known a Canadian she didn't like. We thought it very foolish of her.—Mrs. Smith appeared to have a *prejudice* in Jane's favor when she picked her for the leading part in the play. Jane did not do well in the tryouts.
2. Damage; harm; injury.—When the labor dispute was settled, the company agreed to resume operations without *prejudice* to the men who had gone on strike. They would not be penalized for striking.

pre·mi·um (PREE-mee-əm) *n. premiums.* 1. A prize; a reward.—As a *premium* for buying that soap, you get a free bath towel.
2. A payment for insurance.—Father pays monthly *premiums* on his insurance.

pre·paid (pree-PAYD) *adj.* Paid for beforehand.—The package was *prepaid.*

prep·a·ra·tion (prep-ə-RAY-shən) *n. preparations.* 1. A thing or things done to get ready.—The *preparations* for the picnic are almost finished.—High school is often a *preparation* for college.
2. Something mixed or prepared.—A *preparation* may be a medicine, a food, or anything that is gotten ready for some special use.

pre·pare (pri-PAIR) *v. prepares, prepared, preparing.* 1. Get ready.—Mary *prepares* to go to school early.
2. Make ready. — Mother *prepares* Baby's breakfast.

prep·o·si·tion (prep-ə-ZISH-ən) *n. prepositions.* A connective word showing relationship. In the phrases "playing in the park," "safe among friends," and "made of steel," the words "in," "among," and "of" are *prepositions.*

pre·scribe (pri-SKRYB) *v. prescribes, prescribed, prescribing.* Order the use of; suggest as a cure, treatment, or procedure; advise.—The doctor *prescribed* a new medicine for the baby. He wrote out an order for us to take to the druggist.—Father *prescribed* less television and an earlier bedtime as one remedy for Bob's low grades.

pre·scrip·tion (pri-SKRIP-shən) *n. prescriptions.* 1. An order or direction, usually written by a doctor, giving a druggist an order for pills or medicine for a certain person.—The doctor wrote a *prescription* for my cough.
2. The medicine itself.—Did the drugstore deliver the *prescription?*

pres·ence (PREZ-ənss) *n.* 1. State or condition of being in a place or of being present.—The clown's *presence* at the circus meant fun for the children.
2. Place where someone is.—It is rude and thoughtless to gossip about someone in his *presence.*—He was ushered into the queen's *presence.*

pres·ent (PREZ-ənt) *n. presents.* 1. A gift.—Baby received a *present* on her birthday.
2. This time; the time in which we are living now; this moment.—In history class we study what man has done from times long past right up to the *present.*
—*adj.* 1. Existing or happening at this moment; now.—Mary isn't home at the *present* time. She isn't home now.
2. On hand; here.—All the children in the class are *present* today. None are absent.

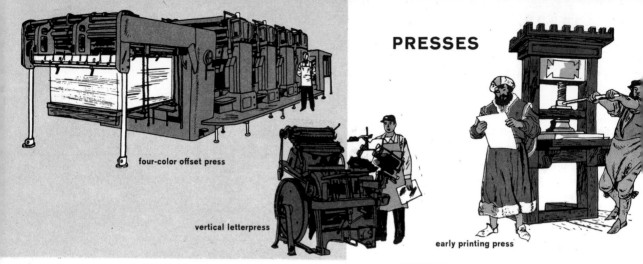

four-color offset press

vertical letterpress

PRESSES

early printing press

pre·sent (pri-ZENT) *v. presents, presented, presenting.* 1. Introduce.—Mary *presented* her friend to the teacher.
2. Send in; give.—The dentist *presented* his bill for the work he had done.—The class *presented* a play.—Jim *presented* his idea to the class.
3. Show; have.—Mary *presents* a neat appearance.
—When a soldier *presents arms*, he brings his gun up in front of him with the trigger away from his body and the barrel of the gun pointing upward.

pres·ent·ly (PREZ-ənt-lee) *adv.* Before long; soon. — Mother said that Father would be home *presently*.

pre·serve (pri-ZERV) *n. preserves.* 1. A kind of jelly with the whole fruit left in.—Strawberries and sugar boiled together make strawberry *preserve* or *preserves*.
2. Place where wild animals are protected.—Hunters are not allowed in the game *preserve*.
—*v. preserves, preserved, preserving.* 1. Keep from spoiling; save.—Mother cans fruits and vegetables to *preserve* them.
2. Keep up; keep in good repair.—The government is *preserving* the Colonial mansion as a museum.
3. Protect from harm or extinction.—An effort is now being made to *preserve* the animals of Africa from being entirely killed off by hunters.

pre·side (pri-ZYD) *v. presides, presided, presiding.* Have charge (of a meeting or group).—Bob will *preside* at the class meeting.

pres·i·dent (PREZ-ə-dənt) *n. presidents.* 1. The chief officer of a business firm, a union, a club, or other organization.
2. (Sometimes spelled with a capital "P.") The head of the government in a republic, such as the *President* of the United States.

press (PRESS) *n. presses.* 1. A printing machine.—City newspapers are printed on big *presses*.
2. Any machine that works by squeezing or pressing.
3. Newspapers. — The story of the accident will be printed in the morning *press*.
4. Reporters.—The *press* turned out in full force for the society wedding.
5. Pressure; push.—Mr. Smith couldn't come because of the *press* of work at his office.
—*v. presses, pressed, pressing.* 1. Push.—*Press* the button and the elevator will stop.
2. Hug.—Father *pressed* the lost child to him.
3. Urge; ask.—Because the money was due, Father *pressed* the man to pay it.
4. Push with all one's weight and force.—Bob *pressed* against the door to open it.
5. Iron.—Mother *pressed* my dress.
6. Squeeze. — Grapes are *pressed* to make wine.

pres·sure (PRESH-er) *n. pressures.* 1. A pressing against or on; the pushing force of surrounding things.—The eggs were broken by the *pressure* of other groceries.
2. The pressing of demands upon one. — Working under *pressure* to hurry or to do better than others is not easy.
3. A physical sense of tightness and discomfort.—Sinus trouble brings a feeling of *pressure* or pain around nose and eyes.

pre·sume (pri-ZOOM *or* -ZYOOM) *v. presumes, presumed, presuming.* 1. Suppose.—I *presume* you asked your mother if you might go.
2. Dare.—The boy *presumed* to ask his teacher to give the class a holiday.
—*presumption, n. presumptions.*

pre·tend (pri-TEND) *v. pretends, pretended, pretending.* 1. Make believe.—The opossum *pretends* that he is dead to fool his enemies.
2. Claim.—Bob doesn't *pretend* to be a good speller.

pret·ty (PRIT-ee) *adj. prettier, prettiest; prettily, adv.* Quite beautiful.—Baby is *pretty.* —*adv.* Rather; fairly.—It is *pretty* cold today.

pre·vent (pri-VENT) *v. prevents, prevented, preventing.* 1. Stop.—The work of the fireman *prevented* the fire from spreading.
2. Keep from happening.—Bob's quick thinking *prevented* an accident.
3. Hinder; interfere. — Father said nothing would *prevent* him from calling.
—*prevention, n. preventions.*

pre·vi·ous (PREE-vee-əss) *adj.; previously, adv.* Just before; earlier.—You will find pictures of presses on the *previous* page, on the page before this.

prey (PRAY) *n.* 1. Any animal that is caught by another animal for food.—Chickens are the *prey* of hawks.
2. Victim or victims.—Poor people are sometimes the *prey* of moneylenders who charge high interest.
—*v. preys, preyed, preying.* 1. Use (another animal) for food.—Hawks *prey* upon chickens and field mice.
2. Make a victim, or victims, of.—Moneylenders may *prey* upon poor people.
—*Prey upon* also means be a constant threat to in any way; feed on; gnaw. — The old woman's illness *preys upon* her mind; it worries her and does her harm.

price (PRYSS) *n. prices.* 1. The amount of money a thing costs.—The *price* of my shoes was five dollars.
2. Cost of any kind.—Illness is often the *price* of overeating.
—*v. prices, priced, pricing.* 1. Ask the price of. —Father *priced* the watermelons. The man told him they were sixty-five cents each.
2. Set a price on.—The man *priced* the bicycle at thirty dollars. That was the amount he wanted for it.

price·less (PRYSS-ləss) *adj.* So valuable that a price can hardly be set.—Many great and famous paintings are *priceless.*

prick (PRIK) *n. pricks.* 1. Sticking, or the feeling of being stuck, with something sharp and slender.—The *prick* of the needle hurt.
2. A little hole made by something sharp.— The *prick* on Mother's finger shows.
3. A hurt, as of conscience or regret.—A *prick* of conscience kept Mary from taking a piece of cake while Mother was out.
—*v. pricks, pricked, pricking.* 1. Make a little hole in with a pin, needle, or similar type of pointed instrument; stick.—Mother *pricked* her finger with the needle.

2. Hurt or bother emotionally.—Mary's conscience *pricked* her.
3. Point (upward).—Fido *pricked* up his ears at the sound of footsteps.

pride (PRYD) *n.* 1. A feeling of happiness at being thought well of, or having something one has done, or owns, thought well of.— Mother takes *pride* in keeping our house neat and clean.
2. A thing one is proud of.—Grandfather's garden is his *pride* and joy.
3. High opinion of oneself; respect for oneself.—Jack's *pride* wouldn't let him admit his fault.
—*v. prides, prided, priding.* Grandmother *prides* herself on her cookies. She thinks they are very good.

priest (PREEST) *n. priests.* A minister or clergyman in the Roman Catholic church, the Episcopal church, and certain other religious groups.

pri·ma·ry (PRY-mair-ee) *n. primaries.* Election to choose one of several people in the same party to be a candidate.
—*adj.; primarily, adv.* 1. First in time or first in order.—The *primary* grades in school are the first grades above the kindergarten.
2. Main; most important.—The *primary* reason that Mother visited the school was to meet Mary's new teacher. — The *primary* colors are red, yellow, and blue. They form the basis for mixing other colors.

prime min·is·ter (prym MIN-iss-ter) *prime ministers.* The chief official of the government in many countries.

prim·er (PRIM-er) *n. primers.* A first book.— Children learn to read from a *primer.* After the *primer,* they try the first reader.

prim·i·tive (PRIM-ə-tiv) *adj.* Referring to, or like, people or things of the earliest times on the earth; crude and simple; ancient.—The cave men were *primitive* people. They lived a rough and simple life. — *Primitive* dishes were made of clay. — When the boys go camping, they live in a *primitive* way.

prim·rose (PRIM-rohz) *n. primroses.* A plant that has yellow and pink flowers.

prince (PRINSS) *n. princes.* 1. The son of a king, or the son of a king's son.
2. A nobleman of the highest rank, having royal blood.

prin·cess (PRIN-səss) *n. princesses.* The daughter of a king or queen or of their son, or the wife of a prince.

prin·ci·pal (PRIN-sə-pəl) *n. principals.* 1. The head of a school.
2. An amount of money which a person owns and puts into a business or a bank so that it will earn more money for him.
—*adj.; principally, adv.* Chief; main.—One of the *principal* reasons for going to school is to gain knowledge and learn how to use it.

prin·ci·ple (PRIN-sə-pəl) *n. principles.* 1. One of the rules or beliefs by which people live.—Treating people as you would like to have them treat you is a good *principle.*
2. Uprightness. — Mr. Smith is a man of *principle.*
3. The idea on which something is based; a truth or fact which makes it possible to do many things.—Bob explained to the class the *principles* by which a radio works.

print (PRINT) *n. prints.* 1. A line or a mark made by pressing one thing against another, as foot*prints* in the sand, or finger*prints* on the furniture.—No two people have finger*prints* exactly alike.

fingerprints   hand print

2. A finished photograph is a *print* from the negative.
3. A mechanically reproduced copy.

4. Words stamped on paper by a printing press.—I have trouble reading fine *print.*
5. A material covered with a design.—That material is a pretty *print.*
—*v. prints, printed, printing.* 1. Mark by pressing.—Printing presses *print* books. They stamp the letters and pictures onto the pages in ink.
2. A photograph is said to be *printed* when it is put on paper so that you can see it.
3. Form letters the way they appear in books and newspapers, instead of the way they are made in handwriting.—Little children sometimes learn to *print* their names before they learn to write them.

print·er (PRIN-ter) *n. printers.* A person whose work is printing, or setting up type to be printed.

pri·or (PRY-er) *adj.* Coming, being, or happening before something else.

prism (PRIZ-əm) *n. prisms.* A bar of glass or crystal, usually triangular, which bends and separates white light into rainbow colors: red, orange, yellow, green, blue, indigo, and violet.

pris·on (PRIZ-ən) *n. prisons.* A place where people are kept as prisoners to punish them for breaking the law.—The robbers were sent to *prison.*

pris·on·er (PRIZ-ə-ner *or* PRIZ-ner) *n. prisoners.* A person or animal that is held captive or kept shut up against his wishes.—A robin shut up in a cage is a *prisoner.*—Prisoners in a penitentiary have to work.

PRINTING

silk screen printing

enlarged piece of type

lithographer's stone

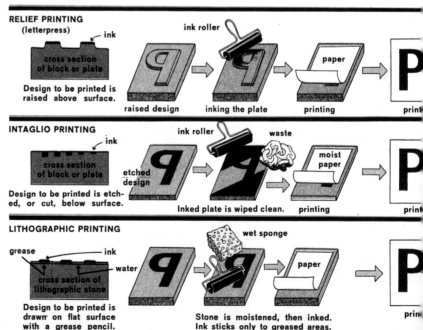

RELIEF PRINTING
(letterpress)

ink

cross section of block or plate

Design to be printed is raised above surface.

raised design   inking the plate   printing

ink roller

paper

P print

INTAGLIO PRINTING

ink

cross section of block or plate

Design to be printed is etched, or cut, below surface.

etched design

ink roller   waste

Inked plate is wiped clean.   printing

moist paper

P print

LITHOGRAPHIC PRINTING

grease   ink

water

cross section of lithographic stone

Design to be printed is drawn on flat surface with a grease pencil.

wet sponge

Stone is moistened, then inked. Ink sticks only to greased areas.

paper

P print

pri·va·cy (PRY-və-see) *n.* 1. The condition of being private or separated from other people.—Hedges or fences between houses insure *privacy* for neighbors who prefer it.
2. Secrecy.—The men discussed their plans in *privacy.*

pri·vate (PRY-vət) *n. privates.* A soldier who holds the lowest rank.—My brother is a *private* in the army.
—adj.; privately, adv. 1. Not for everyone, but only for a certain person or persons. — Our teacher had a *private* talk with Mother. No one else was there to listen.
2. Secret.—What I have to tell you is *private.* It is between us alone.
3. Holding no public office, like that of mayor or governor.—Father is a *private* citizen.

priv·i·lege (PRIV-ə-lij) *n. privileges.* The right to do a special thing.—Our teacher gave us the *privilege* of going home for our books. She let us go.

prize (PRYZ) *n. prizes.* A gift won by doing something better, or by being luckier, than other people.—The teacher gave a pencil as a *prize* to the person who could name the greatest number of flowers.—Bob won a *prize* at the party when he drew the lucky number from the hat.
—v. prizes, prized, prizing. Value highly.—We *prize* this picture. It is worth much to us.
—adj. Fit to win a prize; most valuable.—This lily is Grandmother's *prize* flower.

prob·a·ble (PRAHB-ə-bəl) *adj.; probably, adv.* Likely; likely to happen.—Sickness is the *probable* reason for Mary's absence from school.—Rain is *probable* today.

pro·ba·tion (proh-BAY-shən) *n.* A trial, or chance to show how well one can do.—The man went to work on *probation.* He was given a chance to show that he could do the work well.

prob·lem (PRAHB-ləm) *n. problems.* 1. Something to be worked out; a hard question to be answered.—This is a *problem* in arithmetic: If one apple costs a nickel, how much will six apples cost?
2. Anything that is hard to understand or deal with.—A naughty child sometimes is a *problem.*

pro·ce·dure (prə-SEE-jer) *n. procedures.* A way of doing things.—Bob follows this *procedure* in learning to spell: first he says the word, then he spells it to himself three times, then he writes it three times.

pro·ceed (prə-SEED) *v. proceeds, proceeded, proceeding.* 1. Move forward.—The old man *proceeded* down the road. He went on.
2. Get along according to plans.—Bob and Father are *proceeding* with their model airplanes. They are building six of them.
3. Come forth. — The wedding party *proceeded* from the church.

pro·ceed·ing (prə-SEE-ding) *n. proceedings.* Action; activity; things said or done.— Mary gave a report of the *proceedings* at the meeting.

pro·ceeds (PROH-seedz) *n. pl.* Money received for something; profit.—The *proceeds* from the fair were three hundred dollars.

proc·ess (PRAHSS-ess) *n. processes.* Plan or method. — What *process* is used in making jelly? What steps are taken in making it? What is done first, second, third, and so on?
—v. processes, processed, processing. Treat something in a special way.—Manufacturers *process* cheese to make it easy to spread or use in a sandwich.

pro·ces·sion (prə-SESH-ən) *n. processions.* The moving forward of persons or things in an orderly way.—A circus parade is a *procession.* — Children marching along in a line make a *procession.*

pro·claim (proh-KLAYM) *v. proclaims, proclaimed, proclaiming.* Announce or declare publicly. — The President *proclaimed* a national day of mourning for the dead hero.
—proclamation, n. proclamations.

prod·uce (PRAHD-ooss *or* PROH-dooss *or* -dyooss) *n.* Crops grown on a farm. — The farmer takes his *produce* to market.

pro·duce (prə-DOOSS *or* -DYOOSS) *v. produces, produced, producing.* 1. Show or exhibit something.–The children *produced* a play. They put it on for others to see.–Mary *produced* the pieces of glass as proof that the vase was broken.
2. Make or manufacture; create.–Factories *produce* thousands of automobiles a week.
3. Grow or cause to grow.–Seeds *produce* plants.–Farmers *produce* crops.
4. Cause; bring about.–When Mary works at anything she usually *produces* results.

pro·duc·er (prə-DOO-ser *or* prə-DYOO-ser) *n. producers.* 1. A person who makes or grows things to sell.–The man is a *producer* of corn.
2. A person who produces a moving picture or play.–Uncle Robert is a *producer.* His business is having plays shown on a stage.

prod·uct (PRAHD-ukt) *n. products.* 1. A thing that is grown or made.–Cars are manufactured *products.*–Foods are *products* of the farms.
2. In a problem in multiplication, the answer you get by multiplying two or more numbers together. $2 \times 9 = 18$. The answer, 18, is the *product* of 2 times 9.

pro·duc·tion (prə-DUK-shən) *n. productions.* 1. The act of producing or making something. – *Production* is better in well-lighted factories. More goods are made in less time.
2. Anything produced or brought out, especially something literary or artistic. – The movie we saw last night was a fine *production.*

pro·fan·i·ty (prə-FAN-ə-tee) *n. profanities; profane, adj.* Language used in contempt of God; swearing.

pro·fes·sion (prə-FESH-ən) *n. professions; professional, adj.* A kind of work or occupation for which people must have a special education.–The work of a doctor, dentist, minister, or teacher is a *profession.*–William is planning to go to law school because he hopes to enter the law *profession.*

pro·fes·sor (prə-FESS-er) *n. professors.* One of the higher-ranking teachers in a college or university.

pro·file (PROH-fyl) *n. profiles* and *adj.* An outline picture of anything; or, particularly, the picture of the side view of a person's face.–Ellen painted a *profile* view of Tommy.

prof·it (PRAHF-it) *n. profits.* 1. A gain; money made.–Jack's *profit* from selling papers last week was $1.25. That was the amount of money he had left after all his expenses were paid.
2. Benefit, use, or good.–What *profit* is there in working till you are overtired?
–*v. profits, profited, profiting.* 1. Gain money from business.–Mr. Smith *profits* enormously, considering how little money he has to put into his business.
2. Benefit. – You will *profit* from listening closely in class.

pro·found (prə-FOWND) *adj.; profoundly, adv.* 1. Having deep meaning or understanding; scholarly. – *Profound* books require careful reading.
2. Intense; deep; extreme.–The parents expressed *profound* gratitude when their lost child was returned to them.

pro·gram (PROH-gram) *n. programs.* 1. A list of the things that are going to happen.– A *program* for the concert told what was to be played and by whom.
2. A plan of action.–The President explained his farm *program.*
3. A performance.–The parents enjoyed the assembly *program.*

prog·ress (PRAHG-rəss *or* PROH-gress) *n.* 1. Movement forward.–A turtle makes slow *progress.*
2. Improvement; movement forward.–Have you made any *progress* in your work?

pro·gress (prə-GRESS) *v. progresses, progressed, progressing.* Go forward; advance.– Jim *progressed* quickly in school.

pro·gres·sive (prə-GRESS-iv) *adj.; progressively, adv.* 1. Favoring improvements and movement forward.–A *progressive* city makes improvements and carries out new ideas.
2. Happening step by step.–His *progressive* loss of weight showed that something was seriously wrong.

pro·hib·it (proh-HIB-it) *v. prohibits, prohibited, prohibiting.* Not allow by law; forbid. –The sign said "Smoking *Prohibited.*"
–*prohibition, n. prohibitions.*

proj·ect (PRAHJ-ekt) *n. projects.* A plan or design for something that is to be done; an idea all worked out.–Building a houseboat is Father's summertime *project.*

pro·ject (prə-JEKT) *v. projects, projected, projecting.* 1. Point forward; stick out.–The porch roof *projects* a little to keep the rain from blowing into the porch.

2. Cast or throw upon a flat surface.—Father *projected* the shadow of his hand onto the wall in the shape of a donkey's head.

pro·jec·tion (prə-JEK-shən) *n. projections.*
1. A part that juts out.—Jack stood on the rocky *projection* high above the valley.
2. The projecting of something onto a flat surface.—The film's *projection* was not clear.

pro·jec·tor (prə-JEK-ter) *n. projectors.* An apparatus or machine used to throw still or moving pictures on a screen.

movie projector
slide projector

pro·long (prə-LAWNG) *v. prolongs, prolonged, prolonging.* Make longer; increase in length.—The teacher said she would not *prolong* her talk, but would leave time for us to ask questions.

prom·i·nent (PRAHM-ə-nənt) *adj.; prominently, adv.* 1. Sticking out; standing out.—A long nose is a *prominent* nose.
2. Well-known; noted.—A group of *prominent* businessmen is trying to get the city to build the playground.

prom·ise (PRAHM-iss) *n. promises.* 1. A person's statement or word that he will surely do something.—Bob gave me his *promise* to be here at nine o'clock.
2. Something which shows hope of future success.—She shows *promise* in ballet.
—*v. promises, promised, promising.* 1. Make a promise.—Bob *promised* to be here at nine.
2. Seem likely.—This *promises* to be a hot summer.

pro·mote (prə-MOHT) *v. promotes, promoted, promoting.* 1. Raise in rank, position, grade.—Bob was *promoted* from the fourth grade to the fifth.
2. Help to happen successfully.—The boys are *promoting* the Red Cross drive by giving a benefit baseball game.
—*promotion, n. promotions.*

prompt (PRAHMPT) *v. prompts, prompted, prompting.* 1. Cause; lead.—The good weather *prompted* us to go outside.
2. Remind. — The teacher *prompted* Mary when she forgot her lines in the play.
—*adj.* On time.—Bob is always *prompt.*

prong (PRAWNG) *n. prongs.* A pointed projection, as on a fork or antler.—The fish was caught on one of the hook's two *prongs.*

pro·noun (PROH-nown) *n. pronouns.* A word used instead of the name of something or someone.—The word "you" is a *pronoun* used instead of your name.—The word "he" is a *pronoun* used in speaking of a man or a boy.

pro·nounce (prə-NOWNSS) *v. pronounces, pronounced, pronouncing.* 1. Speak the sounds of.—The word "quay" is *pronounced* just like the word "key."
2. Declare officially.—The jury *pronounced* the man innocent.

pro·nun·ci·a·tion (prə-nun-see-AY-shən) *n. pronunciations.* The sound of a spoken word; the act of speaking sounds.—The *pronunciation* of the word "quay" is the same as the *pronunciation* of the word "key."

proof (PROOF) *n. proofs.* That which shows the truth of something.—Bob offered *proof* that he had been in Washington. He showed a photograph of himself in front of the Capitol.
—*adj.* Safe or protected (against something).— This coat is *proof* against water. Water will not come through it. It is water*proof.*

prop (PRAHP) *n. props.* A stick or the like that leans against something to hold the thing up.

—*v. props, propped, propping.* Hold up or support with a prop or props.—Father *propped* up the fence with poles until he could have time to repair it.

prop·a·gan·da (prahp-ə-GAN-də) *n.* 1. A systematic and organized effort to spread ideas and opinions for the purposes of a person or group.—Among the tools of the dictator's *propaganda* were the nation's strictly censored books, magazines, and newspapers.
2. The ideas and opinions spread.—It is important to learn to distinguish truth from *propaganda* in reading anything.

pro·pel (prə-PEL) *v. propels, propelled, propelling.* Drive, push, or force forward; cause to move ahead.–I wonder what *propels* the human cannon balls at the circus.–Huge propellers *propel* the plane.

pro·pel·ler (prə-PEL-er) *n. propellers.* A device with curved blades that whirl around. *Propellers* are turned by engines and are used on boats and aircraft. The whirling blades push the water or air and thus make the boat or aircraft move.

prop·er (PRAHP-er) *adj.; properly, adv.* According to rule; correct.–It is *proper* to drive on the right side of the street.
–A *proper noun* is the name of a certain person, place, or thing. *Proper nouns* always begin with capital letters.–Chicago, Mary, and America are *proper nouns.*

prop·er·ty (PRAHP-er-tee) *n. properties.* 1. That which is owned, especially land and buildings.–The *property* along the river has been worth more since the park was made.–The bicycle is Bob's *property.* It belongs to him.
2. Special quality of something.–Among the *properties* of glass is the *property* of being transparent.
3. Item used in a play, such as a letter, a handkerchief, a glass.

proph·e·sy (PRAHF-ə-sy) *v. prophesies, prophesied, prophesying.* Predict; tell beforehand.–The old man *prophesied* that there would be a war.

proph·et (PRAHF-ət) *n. prophets.* 1. A person who predicts the future.–Bob was a good weather *prophet.* He said it would snow, and it did.
2. A man who speaks for God.–Jeremiah and Paul are two of the *prophets* in the Bible.

pro·por·tion (prə-POR-shən) *n. proportions.* 1. A part.–A great *proportion* of the earth's surface is under water.
2. The relation between parts.–A normal person's body grows in proper *proportions.* The size of each part is properly related to the size of the whole body.
3. Numerical relation. – The *proportion* of boys to girls in our school is two to one. There are twice as many boys as girls.

pro·pose (prə-POHZ) *v. proposes, proposed, proposing.* 1. Suggest; put forward as a thing to do.–Bob *proposed* that the class have a picnic.
2. Ask to marry.–The young man *proposed* to the young woman.
–*proposal, n. proposals.*

prop·o·si·tion (prahp-ə-ZISH-ən) *n. propositions.* Something suggested or proposed.

pro·pri·e·tor (prə-PRY-ə-ter) *n. proprietors.* The owner and manager of a business.–The *proprietor* of the store gave us a box of candy.

prose (PROHZ) *n.* Ordinary writing (not in the form of poetry or verse). *Prose* does not have the rhythm and rhyme of poetry.

pros·e·cute (PRAHSS-ə-kyoot) *v. prosecutes, prosecuted, prosecuting.* Take to a law court; bring to trial.–The man was *prosecuted* for stealing the car.

pros·pect (PRAHSS-pekt) *n. prospects.* 1. Something looked forward to.–The *prospect* of getting a better job pleased Father.
2. A view. – The *prospect* from our front porch is very beautiful.
3. A person who may be suitable for a purpose or respond to a request.–David may be a *prospect* for our club.

pros·pec·tor (PRAHSS-pek-ter) *n. prospectors.* A person who seeks gold, oil, diamonds, and such things by searching for them in various regions.–The old *prospector* found a pocket of gold in the hills.

pros·per (PRAHSS-per) *v. prospers, prospered, prospering.* Do well; be successful.–Uncle Jim's new store is *prospering.*

pros·per·i·ty (prahss-PAIR-ə-tee) *n.* Good fortune; wealthy condition.–A man who has a good job and all he needs for comfortable living has *prosperity.*

pros·per·ous (PRAHSS-per-əss) *adj.; prosperously, adv.* Successful; well off. – The *prosperous* businessman gave a great deal of money to the playground fund.

pro·tect (prə-TEKT) *v. protects, protected, protecting.* 1. Guard; keep from danger.–The policemen *protect* us from criminals.
2. Shelter; keep from discomfort.–A raincoat *protects* you from the rain.

pro·tec·tion (prə-TEK-shən) *n.* 1. Keeping from danger.–The job of the Safety Patrol is the *protection* of children from traffic.
2. That which keeps from harm, or protects.
–A raincoat is a *protection* against rain.

pro·te·in (PROH-teen *or* PROH-tee-ən) *n. proteins.* A substance vital to all living animal and plant cells.—*Proteins* are found in milk, eggs, meat, and fish.

pro·test (prə-TEST) *v. protests, protested, protesting.* 1. Speak against; object.—The boy *protested* his low mark. He was sure he had done better, and said so.
2. Declare strongly.—The prisoner *protested* his innocence.

Prot·es·tant (PRAHT-iss-tənt) *n. Protestants* and *adj.* A member of any Christian church or sect other than the Roman Catholic and Greek Orthodox Churches.

pro·to·plasm (PROH-tə-plaz-əm) *n.* The living matter in all animal and plant cells. *Protoplasm,* seen under a microscope, has a colorless and jellylike appearance.

pro·trac·tor (proh-TRAK-ter) *n. protractors.* An instrument used for measuring angles and for drawing them accurately. *Protractors* are used by engineers, architects, mathematicians, and others.

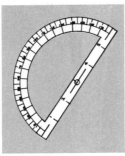

proud (PROWD) *adj. prouder, proudest; proudly, adv.* 1. Having a high regard for oneself or one's family, possessions, etc.—The boy was too *proud* to borrow carfare.
2. Conceited; having too high an opinion of oneself.—The *proud* boy annoyed others because he boasted a great deal.

prove (PROOV) *v. proves, proved, proving.* 1. Make certain the truth of.—The photograph of Bob in front of the Capitol *proved* that he had been in Washington.
2. Test and find as hoped for or believed to be.—Jane *proved* her subtraction answer by addition.—John *proved* himself in the game.

prov·erb (PRAHV-erb) *n. proverbs.* An old saying that gives advice.—"A stitch in time saves nine" is a *proverb.*

pro·vide (prə-VYD) *v. provides, provided, providing.* 1. Supply.—I will *provide* the ice cream if you will *provide* the cake.
2. Give as a condition. — The rules *provide* that no one over ten may enter the contest.
3. Prepare (for a situation) beforehand.— Father has *provided* for his old age.

prov·ince (PRAHV-inss) *n. provinces.* 1. A large division of a country.—Ontario is one of the *provinces* of Canada.

2. A section of a country far from the main city.—People from the *provinces* attended the great fair in the capital city.

pro·vi·sion (prə-VIZH-ən) *n. provisions.* 1. A given condition.—One of the *provisions* of the rules is that no one over ten may enter the contest.
2. A preparing; a making ready ahead of time.—The town had made *provision* for a heavy snowfall, and the plows started to work as soon as the storm began.
3. (In the plural) A supply, usually of things to eat and drink.—The campers have plenty of *provisions.*

pro·voke (prə-VOHK) *v. provokes, provoked, provoking.* 1. Bring on; be the cause of.— Harsh words *provoke* anger.
2. Annoy; make angry.—Bob's bad behavior *provoked* the teacher.

prow (PROW) *n. prows.* The very front part of a ship, plane, or airship.—The *prow* of the ship cut through the water.

prowl (PROWL) *v. prowls, prowled, prowling.* 1. Rove or wander about looking for food.—The hungry dog *prowled* about the alley.
2. Sneak about. — The man *prowled* about looking for something to steal.

pru·dence (PROO-dənss) *n.; prudent, adj.; prudently, adv.* Wise carefulness.—Bob shows *prudence.* He is not at all reckless.

prune (PROON) *n. prunes.* A kind of dried plum.

—*v. prunes, pruned, pruning.* Cut off (parts of plants). — The farmer *prunes* the dead branches of his trees.

pry (PRY) *v. pries, pried, prying.* 1. Try to find out about other people's affairs.—Nobody likes a person who is always *prying.*

2. Force with something used as a lever. — Mother *pried* the top off the jar with a knife.

psalm (SAHM) *n. psalms.* 1. A sacred song or poem.

2. (Spelled with a capital "P.") One of the poems in a part of the Bible known as "The Book of *Psalms.*"

psy·chi·a·trist (sy-KY-ə-trist) *n. psychiatrists.* A medical doctor who specializes in psychiatry, or the treatment of mental difficulties and diseases.

psy·chi·a·try (sy-KY-ə-tree) *n.* The science or practice of treating diseases, difficulties, or disorders of the mind.

psy·chol·o·gist (sy-KAHL-ə-jist) *n. psychologists.* A person who specializes in psychology, or the study of the mind.

psy·chol·o·gy (sy-KAHL-ə-jee) *n.* The science or study of the mind. *Psychology* deals with the mental functions of higher animals, especially those of human beings.

pub·lic (PUB-lik) *n.* The people as a whole. —The mayor of the city asked the *public* not to waste food.

—*adj.; publicly, adv.* 1. Of or for all the people. —A *public* park is open to everyone.

2. Governmental.—The mayor holds *public* office.

pub·li·ca·tion (pub-lə-KAY-shən) *n. publications.* 1. The act of telling or announcing something to the public, as in a newspaper or magazine.—This news is for *publication.*

2. A book, magazine, or paper printed to sell to the public.

3. The printing and sale to the public of a book, magazine, or similar printed matter.

pub·lic·i·ty (pub-LISS-ə-tee) *n.* Condition of being noticed by the people; public notice. —The flyer received much *publicity* through radio, television, and newspapers. People heard much about him.

pub·lish (PUB-lish) *v. publishes, published, publishing.* 1. Make known to the public.— The newspaper *published* the news of the accident on the day after it happened.

2. Make up and print books, magazines, etc., to sell to the public.

pub·lish·er (PUB-lish-er) *n. publishers.* A man or a company whose business is making up, printing, and selling books, magazines, newspapers, and other such publications.

pud·ding (PUHD-ing) *n. puddings.* A sweet, soft dessert, such as cornstarch *pudding,* tapioca *pudding,* or bread *pudding.*

pud·dle (PUD-l) *n. puddles.* A small pool of water.—Mary fell into a mud *puddle* and got her dress muddy.

pueb·lo (PWEB-loh) *n. pueblos.* An Indian village of the southwestern United States, especially one of those in New Mexico or Arizona. The houses in a *pueblo* are usually built of stone or adobe.

pug (PUG) *n. pugs* and *adj.* A small, tan, short-haired dog that has a turned-up nose and a curly tail.

pull (PUHL) *n. pulls.*
1. A drawing towards. —The man gave a *pull* on the string and it broke.

2. A strenuous climb.—The old car had a hard *pull* up the hill.

—*v. pulls, pulled, pulling.* 1. Use force to move or draw toward one; drag.—The horse *pulled* the cart up the hill.—Father *pulled* a dollar from his pocket.

2. Move.—The train *pulled* out of the station.

pul·let (PUHL-ət) *n. pullets.* A young hen.

pul·ley (PUHL-ee) *n. pulleys.* A wheel with the rim hollowed out so that a rope or chain can run on it without slipping off. *Pulleys,* usually several together, are used to lift heavy objects.

Pull·man (PUHL-mən) *n. Pullmans* and *adj.* A railroad car with berths which can be made up at night for people to sleep in.

pulp (PULP) *n.; pulpy, adj.* 1. The soft, juicy part of fruit.
2. Paper, wood, cloth, or anything else ground up very fine and mixed with enough water to make a paste.

pul·pit (PUHL-pit) *n. pulpits.* A platform where a minister stands to preach.

pulse (PULSS) *n. pulses.* 1. Beating of the heart.—The nurse listened to the boy's *pulse.*
2. Any regular beating or throbbing like that of the heart.—The boys heard the *pulse* of the motor in the steamship.
—*v. pulses, pulsed, pulsing.* Beat regularly, as a heart.—The machines *pulsed* steadily in the great factory.

pu·ma (PYOO-mə) *n. pumas.* A large American wildcat, also called a mountain lion.

pump (PUMP) *n. pumps.* 1. A machine for forcing liquid or gas through a pipe or hose from one place to another.—The car drew up to the gasoline *pump.*

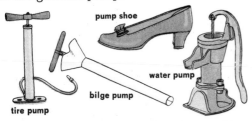

tire pump
pump shoe
water pump
bilge pump

2. A kind of low shoe without laces.—Many girls wear *pumps* to dance in.
—*v. pumps, pumped, pumping.* 1. Fill with a pump.—Bob *pumped* up his bicycle tires.
2. Move, as by a pump.—One's heart *pumps* blood to all parts of the body.
3. Question (a person) continuously to draw out a secret.—Mary had a secret, but the others could not *pump* it out of her.

pump·kin (PUMP- *or* PUNG-kin) *n. pumpkins.* A large yellow fruit that grows on a vine on the ground.

punch (PUNCH) *n. punches.* 1. A blow.—One boxer gave the other a *punch* in the nose.
2. A drink made by mixing fruit juices and other liquids.
3. A tool used to make holes.—Mary made holes in the paper with a paper *punch.*
—*v. punches, punched, punching.* Hit; strike.
—One boxer *punched* the other.

punc·tu·al (PUNGK-choo-əl) *adj.; punctually, adv.* Exactly on time; prompt; not late.
—Tom is always *punctual* for his appointments. He never keeps anyone waiting.

punc·tu·ate (PUNGK-choo-ayt) *v. punctuates, punctuated, punctuating.* Divide up with commas, periods, question marks, etc., to make for easier reading and understanding.—The teacher told us to *punctuate* our stories.

punc·tu·a·tion (pungk-choo-AY-shən) *n.* Dividing up with marks such as the period and the comma, to make for easier reading and understanding.—Mary made three mistakes in *punctuation.*

pun·ish (PUN-ish) *v. punishes, punished, punishing.* Bring pain or unpleasantness to a person for some wrong done.—Some parents *punish* their children by spanking them.

pun·ish·ment (PUN-ish-mənt) *n. punishments.* The act of giving pain or taking away pleasure from one who has done wrong. — Spanking children is *punishment.*—Taking away a person's freedom is *punishment.*

punt (PUNT) *n. punts.* A kick of a football made by holding the ball out, dropping it, and kicking it before it touches the ground.—Our fullback made a long *punt.*
—*v. punts, punted, punting.* Kicking a football in this manner.

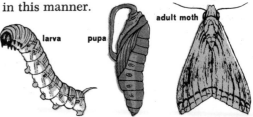

larva
pupa
adult moth

pu·pa (PYOO-pə) *n. pupae* or *pupas.* The stage through which some insects pass between the larva and the fully grown form. *Pupas* are often found in cocoons.

pu·pil (PYOO-pəl) *n. pupils.* 1. A boy or girl who is in school or studying under a teacher. —There are thirty *pupils* in our class.
2. The dark center of the eye.

pup·pet (PUP-it) *n. puppets.* A doll moved by strings or by hand on a tiny stage.

pup·py (PUP-ee) *n. puppies.* Some baby animals, especially baby dogs and foxes, are called *puppies* or pups. —Father bought a new *puppy* for Sally.

pur·chase (PER-chəss) *n. purchases.* Anything bought.— Mother's *purchase* was a dress.
—*v. purchases, purchased, purchasing.* Buy.— Mother went shopping to *purcha*se a dress.

pure (PYUHR) *adj.; purely, adv.* 1. Clean and clear; not mixed with dirt or other unwanted things.—This water is *pure.*
2. Only; not including anything else.—The joke was played in *pure* fun, in fun only.

pu·ri·fy (PYUHR-ə-fy) *v. purifies, purified, purifying.* Make pure or clean.—The city *purifies* our drinking water.

pur·ple (PER-pəl) *n.* and *adj.* A dark, rich color that can be made by mixing red and blue together.— Some flowers, such as violets, are *purple.*

pur·pose (PER-pəss) *n. purposes; purposely, adv.* 1. An aim. —What is your *purpose* in going to school?
2. Deliberate intention.—You dropped your handkerchief on *purpose.* You meant to.

purr (PER) *n. purrs.* A humming sound.—I heard the *purr* of the cat.
—*v. purrs, purred, purring.* Make a low, humming sound.—The cat *purrs* when she is very comfortable.

purse (PERSS) *n. purses.* 1. A pocketbook; a small bag to carry money and other things in.
2. A sum of money put up as a prize in such events as boxing and horse racing. — The men fought for a *purse* of $10,000.

—*v. purses, pursed, pursing.* Pucker up.—When Baby cries, she *purses* her lips.

pur·sue (per-SOO *or* -SYOO) *v. pursues, pursued, pursuing.* Chase.—The policeman *pursued* the speeding automobile.

pur·suit (per-SOOT *or* -SYOOT) *n. pursuits.* 1. A chase.—The policeman is in *pursuit* of the speeding automobile.
2. Work; occupation.—What is your father's *pursuit?*

pus (PUSS) *n.* The yellowish-white matter that is found in boils and some other sores.

push (PUHSH) *n. pushes.* A shove.—We gave the car a *push* to see if we could start it.
—*v. pushes, pushed, pushing.* 1. Use force to move something away from one.—The boys *pushed* the automobile to start it.
2. Shove. — The policeman *pushed* through the crowd.

put (PUHT) *v. puts, put, putting.* 1. Place; lay.—*Put* the basket on the table.
2. Cause to change in place, feeling, or condition.—Mother *put* the cat out.

putt·er (PUT-er) *n. putters.* A golf club used for knocking the ball into the hole.
—*v. putters, puttered, puttering.* Keep busy but not get very much done.—Father *putters* in the garden on summer evenings.

puz·zle (PUZ-əl) *n. puzzles.* A problem to be worked out.—There is a crossword *puzzle* in the paper every morning.
—*v. puzzles, puzzled, puzzling.* Confuse.—The teacher was *puzzled* over the girl's behavior. The girl's behavior *puzzled* the teacher. She didn't know what to think about it.

pyr·a·mid (PIR-ə-mid) *n. pyramids.* 1. Any object that has a flat bottom and three or more sides that form triangles and meet at one point on top.

2. The massive structures built in ancient Egypt and used for tombs. The three great *pyramids* near Cairo are usually referred to as the *Pyramids,* spelled with a capital "P."

Q q

Q, q (KYOO) *n. Q's, q's.* The seventeenth letter of the alphabet.

quack (KWAK) *n. quacks.* 1. The cry of a duck.—A sheep says "Baa, baa." A duck says "Quack, quack."
2. A person who fools others by pretending to know much about something about which he knows little or nothing.—The doctor who gave the sick old lady sugar pills was not a real doctor. He was a *quack.*
—*v quacks, quacked, quacking.* Make a sound like a duck.—The duck *quacked* loudly when Bill chased it.

quad·rant (KWAHD-rənt) *n. quadrants.* 1. One of the four quarters of a circle; an arc of ninety degrees. 2. An instrument used in navigation and astronomy. A *quadrant* is used to measure heights.

qua·drille (kwə- *or* kə-DRIL) *n. quadrilles.* 1. A square dance with four couples. The couples form a square and follow the directions of a person who calls out the different kinds of steps.
2. The music for such a dance.

quad·ru·ped (KWAHD-ruh-ped) *n. quadrupeds.* An animal with four feet. Horses, dogs, cattle, sheep, and many other animals are *quadrupeds.*

quad·ru·ple (KWAHD-roo-pəl) *n. quadruples.* An amount that is four times as great as another.—Eight is the *quadruple* of two. Eight is four times two.
—*adj.* 1. Four times as much, or four times as many.
2. Made up of four. — It is supposed to be good luck to find a *quadruple-* or four-leaved clover.

quad·ru·plet (kwahd-ROOP-lit) *n. quadruplets.* One of four children born to one mother at the same time. — Mrs. Ralph Jones had *quadruplets.*

quail (KWAYL) *n. quails.* A plump game bird sometimes called a bobwhite.— Father hunts *quail.*
—*v. quails, quailed, quailing.* Shrink with fear and dread.— Jack *quailed* at the thought of swimming the icy creek.

quaint (KWAYNT) *adj.; quaintly, adv.; quaintness, n.* Odd, strange, or old-fashioned, but interesting and charming.—Grandmother has a *quaint* velvet jacket like those worn years ago.

quake (KWAYK) *v. quakes, quaked, quaking.* Tremble; shake.—Mary *quaked* with excitement as the time drew near for her party.

Quak·er (KWAY-ker) *n. Quakers.* A member of the Society of Friends, a Christian religious group.

qual·i·fy (KWAHL-ə-fy) *v. qualifies, qualified, qualifying.* Be able or well suited. — Mary's teacher believes Mary is *qualified* to enter the musical contest.
—*qualification, n. qualifications.*

qual·i·ty (KWAHL-ə-tee) *n. qualities.* 1. Grade or degree of excellence.—A good *quality* of shoe leather will wear better than a poor *quality.*
2. Characteristic.—Jack's best *qualities* are honesty and truthfulness.
3. Merit or good value.—Mother would rather buy one dress of good *quality* than three dresses of poor material.

quan·ti·ty (KWAHN-tə-tee) *n. quantities.* 1. Amount.—The United States imports a large *quantity* of coffee.
2. A large number. — Grandmother baked *quantities* of cookies for the holidays.

quar·an·tine (KWOR- *or* KWAHR-ən-teen) *n.* A ship is in *quarantine* in the harbor. No one is allowed to leave until doctors make sure that the people on it have no disease which might be spread to others on land.
—*v. quarantines, quarantined, quarantining.* Keep away from others because of illness.— The children who had scarlet fever were *quarantined.*

quar·rel (KWOR- *or* KWAHR-əl) *n.* quarrels; quarrelsome, *adj.* Dispute or disagreement.—Jack and Bill are friends again after their *quarrel.*

—*v.* quarrels, quarreled, quarreling. 1. Disagree or argue angrily.—The boys *quarreled* over the bicycle.

2. Find fault. — Jack is always *quarreling* with the decisions of the umpire.

quar·ry (KWOR- *or* KWAHR-ee) *n.* quarries. 1. A place in the ground from which stone is dug.—There are many marble *quarries* in the state of Vermont.

2. A hunted bird or animal. — The dogs growled as if they knew they would find their *quarry* in the tree. And sure enough, the raccoon they were hunting was clinging to the highest branch.

—*v.* quarries, quarried, quarrying. Dig from a quarry.—Marble is *quarried* in Vermont.

quart (KWORT) *n.* quarts. A unit for the measurement of liquids.—Milk and other liquids are measured by the space they fill. Two pints make a *quart.* Four *quarts* make a gallon.

quar·ter (KWOR-ter) *n.* quarters. 1. One of four equal parts; one fourth.—If you divide a pie into four equal parts, each part is one fourth, or one *quarter.*

2. A section or region.—We visited the French *quarter* of the city.

3. Each of the four monthly phases of the moon. They are called: new moon, first *quarter,* full moon, and last, or fourth, *quarter.*

4. (In the plural) A place to live.—The troops moved into new *quarters.*

—*v.* quarters, quartered, quartering. 1. Provide living space for.—After the flood, many families were *quartered* in hotels.

2. Divide into four equal parts. — Mother *quartered* the orange for Sally.

quar·ter·ly (KWOR-ter-lee) *n.* quarterlies. A magazine published four times a year.

—*adj.* and *adv.* Happening or being done four times a year, or every three months.—Some people pay their income taxes *quarterly.*

quar·tet (kwor-TET) *n.* quartets. 1. A group of four persons or four things.—Four persons who sing together or play musical instruments together are a *quartet.*

2. A piece of music written for four voices or instruments.—Four boys sang a *quartet.*

quartz (KWORTSS) *n.* A kind of mineral that is made up of very hard crystals. *Quartz* is colorless, pink, yellow, brown, green, or purple.

quay (KEE) *n.* quays. A wharf or landing place where boats can load and unload.—The merchant went down to the *quay* every day to watch for his ship.

queen (KWEEN) *n.* queens; queenly, *adj.* 1. A woman ruler, or the wife of a king.

2. A girl or woman who is chosen to be the most important one at some special event, or one who is very popular. — Mary was chosen *Queen* of the May.

3. A fully developed female bee or ant. — The *queen* insect lays the eggs.

4. A playing card that has the picture of a queen on it.

queer (KWIR) *adj.* queerer, queerest; queerly, *adv.*; queerness, *n.* Peculiar or strange; odd.—The man had a *queer* feeling of uneasiness as he stepped through the doorway of the old house.

quench (KWENCH) *v.* quenches, quenched, quenching. Extinguish or put out; put an end to.—Cool water will *quench* your thirst better than soda pop.—Rain *quenched* the forest fire.

que·ry (KWIR-ee) *n.* queries. A question.—"Where are you going?" is a *query.*
—*v.* queries, queried, querying. Inquire; ask a question. — "What is your name?" *queried* Sally.

quest (KWEST) *n.* quests. 1. A search or hunt for something.—The hunters went into the forest in *quest* of deer.
2. A search undertaken as a mission by a knight.—Sir George vowed to kill the dragon and set out in *quest* of the beast right away.

ques·tion (KWESS-chən) *n.* questions. 1. A sentence that asks something. — Sally asks many *questions,* because there are many things she wants to know.
2. Subject or problem.—At the meeting tonight, the people will discuss the *question* of improving the playgrounds.
3. A doubt or uncertainty.—If there is any *question* of the safety of the ice, do not go skating.
—*v.* questions, questioned, questioning. 1. Ask. —The teacher *questioned* us about the lost book.
2. Be uncertain of, or doubt.—No one can *question* Jack's honesty.

ques·tion·naire (kwess-chən-AIR) *n.* questionnaires. A list of questions designed to find out something specific, such as why you buy a certain brand of soap or what kind of TV programs you prefer.

queue (KYOO) *n.* queues. 1. A long braid of hair that hangs down the back. For this meaning, this word is also spelled "cue."
2. A waiting line, as at a store counter or ticket booth.—When a good movie is in town, people often have to stand in *queues* to get tickets.

quick (KWIK) *n.* 1. Deep and sensitive part. —Mary bit her nails to the *quick.*
2. People who are alive.—When Father got over his cold, he said he felt like one of the *quick* again; he felt really alive.
—*adj.* quicker, quickest. 1. Fast or rapid; swift.

—The magician was so *quick* that we could not follow his movements.
2. Hasty or unthinking.—Jack's worst fault is his *quick* temper.

quick·en (KWIK-ən) *v.* quickens, quickened, quickening. 1. Hasten or move faster; hurry. —Jack *quickened* his steps as the rain began to fall.
2. Arouse or excite.—The man's story *quickened* Ed's interest in him.

quick·ly (KWIK-lee) *adv.* Fast; hastily; with speed; rapidly.—We must pack *quickly* if we hope to catch the train.

quick·ness (KWIK-nəss) *n.* Speed; swiftness.—Bob's *quickness* in the football game surprised the other team.

quick·sand (KWIK-sand) *n.* quicksands. A very deep mass of soft, wet sand that is dangerous because a man or animal can sink into it completely, quickly, and easily.

quick·sil·ver (KWIK-sil-ver) *n.* Mercury, a silver-white metal. *Quicksilver,* or mercury, is the only metal that is fluid at normal temperatures. It is used in thermometers because it expands when it is heated and so moves up the glass tube.

qui·et (KWY-ət) *n.* Stillness and peace.—The *quiet* of the country is restful to Grandmother after a week in the city.
—*v.* quiets, quieted, quieting. Silence and soothe, or calm down.—The teacher *quieted* the excited boy.
—*adj.* quieter, quietest; quietly, *adv.* 1. Silent and still; calm.—The garden was so *quiet* that we could hear the bees humming.
2. Motionless.—There was no breeze, and the leaves were *quiet.*
3. Restful and peaceful.—We spent a *quiet* day in the country.
4. Gentle; mild.—Mother has a *quiet* manner.
5. Not bright or flashy.—Grandmother wore a *quiet* lavender dress.

qui·et·ness (KWY-ət-nəss) *n.* Stillness; calmness.—The *quietness* in the country is restful to Grandmother.

quill (KWIL) *n.* quills. 1. A large, stiff feather taken from the wing or tail of a goose, duck, or other fowl.
2. A pen made from a sharpened feather.—In the picture in our classroom, Columbus is drawing a map with a *quill.*
3. A stiff hair or spine.—Porcupines' bodies are covered with *quills.*

quilt (KWILT) *n. quilts.* A stuffed or filled bed cover used for warmth. – Grandmother stuffs her patchwork *quilts* with cotton.

–v. quilts, quilted, quilting. Make a quilt; sew together, with fine stitches, two layers of cloth with something soft inside.–Mother is *quilting* a bathrobe for Sally.

quince (KWINSS) *n. quinces.* 1. A golden-yellow apple-shaped fruit that has a strong smell and a sour taste. *Quinces* are used in jelly and marmalade. 2. The shrub or small tree on which the fruit grows. The flowering *quince* has many branches, full leaves, and large white or pink flowers.

qui·nine (KWY-nyn) *n.* A bitter medicine used in treating malaria and other sicknesses.

quin·tu·plet (kwin-TUP-lət *or* kwin-TOO-plət *or* kwin-TYOO-plət) *n. quintuplets.* 1. Five things of a kind. 2. One of five animals or children born to the same mother at the same time.

quit (KWIT) *v. quits, quitted, quitting.* 1. Stop; halt.–The farmer *quits* work at eight o'clock. 2. Leave.–Bob *quit* his summer job to go back to school.

quite (KWYT) *adv.* 1. Fully; entirely; completely.–The story is not *quite* finished. 2. Truly; really.–Mary's cold is *quite* bad. 3. More than a little.–Bob was *quite* disappointed by the results of the game. 4. Very much of.–You have *quite* a suntan.

quiv·er (KWIV-er) *n. quivers.* A case for carrying arrows. – Robin Hood wore a *quiver* over his shoulder.

–v. quivers, quivered, quivering. Tremble or shiver gently. – The leaves *quivered* in the breeze.

quiz (KWIZ) *n. quizzes.* A test or examination.–Our teacher gave us a *quiz* in arithmetic.
–v. quizzes, quizzed, quizzing. Ask questions of.–It is not polite to *quiz* others about their private affairs.
–adj. Bob likes to test himself on the *quiz* section in the magazine.

quoit (KWOIT) *n. quoits.* A ring of flattened metal that is used in playing a game. The game is played by pitching the metal *quoits* at a peg in the ground to see who can get the *quoit* on or nearest the peg.

quo·rum (KWOR-əm) *n. quorums.* The minimum number of members who must be present before a meeting can be held or a vote can be taken. The rules of a club tell how many club members are needed to make a *quorum.*

quo·ta (KWOH-tə) *n. quotas.* A set share; a determined part; a certain percentage of a total.–Everyone was given ten tickets to sell. If anyone sold his *quota*, that is all ten tickets, he would be rewarded with a free ticket for himself.

quo·ta·tion (kwoh-TAY-shən) *n. quotations* and *adj.* The exact words spoken or written by one person when repeated by another person.–Bob said to him, "I would like to go to the ball game." The words in *quotation* marks are a *quotation.* The marks (". . ."), before the word I and after the word game, are *quotation* marks. They show the beginning and the end of the *quotation.*–"The Lord is my shepherd; I shall not want" is a *quotation* from the Bible.

quote (KWOHT) *n. quotes.* A quotation; the exact words spoken or written by one person and repeated by another.–Father answered with a *quote* from Shakespeare.
–v. quotes, quoted, quoting. 1. Repeat exactly what someone else has said or written. – Father likes to *quote* things he has read. 2. Name the price of.–The farmer *quoted* twenty-five dollars for his load of hay.

quo·tient (KWOH-shənt) *n. quotients.* The answer or number which you get after working a problem in division.–In 12 ÷ 3 = 4, the *quotient* is 4.

R r

R, r (AHR) *n. R's, r's.* The eighteenth letter of the alphabet.

rab·bi (RAB-y) *n. rabbis.* A pastor of the Jewish faith.

rab·bit (RAB-it) *n. rabbits.* A small, swift animal with soft fur, long ears, and a short, puffy tail. The *rabbit* belongs to the hare family. It has strong hind legs for jumping.

showshoe rabbit   cottontail rabbit

jack rabbit   Belgian hare

ra·bies (RAY-beez) *n.* A disease which makes dogs and other animals go mad. If a person is bitten by a mad dog, he too may get *rabies.*

rac·coon or **ra·coon** (rə-KOON) *n. raccoons* or *racoons.* A small fur-bearing animal that lives in trees and moves about mostly at night.

race (RAYSS) *n. races.* 1. A contest of speed. —There are auto *races*, foot *races*, horse *races*, swimming *races*, and many other kinds.
2. A large group of people with the same skin color, kind of hair, and other common traits.

children of different races

3. The stream of water which turns a water wheel.—The strong, fast current of water that turns a mill is a mill *race.*
—*v. races, raced, racing.* 1. Run in competition.—I will *race* you boys to the corner.
2. Run fast.—Father *raced* the motor of his car. He made it go fast while the car stood still.—The horse *raced* across the pasture.

rac·er (RAY-ser) *n. racers.* A person, animal, or thing that races. An automobile, a horse, a boat, or a person that takes part in a race is a *racer.*

rack (RAK) *n. racks.* 1. A framework that is used as a holder, such as a toothbrush *rack*, a towel *rack*, a *rack* to drain dishes on, a shoe *rack*, or a hat *rack.*

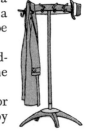

2. A box made of slats.—Grandfather puts the hay for the horses in a feed *rack.*
3. A device used long ago for torturing or hurting people by stretching their limbs.

rack·et (RAK-it) *n. rackets.* 1. A loud, confused noise.—The children made so much *racket* playing circus that Mother didn't hear the bell ring.
2. A bat with a long handle and a flat oval frame laced tightly with strong cord.—Tennis and some other games are played by hitting a ball with a *racket.*
3. A dishonest scheme or plan for getting people's money.

ra·dar (RAY-dahr) *n.* An instrument which uses radio waves for detecting standing or moving objects that can't be seen. *Radar* can determine an object's distance, speed, and direction of travel. It is a valuable aid to sea and air navigation.

ra·di·ant (RAY-dee-ənt) *adj.; radiantly, adv.* Shining; bright; brilliant and joyous.—Sally has a *radiant* smile. Her whole face lights up with joy when she smiles.

ra·di·ate (RAY-dee-ayt) *v. radiates, radiated, radiating.* 1. Send forth rays of. — The radiator *radiates* heat.—The bride's face *radiated* joy.
2. Come forth in rays.—Heat *radiating* from the hot water pipes warmed the garage.
3. Spread out from a central point.—The spokes of a wheel *radiate* from the hub.

ra·di·a·tion (ray-dee-AY-shən) *n.* 1. Sending out and spreading rays, such as those of light, heat, and electricity. — Uncontrolled atomic *radiation* can destroy all life in a wide area.
2. The rays sent out.—Thick walls of lead and concrete protect workers in atomic laboratories from dangerous *radiation.*

ra·di·a·tor (RAY-dee-ay-ter) *n. radiators.* A heater made up of tubes or pipes through which hot water or steam passes. *Radiators* are used to heat houses.

ra·di·o (RAY-dee-oh) *n. radios* and *adj.* 1. A way of sending sounds over a long distance by means of electrical waves, without connecting wires. One instrument, called the "transmitter," receives sounds and sends them out in the form of the waves. Another instrument, called the "receiver," receives the waves and changes them back into sound.
2. A *radio* transmitter.
3. A *radio* receiver.
4. A message sent by radio.
—*v. radio, radioed, radioing.* Send or despatched by radio.—The ship *radioed* a message for help.

ra·di·o·ac·tive (ray-dee-oh-AK-tiv) *adj.* Sending out rays from an atomic nucleus. Uranium and radium are both *radioactive* elements.

rad·ish (RAD-ish) *n. radishes.* A vegetable that grows in the ground like a carrot or a turnip. *Radishes* are round or long, red or white, and are eaten raw. Some *radishes* have a sharp taste.

ra·di·um (RAY-dee-əm) *n.* A highly radioactive metallic element. *Radium* was discovered by Professor and Madame Pierre Curie in 1898. It is used in the treatment of cancer and certain other diseases.

ra·di·us (RAY-dee-əss) *n. radii.* 1. A straight line drawn from the center of a circle or sphere to the outside rim or circumference.
2. The length of this line.—The circle has a two-inch *radius*.
3. Area of a circle with a radius of a certain length.—In looking for the lost child the police searched the area within a *radius* of ten miles from his home.

raf·fle (RAF-əl) *n. raffles.* A way of raising money by selling chances on a prize to many people. The prize is given to the holder of the winning ticket.
—*v. raffles, raffled, raffling.* Sell by selling chances.—We *raffled* a quilt to get money for the playground. We sold it by selling chances on it.

raft (RAFT) *n. rafts.* A platform of boards, logs, etc., fastened together, which float on the water like a boat.

rubber raft   log raft

raft·er (RAF-ter) *n. rafters.* One of the large crosswise beams or timbers that hold up the roof of a building.

rag (RAG) *n. rags.* 1. A piece of used cloth.— Mother often uses *rags* for cleaning.
2. Old, torn clothing.—At midnight, Cinderella's ball gown turned to *rags*.

rage (RAYJ) *n. rages.* 1. Wild anger.—Jack was in a *rage* over the theft of his bicycle.
2. A fashion or fad.—Hair ribbons are all the *rage*. All the girls are wearing them.
—*v. rages, raged, raging.* Act wildly. — The accused prisoner *raged* like a mad person.

rag·ged (RAG-id) *adj.* 1. Torn in pieces. — After the football game, Jack's clothes were all *ragged*.
2. Dressed in ragged clothing.—The tramp was *ragged*.
3. Rough, or not regular.—The rocks along the cliff are sharp and *ragged*.

RAILROADS

Tom Thumb 1829
Rocket 1829
DeWitt Clinton 1831
Best Friend of Charleston 1830

rag·weed (RAG-weed) *n. ragweeds.* A common weed. The fine pollen from its blossoms gives some people hay fever.

raid (RAYD) *n. raids.* 1. A swift attack.—The enemy airplanes made a sudden night *raid* on the city.
2. The policemen made a *raid* on the gambling club. They forced their way in and captured the gamblers.
—*v. raids, raided, raiding.* 1. Make an attack on.—The airplanes *raided* the city.
2. Break into and seize property from.—The burglars *raided* the store.

rail (RAYL) *n. rails.* 1. A slender bar of wood or metal.—Streetcars and trains run on tracks made of metal *rails.*—Some fences are made of wooden *rails.*
2. A bar in a railing.—Baby's crib has *rails* around the sides.
—*v. rails, railed, railing.* Complain or scold bitterly.—From way down the street we could hear the woman *railing* at her husband for his laziness.

rail·ing (RAY-ling) *n. railings.* An enclosure or fence made of rails.—Father put a *railing* around the porch so that the baby would not fall off.

rail·road (RAYL-rohd) *n. railroads.* 1. A track for trains, made of steel rails fastened to wooden ties with spikes.
2. A system of train tracks, trains, stations, and the body of men in charge of them.—Uncle Jim works for the *railroad.*

rail·way (RAYL-way) *n. railways.* 1. A railroad.
2. Any track made of rails for wheels to run on.

rain (RAYN) *n. rains; rainy, adj.* 1. Water which falls from clouds.—Drops of *rain* beat against my face.
2. A fall of rain.—We had a heavy *rain.*
3. A shower of anything falling like rain.—A *rain* of petals came from the apple tree.
—*v. rains, rained, raining.* 1. Fall in drops from the clouds.—It *rained* today.
2. Fall like rain.—Rice and bits of colored paper *rained* on the bride and groom.

rain·bow (RAYN-boh) *n. rainbows.* A large arch or bow of colors which often is seen in the sky opposite the sun during a light rain. It is caused by the sun shining through raindrops.

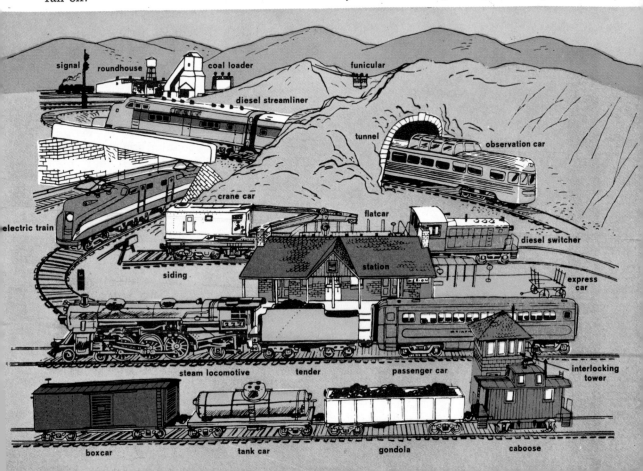

signal   roundhouse   coal loader   funicular   diesel streamliner   tunnel   observation car   crane car   flatcar   diesel switcher   electric train   siding   station   express car   steam locomotive   tender   passenger car   interlocking tower   boxcar   tank car   gondola   caboose

rain·coat (RAYN-koht) *n. raincoats.* A waterproof coat to keep the rain off.—When it rains, Bob wears his *raincoat.*

Japanese raincoat   fisherman's raincoat

fireman's raincoat

rain·drop (RAYN-drahp) *n. raindrops.* One drop of water falling from the clouds.

rain·fall (RAYN-fawl) *n. rainfalls.* 1. A shower of rain.—Today we had a heavy *rainfall.*
2. The total amount of rain that falls in a particular place during a month, year, etc.—The *rainfall* in Oregon is greater than the *rainfall* in Arizona.

rain·storm (RAYN-storm) *n. rainstorms.* A rainfall, sometimes with wind.—On our way home from school we were caught in a *rainstorm.*

raise (RAYZ) *n. raises.* Increase in wages.—Father got a *raise* of twenty dollars a week when he got his promotion.
—*v. raises, raised, raising.* 1. Lift, bring, or put up.—The witness *raised* his right hand.
2. Pick up.—When Tom *raised* the stone, he found a frog under it.
3. Erect or build.—The city *raised* a monument in honor of its soldiers.
4. Breed; bring up. — Grandfather *raises* cows.
5. Grow. — Grandmother *raises* vegetables and flowers.
6. Get together or collect from different places. — The poor family could not *raise* enough money to pay the rent.
7. Bring up for attention.—Bob *raised* the question of buying more books for the school library.
8. Stir up.—The speaker's remarks *raised* excitement in the crowd.
9. Increase; make higher.—The painter has *raised* his price for painting a room.

rai·sin (RAY-zən) *n. raisins.* A special kind of grape that has been dried.—Grandmother puts *raisins* on cookies and in rice pudding.

rake (RAYK) *n. rakes.* A gardening tool with a long handle and a cross rod with comblike teeth in it.

—*v. rakes, raked, raking.* 1. Comb up; gather together.—Sally likes to *rake* the leaves in the yard. She likes to use the rake.
2. Search through thoroughly.—Mary *raked* the contents of the old trunk trying to find a costume to wear.

ral·ly (RAL-ee) *n. rallies.* A large, informal meeting of people to get them enthusiastic about something.—We held a *rally* to raise money for the playground.
—*v. rallies, rallied, rallying.* 1. Start to improve or take a turn for the better.—The sick boy *rallied* after the doctor had cared for him.
2. Get together.—Bob tried to *rally* enough boys for a ball team.
3. Gather in numbers to help.—The townspeople all *rallied* to the scene of the fire.

ram (RAM) *n. rams.* 1. A male sheep.—Some *rams* have horns.
2. A machine for knocking down walls.—The battering *ram* was used in the Middle Ages for besieging castles.
—*v. rams, rammed, ramming.* 1. Strike or crash into.—An auto behind us *rammed* our car.

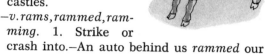

2. Crush or drive down firmly.—The janitor *rammed* the paper into the barrel.

ram·ble (RAM-bəl) *n. rambles.* A stroll or walk for pleasure. — The girls went for a *ramble* in the woods.
—*v. rambles, rambled, rambling.* 1. Wander aimlessly.—We *rambled* about the woods.
2. Talk first of one thing and then another.—The teacher told the children not to *ramble* when they made their two-minute speeches, but to keep to the point.
3. Grow in a wandering, untrained fashion.—Vines *rambled* over the porch.

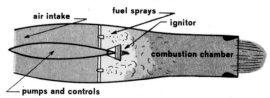

air intake   fuel sprays
ignitor
combustion chamber
pumps and controls

ram-jet (RAM-jet) *ram-jets.* A special type of jet engine used in certain jet-propelled aircraft. The *ram-jet* operates by continuously burning fuel mixed with air that is "rammed" into the engine by the forward motion of the plane.

ramp (RAMP) *n.* ramps. A slanting passage-way joining two places, one of which is higher than the other.—We walked up the *ramp* in the stadium.

ram·page (RAM-payj) *n.* rampages. Violent behavior. — The wild bull kicked down the barn door and broke through the fence in its *rampage*.

ram·part (RAM-pahrt) *n.* ramparts. A broad, high, protecting wall made of earth, some-times with watchtowers on the top.—Francis Scott Key watched the *ramparts* of Fort Mc-Henry to see if the flag was still flying there as he wrote "The Star-Spangled Banner."

ram·shack·le (RAM-shak-əl) *adj.* Shaky; ready to fall apart; rickety.—The *ramshackle* hut was blown down during the storm.

ran (RAN) *v.* One form of the verb *run*.—The child *ran* to his mother.

ranch (RANCH) *n.* ranches. Large farm for raising cattle, sheep, or horses.—The cowboy lived on a *ranch*.

ranch·er (RANCH-er) *n.* ranchers. A man who works on, owns, or runs a ranch or big stock farm.

ran·dom (RAN-dəm) *adj.* Without specific plan or purpose; chance.—My seeing Bill in the store was just a *random* meeting.

—*At random* means haphazardly, or in an un-organized way.—The children ran about *at random*.

rang (RANG) *v.* One form of the verb *ring*.—The teacher *rang* the bell.

range (RAYNJ) *n.* ranges. 1. Row or chain of mountains or hills. — The Rockies are the highest mountain *range* in North America.
2. A stove to cook on.
—Mother has a new electric *range*.
3. Reach.—The gun's *range* is a thousand yards.—Bob was care-ful to stay out of *range* of the angry bear.

4. Number or variety.—The books in the store covered a wide *range* of subjects.
5. Unfenced land where cattle graze, or eat grass.

—*v.* ranges, ranged, ranging. 1. Wander or roam.—In the days of the early settlers, buf-faloes *ranged* the prairies.
2. Extend.—The price of baseballs *ranged* from fifty cents to four dollars.

rang·er (RAYN-jer) *n.* rangers. 1. A person whose duty is to watch over a forest and aid in putting out fires that may start.
2. A member of a group of armed men whose duty is to patrol a certain part of the country.

rank (RANGK) *n.* ranks. 1. A row.—The sol-diers marched in *ranks* of four, side by side.
2. Standing or class.—A sergeant's *rank* is above that of a corporal.

—*v.* ranks, ranked, ranking. 1. Have a certain standing. — A corporal *ranks* lower than a sergeant.
2. List in order.—The students were *ranked* according to their grades.

—*adj.* ranker, rankest. Strong and disagreeable in odor and taste.—Butter and other fats that stand a long time sometimes become *rank*.

ran·sack (RAN-sak) *v.* ransacks, ransacked, ransacking. 1. Search through thoroughly.—Mother *ransacked* the clothes closets, but she couldn't find her green dress.
2. Rob or plunder. — The band of outlaws *ransacked* the town.

ran·som (RAN-səm) *n.* ransoms. Money paid to free a person who has been kidnaped or captured.—The rich man paid a *ransom* of twenty-five thousand dollars to free his son.

—*v.* ransoms, ransomed, ransoming. Pay ran-som for.—The prince offered to *ransom* his men, who were prisoners of the enemy.

rap (RAP) *n.* raps. Light knock.—I heard a *rap* on my window.

—*v.* raps, rapped, rapping. 1. Tap, or hit light-ly and quickly.—On Halloween the children *rapped* on the neighbors' windows.
2. Speak sharply. — The lawyer *rapped* out the questions.

rap·id (RAP-id) *adj.; rapidly, adv.* Fast or quick. — After the race, Bob could feel the *rapid* beating of his heart.

rap·ids (RAP-idz) *n. pl.* A place in a river where the water flows very fast over rocks, but not in a falls.—The boys went through the *rapids* in their canoe.

rap·ture (RAP-cher) *n. raptures.* Great joy and delight.—The family's *rapture* at their son's return was great.

rare (RAIR) *adj. rarer, rarest; rarely, adv.* 1. Seldom to be found.—This piece of china is valuable because it is so *rare.* There are very few of its kind.—The birth of quintuplets is *rare.*
2. Cooked only a short time, so as to be still juicy and pink (of meat).—Mother likes her meat well-done. Father likes it *rare.*

ras·cal (RASS-kəl) *n. rascals.* 1. Mean, wicked, tricky person.—The *rascals* who sold land they did not own were arrested as they tried to leave town.
2. Mischievous or trouble-making child or young person.—Grandmother told us Father was a *rascal* when he was a little boy.

rash (RASH) *n. rashes.* A breaking out of red spots on the skin.—A *rash* may be a sign of measles.
—*adj. rasher, rashest; rashly, adv.* Reckless.—It is *rash* to promise to do more than you are sure you can do.

rasp·ber·ry (RAZ-bair-ee) *n. raspberries* and *adj.* A small, seedy berry that grows on a bush. *Raspberries* are usually red, but may be black, purple, or yellow. — *Raspberry* jam has many little seeds in it.

rat (RAT) *n. rats.* An animal that looks like a

large mouse. *Rats* gnaw with their sharp teeth. *Rats* are pests, and often carry diseases.

rate (RAYT) *n. rates.* 1. Amount; degree. — The plane flew at the *rate* of three hundred miles·an hour. At that speed it could go three hundred miles in one hour.—The *rate* of interest on the loan will be six per cent. You will have to pay six dollars a year for each hundred dollars you borrow.
2. A price.—The theater *rates* are higher for the evening show than for the afternoon show.
3. Rank.—The hotel was first-*rate.*
—*v. rates, rated, rating.* 1. Set a value on.—The real-estate agent *rated* the house at ten thousand dollars.
2. Rank or consider.—Bob is generally *rated* the best student in his class.
—*At any rate* means anyway.—*At any rate,* we reached home before the rain started.

rath·er (RATH-er) *adv.* 1. More gladly; with more willingness.—I'd *rather* travel by train than by muleback.
2. Somewhat. — Mother is *rather* worried about Baby's cold.
3. Instead.—The bear is not dead; *rather,* it is asleep.
—*Rather than* means instead of.—The road runs northeast, *rather than* directly north.

rat·i·fy (RAT-ə-fy) *v. ratifies, ratified, ratifying.* Approve formally.—The Senate is expected to *ratify* the new treaty.

ra·tio (RAY-shoh *or* RAY-shee-oh) *n. ratios.* Numerical relation; proportion.—The boys in the class outnumbered the girls in the *ratio* of three to two. This means that for every three boys in the class there were two girls.

ra·tion (RASH-ən *or* RAY-shən) *n. rations.* 1. The amount of a certain article each person may have.—During the war doctors were allowed larger *rations* of gasoline than were given to men who drove their cars only for pleasure.
2. A certain amount of food allowed for each day.—The soldiers were given *rations* of chocolate for the march.
—*v. rations, rationed, rationing.* Give out (a supply that is limited) in fair amounts to each person.—Sugar, coffee, and gasoline are some of the articles that are *rationed* in most countries during wartime.

ra·tion·al (RASH-ən-əl) *adj.; rationally, adv.* 1. Able to think clearly and sensibly.—Father is a *rational* man.
2. Reasonable; intelligent; sensible. — John offered a *rational* excuse for his absence.
3. Based on reason; of reason. — That is a foolish argument, not a *rational* one.

rat·tle (RAT-l) *n. rattles.* 1. The sound of something shaking.—We heard the *rattle* of the screen door during the storm.
2. A toy that makes a noise when shaken.—Baby likes to throw her *rattle* out of the carriage.
3. Organ at the end of a rattlesnake's tail.
—*v. rattles, rattled, rattling.* Make the sound of something loose being shaken. — The wind makes the windows *rattle.*

rat·tle·snake (RAT-l-snayk) *n. rattlesnakes.* A kind of poisonous snake. Its tail has rattles, or loose rings, that make a rattling noise when the tail moves.

rav·el (RAV-əl) *v. ravels, raveled* or *ravelled, raveling* or *ravelling*. Separate or become separated into threads or yarn.—Mother hemmed the towel so that it would not *ravel*.

ra·ven (RAY-vən) *n. ravens*. A very shiny black bird somewhat like the crow, but larger.
—*adj*. Black and shiny. —Snow White had white skin, red lips, and *raven* hair.

ra·vine (rə-VEEN) *n. ravines*. A deep, narrow hollow made by running water. — We stood on the cliff and looked down into a *ravine*.

raw (RAW) *adj. rawer, rawest*. 1. Not cooked. —Cabbage can be eaten *raw*.
2. Not ready to use (of materials).—Cotton as it comes from the fields and logs as they come from the woods are *raw* materials.
3. Cold and wet (of weather).—A *raw* March wind was blowing.
4. Not trained, or not experienced.—Many *raw* sailors become seasick.
5. Sore from having the skin scraped off.—The *raw* sore on Mary's knee was caused by her falling on the sidewalk.

ray (RAY) *n. rays*. 1. Narrow beam, as of light.—A *ray* of light shone through the hole.
2. A faint sign (of hope).—Jack can always see a *ray* of hope when things look bad.
3. One of many lines extending from a center in all directions.— Sally's picture of the sun was a big circle with *rays* around it.
4. A kind of flat fish.

ray·on (RAY-ahn) *n*. A smooth, soft cloth woven of threads made from wood. *Rayon* looks something like silk.

raze (RAYZ) *v. razes, razed, razing*. Destroy or tear down.—The workmen *razed* the old building. They tore it down to the ground.

ra·zor (RAY-zer) *n. razors*. A sharp-bladed tool used by men for shaving. Some *razors* have folding blades; some are of a safety type in which the blade is partly covered; others have blades operated by electricity.

safety razor electric razor

straight razor

reach (REECH) *n. reaches*. 1. A stretching of the arms.—Baby made a sudden *reach* for Father's hat.
2. Range.—The frightened boy kept out of *reach* of the growling dog.
3. A long expanse, especially of water.—The steamboat pilot entered the long *reach* of rapids with caution.
—*v. reaches, reached, reaching*. 1. Thrust or push out (one's hands or arms). — Baby *reached* to Mother to be taken out of her crib.
2. Extend.—A branch of the tree *reached* to the window.
3. Get to or arrive at.—We *reached* school.
4. Impress or have influence on.—The teacher tried to *reach* Bill by appealing to his sense of fair play.

re·act (ree-AKT) *v. reacts, reacted, reacting*.
1. Act in response to something. — John *reacted* strangely to his election as class president. He didn't seem happy at all.
2. Act automatically in response to something.—When you touch a hot iron, you *react* by pulling your hand back.
3. Cause (something or someone) to act in response. — Acid *reacts* on litmus paper by turning it red.
—*reaction, n. reactions*.

read (REED) *v. reads, read, reading*. 1. Look at and get meaning from (something written or printed).—You are now *reading* this dictionary.—We may *read* by saying words aloud or by thinking of them silently.—We *read* music by singing or playing an instrument while looking at the notes.
2. Understand or get the meaning of.—When we understand a map, we can *read* it.—When we understand a speedometer on a car, we can *read* it.
3. Predict, or tell beforehand.—The weather man *reads* the weather. He tells beforehand what kind of weather we will have.
4. Show or indicate.—The gas meter *reads* ten units of gas used. — The speedometer *reads* twenty-five miles per hour.
5. Put a meaning which may not be true (into something).—He *read* jealousy into her letter, but he was mistaken. She was not jealous at all.

read (RED) *v*. One form of the verb *read*.—Have you *read* "Robinson Crusoe"?

read·er (REED-er) *n. readers*. 1. Person who reads.—Mary is quite a good *reader*. She understands books and stories that she reads.
2. A book used to teach reading.—Mary reads from the sixth-grade *reader*.

read·i·ness (RED-ee-nəss) *n.* 1. Condition of being ready or prepared.—Everything is in *readiness* for the picnic.
2. Willing promptness.—The man's *readiness* to work caused his boss to raise his salary.

read·ing (REED-ing) *n.* The act of seeing and getting the meaning of something written or printed.—*Reading* is easy for Mary, so she reads many books.

read·y (RED-ee) *adj.* readier, readiest; readily, adv. 1. Prepared. — When Father comes home, he likes to find his dinner *ready*.
2. Willing.—We are *ready* to take less money for the bicycle now that the tires are worn.
3. Quick.—Jack always has a *ready* answer in arithmetic class.
4. Right at hand, or to be had right away.—The hospital had a *ready* supply of bandages.

re·al (REE-əl) *adj.*; really, adv. Actual and true; not false, imaginary, or artificial.—Sally likes fairy tales. Mary likes stories about *real* people.
—*Real estate* is land and the buildings on it.

re·al·is·tic (ree-ə-LISS-tik) *adj.*; realistically, adv. 1. Looking very real.—The artist drew a *realistic* portrait of the man.
2. Down to earth; concerned with matters as they really are. — Harry is *realistic*. He knows what he can do and plans it well. He does not try to do what is beyond him.

re·al·i·ty (ree-AL-ə-tee) *n.* realities. What is; the truth; the way things actually are.—Mary and Jack like to tease each other, but in *reality* they are very fond of each other.

re·al·ize (REE-ə-lyz) *v.* realizes, realized, realizing. 1. Understand or know; be aware of.—Jack doesn't *realize* that his remarks sometimes hurt people's feelings.
2. Achieve, or make come true or happen.—Grandmother finally *realized* her wish when she moved back to the country.
3. Get as profit from the sale of something.—Bob *realized* five dollars on the sale of his bicycle. He sold it for five dollars more than he paid for it.

realm (RELM) *n.* realms. 1. A kingdom. — The holiday was celebrated throughout the *realm*.
2. Any region.—This story is in the *realm* of fantasy.

reap (REEP) *v.* reaps, reaped, reaping. 1. Cut and gather.—The farmer *reaps* his grain in the summer.
2. Obtain or get in return.—Give happiness to others and you will *reap* happiness.

reap·er (REEP-er) *n.* reapers. A machine for cutting grain, or a person who cuts grain.

re·ap·pear (ree-ə-PIR) *v.* reappears, reappeared, reappearing. Appear or show again; come to be seen again.—The sun went behind a cloud, and then it *reappeared*.

rear (RIR) *n.* The back or end part.—The back yard is at the *rear* of the house.—John was at the *rear* of the parade.
—*v.* rears, reared, rearing. 1. Rise.—The horse *reared* up on his hind legs.
2. Raise or bring up.—Grandmother *reared* three children.
—*adj.* Back; hind.—The *rear* wheels of the car got stuck in the soft earth.

re·ar·range (ree-ə-RAYNJ) *v.* rearranges, rearranged, rearranging. Arrange again; put in different positions. — Mother likes to *rearrange* the furniture.

rea·son (REE-zən) *n.* reasons. 1. Cause of a happening; explanation. — Can you give a *reason* for believing that the earth is round?
2. Thought or good sense.—The angry man did not use *reason* when he hit the policeman.
3. Sanity or senses.—The old miser lost his *reason* when his money was stolen.
4. Power or ability to think.—You must use your *reason* to solve problems in arithmetic.
—*v.* reasons, reasoned, reasoning. 1. Think through or solve.—Mary tried to *reason* out the problem in arithmetic.
2. Argue, or point out the other side of a question.—It is hard to *reason* with Jack when he is angry.

rea·son·a·ble (REEZ-nə-bəl) *adj.*; reasonably, adv. 1. Fair and just.—Our teacher is *reasonable* in the amount of homework she assigns us. — Mary's wish for a new dress seems *reasonable*, since she has outgrown several of her others.
2. Logical; sensible.—The answer to the problem seems too large a figure to be *reasonable*.
3. Moderate.—The price of strawberries is *reasonable* in June. They are not expensive.

reb·el (REB-əl) *n.* rebels. A person who fights against lawful control.—The *rebels* tried to overthrow the government.

re·bel (ri-BEL) *v.* rebels, rebelled, rebelling. Fight against lawful control. — Prisoners sometimes *rebel* and try to escape.

re·bel·lion (ri-BEL-yən) *n. rebellions.* 1. A rising up of people against the government or other authorities.–The discontented citizens started a *rebellion*.

2. Resistance to any authority or restriction. –John's *rebellion* against wearing a tie and jacket to class ended when he found that all the boys wore them.

re·bound (ri-BOWND) *v. rebounds, rebounded, rebounding.* Spring or bounce back. –The ball hit the wall and *rebounded*.

re·call (ri-KAWL) *v. recalls, recalled, recalling.* 1. Remember.–Bill couldn't *recall* which day he was absent.

2. Call back.–The messenger was *recalled*. He was told to come back.

3. Remove (an elected official) from office by a vote.–The mayor was *recalled* for taking bribes.

re·cede (ri-SEED) *v. recedes, receded, receding.* Move or go back; withdraw; slant backward.–The tide is *receding*.–An ape's forehead *recedes* more than a man's.

re·ceipt (ri-SEET) *n. receipts.* 1. A written statement which says that one has received something. — When the insured package came, Mother signed a *receipt* for it.

2. (In the plural) Money received. — The *receipts* from the flower show will be used to buy library books.

3. Act of receiving.–I wrote to Grandmother on *receipt* of her letter.

–v. receipts, receipted, receipting. Mark "Paid." –Mother asked the milkman to *receipt* his bill when she paid him.

re·ceive (ri-SEEV) *v. receives, received, receiving.* 1. Get, or have given or brought to one; accept (something offered).–We *receive* an allowance from Father each week.–We *received* a letter every week from Jack while he was at camp.–Baby *received* a bad bump when she fell.

2. Greet or welcome.–Sally likes to *receive* Mother's guests. She greets them at the door and invites them in.

3. Hold.–We left a box on the porch to *receive* the Christmas packages.

4. Have as an experience.–Mary is *receiving* a good musical education.

5. Change electric waves into sounds or pictures. — This television set doesn't *receive* Channel 8.

re·ceiv·er (ri-SEE-ver) *n. receivers.* 1. A person who gets or accepts.–Bob gave Mother a present for her birthday. Bob was the giver of the present, and Mother was the *receiver*.

2. A thing that receives. — We talk on the telephone through the mouthpiece, and we listen to or receive the message through the *receiver*.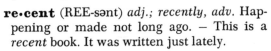

3. A container, or something else that is used to put things in.

re·cent (REE-sənt) *adj.; recently, adv.* Happening or made not long ago. — This is a *recent* book. It was written just lately.

re·cep·ta·cle (ri-SEP-tə-kəl) *n. receptacles.* Anything which serves to hold something. –Vases, boxes, and baskets are *receptacles*.

re·cep·tion (ri-SEP-shən) *n. receptions.* 1. A party at which people are greeted by an honored guest.–After the wedding, there was a *reception*. The bride and groom received many friends.

2. Way of receiving.–They gave me a friendly *reception*. They received me in a friendly way.

3. Condition of receiving.–The *reception* on the radio is poor during a thunderstorm.

re·cep·tion·ist (ri-SEP-shən-ist) *n. receptionists.* A person who is hired by a business firm to receive visitors and clients, usually in an outer office.

re·cess (ri-SESS *or* REE-sess) *n. recesses.* 1. A nook, or hollow space.–Mother put Uncle Jim's trunk in a *recess* in the bedroom wall.

2. A short time during which work stops.–In some schools children have a *recess* in the morning and in the afternoon.

–(ri-SESS) v. recesses, recessed, recessing. Begin a break, recess, or holiday.–School *recessed* in June for the summer vacation.

rec·i·pe (RESS-ə-pee) *n. recipes.* A set of directions telling how a thing, especially a food dish, should be prepared. — This cake was made from a new *recipe*.

re·cit·al (ri-SYT-l) *n. recitals.* 1. A musical entertainment at which one or more persons play, sing, or dance.

2. An account or tale.–The teacher's *recital* of his travels was exciting to the children.

re·cite (ri-SYT) *v. recites, recited, reciting.* 1. Repeat or say aloud from memory.–The children can *recite* many poems.

2. Answer the teacher's questions about a lesson.–Bill, Mary, and John *recited* in social studies class today.

–recitation, n. recitations.

reck·less (REK-ləss) *adj.; recklessly, adv.; recklessness, n.* Very, very careless.—Do not be *reckless* while crossing the street. Do not risk being hurt.

reck·on (REK-ən) *v. reckons, reckoned, reckoning.* 1. Count up. — Jack is *reckoning* the weeks before school is out.
2. Judge or regard.—Mr. Smith is *reckoned* the best man for the job. He is thought to be the best.
—*reckoning, n. reckonings.*

re·cline (ri-KLYN) *v. reclines, reclined, reclining.* Lean back.—I like to *recline* in an easy chair and read.

rec·og·ni·tion (rek-əg-NISH-ən) *n.* 1. Being known or identified. — The books were burned beyond *recognition.*
2. Favorable attention.—The soldier received *recognition* for his bravery. He received many honors in *recognition* of his bravery.
3. Acknowledgment. — The government demanded *recognition* of its treaty rights in the use of the river.

rec·og·nize (REK-əg-nyz) *v. recognizes, recognized, recognizing.* 1. Know; identify from familiarity. — Mother didn't *recognize* my voice over the telephone.
2. Appreciate.—The teacher *recognized* the children's efforts to get their work done.
3. Admit.—Jack *recognized* it was his duty to stay home and help his mother.
4. Show favorable attention as a reward.— The country *recognized* the soldier's bravery by awarding him a medal.

rec·ol·lect (rek-ə-LEKT) *v. recollects, recollected, recollecting.* Remember.—Bob doesn't *recollect* who borrowed the book.
—*recollection, n. recollections.*

rec·om·mend (rek-ə-MEND) *v. recommends, recommended, recommending.* 1. Show favor for.—We *recommend* Mary to act as leader of her group.
2. Suggest or advise. — The doctor *recommended* that Father stay in bed several days. He advised him to do so.

rec·om·men·da·tion (rek-ə-men-DAY-shən) *n. recommendations.* A statement of praise for, or advice about, a person's work, behavior, ability, or the like. — When Jack wanted to get a job selling papers, he asked his teacher for a *recommendation.*

rec·on·cile (REK-ən-syl) *v. reconciles, reconciled, reconciling.* 1. Make up a quarrel or disagreement.—Jack and Mary had a quarrel, but they were *reconciled.*
2. Make content; satisfy.—Ted was *reconciled* to staying at home when he found that Bert was staying home, too.
3. Make agree or correspond.—The newspaper article is all mixed up. It is impossible to *reconcile* it with the facts we know.

re·con·nais·sance (ri-KAHN-ə-sənss) *n. reconnaissances.* The inspecting, observing, or examining of an area, especially for military purposes.—The plane took off on a flight of *reconnaissance.* — I will do some *reconnaissance* on possible picnic spots.

rec·ord (REK-erd) *n. records.* 1. Something written to be kept.—Bob made a *record* of all the things that happened while the teacher was away.
2. A grooved disc that gives back sounds recorded on it. — Mary played a *record* on the phonograph.

3. The things known about a person or thing. — The baseball team's *record* is five games lost and ten won.
4. The best performance.—When a racer goes faster than any other has yet gone, he breaks a *record*, and sets a new *record.*

re·cord (ri-KORD) *v. records, recorded, recording.* 1. Write down in a form that will last.—The teacher will *record* the names of the children in her class. She will write them down in her book to use later.
2. Put in a form that can be saved.—We *record* music on wax discs, records, or on tape, so that it can be played back and heard later on.
3. Show or indicate.—A speedometer on a car *records* the number of miles the car has traveled.

re·cov·er (ri-KUV-er) *v. recovers, recovered, recovering.* 1. Get back again.—Bobby *recovered* his lost dog.
2. Get well.—It will take a long time for the sick man to *recover.*
—*recovery, n. recoveries.*

re-cov·er (ree-KUV-er) *v. re-covers, re-covered, re-covering.* Put a new cover on.—We had a chair *re-covered.* We had new cloth put over it.

rec·re·a·tion (rek-ree-AY-shən) *n.* Any amusement or pastime; any game; relaxation.—Golf, tennis, strolling, swimming, and reading are all forms of *recreation.*

rec·tan·gle (REK-tang-gəl) *n. rectangles.* A plane (flat) figure that has four sides and four perfectly square corners or angles. A square is a *rectangle* with equal sides.

rec·tor (REK-ter) *n. rectors.* A clergyman in charge of a parish or church.—The *rector* is trying to raise funds for his church.

re·cu·per·ate (ri-KOO-pə-rayt *or* ri-KYOOP-er-ayt) *v. recuperates, recuperated, recuperating.* 1. Get well from an illness; recover.—Tom is *recuperating* from the measles.
2. Recover from financial losses.—The business has fully *recuperated.* Now it is earning money.
—*recuperation, n. recuperations.*

red (RED) *n. reds* and *adj.* The color of blood.
—The colors of the American flag are *red,* white, and blue.
—*Reddish* means somewhat red.

Red Cross (RED KRAWSS). A world-wide organization whose purpose is to help people everywhere in time of disaster or misfortune. It cares for the sick and wounded in time of war. It gives help to those who need it during and after floods, fires, earthquakes, and other disasters. The sign of the *Red Cross* is a red cross on a white background.

re·deem (ri-DEEM) *v. redeems, redeemed, redeeming.* 1. Get back by paying an amount owed.—The man *redeemed* his watch at the pawnshop after he found a job.
2. Make good or fulfill.—Do not make a promise you are not sure you can *redeem.*
3. Make up for.—Bill's generosity does much to *redeem* his quick temper.
4. Do well after starting badly.—After walking the first three batters, Hank *redeemed* himself by striking out the next three.

re·duce (ri-DOOSS *or* -DYOOSS) *v. reduces, reduced, reducing.* 1. Make smaller or lower.
—Letting some air out of a toy balloon *reduces* its size.—Charging less money for shoes *reduces* their price.
2. Change to a different form.—A fire soon *reduced* the box to ashes.
3. Bring to a worse condition.—Mary was *reduced* to tears by Jack's teasing.—The family was *reduced* to poverty.
4. Grow thinner by dieting. — Some people often won't eat butter and potatoes because they are trying to *reduce.*

5. Change numbers to their simplest form without altering their value.—You can *reduce* 8/10 by changing it to 4/5.

re·duc·tion (ri-DUK-shən) *n. reductions.* 1. Cutting down on something; making it less.
—After a *reduction* was made in the price of the bicycle, Tim was able to buy it.
2. The amount which is taken off a thing.—The price was lowered from twenty to sixteen dollars. The *reduction* was four dollars.

red-winged black·bird (RED-wingd BLAK-berd) *red-winged blackbirds.* An American blackbird that has a patch of red feathers on each wing.

red·wood (RED-wuhd) *n. redwoods.* A very large, tall tree that grows in California. Its wood is brownish-red. It belongs to the pine-tree family.

reed (REED) *n. reeds; reedy, adj.* 1. A kind of tall grass that grows in marshy places. It has hollow, jointed stems.
2. A strip or cylinder of wood, metal, or other material in the mouthpieces of some wind instruments. Clarinets, English horns, saxophones, and oboes are played with *reeds.*

reef (REEF) *n. reefs.* A ridge of rocks or sand that comes to or nearly to the top of the water in the sea.

reel (REEL) *n. reels.* 1. A very lively and once-popular dance.
2. A big wide-edged wheel or spool that is set into a frame so that it will turn easily.—A fisherman winds his fishing line on a *reel.*
3. A length of something that is wound on a reel.—The men used a huge *reel* of wire.
—*v. reels, reeled, reeling.* 1. Wind on a reel.—The fisherman *reeled* in his fishing line.
2. Recite or say quickly and easily.—Jack can *reel* off his multiplication tables.
3. Whirl, or go round and round.—Bert was so sleepy that the room seemed to *reel.*
4. Sway, or move around dizzily.—The prize fighter *reeled* when he was hit.

re·en·ter (ree-EN-ter) *v. re-enters, re-entered, re-entering.* Go back in.–Mary went out and found it was raining. So she *re-entered* the house to get her umbrella.

re·fer (ri-FER) *v. refers, referred, referring.*
1. Turn to.–We *refer* to the table of contents in a book to find out on which page a story can be found.
2. Send or direct.–The teacher *referred* us to the library for other books on North and South America.
3. Speak about; call attention to.–Our teacher often *refers* to the dangers of crossing the street when the light is red.

ref·er·ee (ref-ə-REE) *n. referees.* 1. A person who acts as a judge of plays made in games and sports such as basketball, football, prize fights, and the like.–The *referee* in a baseball game is called an umpire.–The *referee* in the basketball game blows a whistle every time the ball goes out of bounds.
2. Person who decides who is right and who is wrong.–The boys asked their father to act as *referee* of the argument.
–*v. referees, refereed, refereeing.* Act as referee.–Bob *refereed* the hockey game.

ref·er·ence (REF-er-ənss) *n. references.* 1. A mention, or calling of attention.–The doctor made *reference* to the importance of good teeth. He spoke about it.
2. A person able to describe one's ability or character.–Bob gave his teacher as a *reference* in applying for the job.
3. A statement describing one's abilities or character. – Bob got a *reference* from his teacher.
4. Information to which one can refer, such as in a book or encyclopedia.–A dictionary is a work of *reference.*
5. Regard.–I am writing him in *reference* to the house he has for sale.

re·fill (REE-fil) *n. refills.* Something to replace a filling that is used up.–Grandfather gave Tom a *refill* for his loose-leaf notebook. He gave him a package of new sheets of paper to refill it.
–(ree-FIL) *v. refills, refilled, refilling.* Fill again.–Mary's fountain pen ran dry, and she had to *refill* it.

re·fine (ri-FYN) *v. refines, refined, refining.*
1. Make pure or fit for some special use.–Cotton, sugar, rubber, and other raw materials are *refined* before they are used.
2. Mother is *refined.* She is educated and kind, and has good manners.
–*refinement, n. refinements.*

re·flect (ri-FLEKT) *v. reflects, reflected, reflecting.* 1. Give back (light, heat, etc.)–A mirror *reflects* light. Polished metal *reflects* heat.–When you look into still water or into a mirror, your image, or likeness, is *reflected.*

2. Throw.–Jane's politeness *reflects* credit on her parents.
3. Show the effect of; be a result of.–Jane's politeness *reflects* her parents' good training.
4. Think over carefully.–One should *reflect* on the things he reads.
–*Reflect on* also means throw blame on.–Bad behavior *reflects on* one's training. It brings back blame to one's home or school. It shows that one has had poor training or teaching.
–*reflection, n. reflections.*

re·flec·tor (ri-FLEK-ter) *n. reflectors.* That which reflects light, heat, or the like.–Automobile lights have *reflectors* to throw out the light in one direction.

re·for·est·a·tion (ree-for-iss-TAY-shən *or* ree-fahr-iss-TAY-shən) *n.* Replanting with trees. If we did not have programs of *reforestation,* we would run out of lumber, and many parts of the nation would turn into dust bowls. Trees protect areas from wind, and their roots keep the soil from washing or blowing away.

re·form (ri-FORM) *v. reforms, reformed, reforming.* 1. Improve by doing away with faults; make better.–The teacher *reformed* the mischievous pupil with kindness and understanding.–The candidate promised to *reform* the town government.
2. Correct one's own bad habits; change oneself for the better.–The judge freed the prisoner when he promised to *reform.*
–*reform, n. reforms.*

Ref·or·ma·tion (ref-er-MAY-shən) *n.* The religious movement in the sixteenth century which brought about the formation of the Protestant churches. Until then Christianity was represented in Europe only by the Catholic Church.

re·form·a·to·ry (ri-FORM-ə-tor-ee) *n. reformatories.* An institution to which young lawbreakers are sent to learn to be good citizens.—The young offender is learning a trade at the *reformatory.*

re·fract (ri-FRAKT) *v. refracts, refracted, refracting.* Bend the rays of (light, heat, etc.), causing a change in direction.—By *refracting* light, lenses of different shapes reduce or enlarge an image.

re·frain (ri-FRAYN) *n. refrains.* Chorus.—The song had a merry *refrain.*
—*v. refrains, refrained, refraining.* Keep oneself (from doing something).—Jack cannot *refrain* from laughing when Mary tries to act very grown-up.

re·fresh (ri-FRESH) *v. refreshes, refreshed, refreshing.* Make fresh again.—A swim in the lake *refreshes* one on a hot day.—Rain on a hot day *refreshes* the air.—Before the test Bob *refreshed* his memory by studying.

re·fresh·ment (ri-FRESH-mənt) *n. refreshments.* Food and drink. — Cocoa and sandwiches were the *refreshments* served at the party.

re·frig·er·ate (ri-FRIJ-ə-rayt) *v. refrigerates, refrigerated, refrigerating.* Make or keep cold.—Mother is *refrigerating* the lemonade.
—*refrigeration, n.*

re·frig·er·a·tor (ri-FRIJ-ə-ray-ter) *n. refrigerators.* A box or room for keeping foods cold. Ice is used in some boxes. Others have freezing units in them which are run by electricity or gas.

ref·uge (REF-yooj) *n. refuges.* 1. A place that is safe or protected; a shelter.—The town has a *refuge* for stray animals.
2. Protection from danger; shelter, especially from exposure to the weather. — The fleeing man is seeking *refuge.*—Never take *refuge* under a tree during a thunderstorm. Lightning may strike the tree.

ref·u·gee (REF-yuh-jee) *n. refugees.* A person who is seeking safety and protection, usually by fleeing from one country to another.—Many Jewish *refugees* came to the United States from Germany to escape persecution by the Nazi government.

re·fund (REE-fund) *n. refunds.* A sum paid back.—The store gave Mother a *refund* on the soiled dress.
—(ri-FUND) *v. refunds, refunded, refunding.* Give back.—Mother returned the soiled dress to the store and they *refunded* her money.

ref·use (REF-yooss *or* -yooz) *n.* Garbage, trash, or other waste.—After the picnic, we put the *refuse* in a trash can.

re·fuse (ri-FYOOZ) *v. refuses, refused, refusing.* Decline, or say no.—Mary *refused* to go with us, because she didn't want to walk so far.—When the hungry man asked for a dime, Father couldn't *refuse.*
—*refusal, n. refusals.*

re·gain (ri-GAYN) *v. regains, regained, regaining.* 1. Get back.—Father has *regained* his health.
2. Get back to.—The swimmers *regained* the shore just before the storm.

re·gal (REE-gəl) *adj.; regally, adv.* 1. Of royalty; of a king or queen; royal.—The *regal* procession moved slowly through the church.
2. Splendid; good enough for a king.—The rich man lived in a *regal* manner.

re·gard (ri-GAHRD) *n. regards.* 1. Respect or consideration. — Jack usually has *regard* for the rights of other people.
2. (In the plural) Good wishes.—The teacher sent mother her best *regards.*
3. A look.—The judge fixed the prisoner with a steady, earnest *regard.*
—*v. regards, regarded, regarding.* 1. Look at.—The judge *regarded* the prisoner sternly.
2. Believe to be; consider.—Bob is *regarded* as the best player on the team.
3. Think well of.—We *regard* the new mayor very highly.
—*In regard to* means about or concerning.—We received a letter *in regard to* the lost purse. The letter asked what color the purse was.

re·gat·ta (ri-GAT-ə *or* ri-GAHT-ə) *n. regattas.* A boat race, or a series of boat races (for sailboats, yachts, etc.). — The international *regatta* is a colorful event.

re·gime (rə-ZHEEM) *n. regimes.* 1. A system of government or management.—After the revolution a new *regime* was established.
2. A definite method or plan of living; a system of doing things.—The athlete's *regime* includes a morning hike and an hour more of exercise.

reg·i·ment (REJ-ə-mənt) *n. regiments.* An organized group of soldiers usually commanded by a colonel.
—*v. regiments, regimented, regimenting.* Put (persons) under strict control.—The citizens did not want to be *regimented* in any way by the government.

re·gion (REE-jən) *n. regions.* 1. Section or part of a country; part of the world.—Eskimos live in a cold *region.*
2. Part (of the body).—The ball hit Bob in the *region* of the stomach.
3. Any area.—Astronomers study distant *regions* of the sky.

reg·is·ter (REJ-iss-ter) *n. registers.* 1. A list of people's names kept for some particular purpose.—The school keeps a *register* of the names of its pupils.
2. A screened or grilled opening through which heated or cooled air comes. — Hot air comes into the room from the furnace through a *register.*
3. Range.—The *register* of one's voice is from the lowest note he can sing to the highest one he can sing.—Musical instruments have *registers,* too.
4. Something which makes a record.—The clerk rang up the price on the cash *register.*
—*v. registers, registered, registering.* 1. Have one's name recorded or put on a list.—On the first day of school, forty children *registered.*
2. Show or indicate.—Speedometers *register* the speed at which a car is going.
3. Record. — Father received a letter which had been *registered.* The postmaster had made a record to show that it had passed through the post office and had been delivered.—Mother's and Father's marriage was *registered* at the village church.
4. Express; show. — A good actor must be able to *register* joy, sorrow, fear, and many other feelings by the look on his face.

re·gret (ri-GRET) *n. regrets.* 1. Sorrow; the wish that things could be or could have been otherwise.—It was with much *regret* that Bob parted with his bicycle.

2. (In the plural) A message saying that one is sorry one cannot accept an invitation.—Mary couldn't go to the party; so she sent her *regrets.*
—*v. regrets, regretted, regretting.* Feel sorry.—I *regret* that I lost my dog.

reg·u·lar (REG-yə-ler) *n. regulars.* One who is not a substitute.—Bob is a *regular* on the ball team. He always plays.
—*adj.; regularly, adv.* 1. Even.—The shore around the lake is quite *regular.*—The teeth of the comb are *regular.* They are all the same in size and spacing.
2. Usual or customary.—The *regular* Labor Day holiday comes on the first Monday in September. It comes on the same day again and again.—The *regular* place to store a car is in a garage.
3. Belonging at all times.—Uncle Dave is a *regular* soldier in the army.
4. Usually done in a certain way and in a certain order.—Father is a man of *regular* habits. He does the same things every day at about the same time and in about the same way.
5. Real or complete.—Jack and Mary make a *regular* game of their homework.

reg·u·late (REG-yə-layt) *v. regulates, regulated, regulating.* 1. Control.—The faucet *regulates* the water that comes from it.—The thermostat *regulates* the oil burner so that the house is kept at the desired temperature.
2. Adjust the speed of.—The jeweler *regulated* my watch. He made it keep good time.
3. Organize; adjust. — Mother *regulates* her schedule so that all her work is done by the time Father gets home.
—*regulation, n. regulations.*

re·hearse (ri-HERSS) *v. rehearses, rehearsed, rehearsing.* Practice.—The actors *rehearsed* their parts for the play.
—*rehearsal, n. rehearsals.*

reign (RAYN) *n. reigns.* The length of time one ruler rules a country.—England was prosperous during the *reign* of Queen Elizabeth I.
—*v. reigns, reigned, reigning.* Rule.—The king *reigned* over his people.

rein (RAYN) *n. reins.* 1. A long strip of leather fastened to the part of a horse's bridle that goes through his mouth. A *rein* is used to guide the horse. Pull on the right *rein*  and the horse will turn to the right.

2. Control.—During Mother's absence, Grandmother took over the *reins* of the household. She managed the house.

—*v.* reins, reined, reining. 1. Pull up the reins of.—She *reined* in her horse so that he halted. 2. Restrain; check.—I *reined* in my temper as well as I could.

rein·deer (RAYN-dir) *n. sing.* and *pl.* A kind of deer with large horns or antlers. *Reindeer* live in the North, where it is cold.

re·in·force (ree-in-FORSS) *v.* reinforces, reinforced, reinforcing. Make stronger.—Mother *reinforced* the elbow of Bob's sweater by sewing an extra piece of cloth on it. — The team was *reinforced* with many new players.

re·ject (ri-JEKT) *v.* rejects, rejected, rejecting. 1. Refuse to take.—The teacher *rejected* Bill's paper because it wasn't neat. 2. Throw away or discard.—Mother *rejected* all the buns that were burned. 3. Refuse to consider.—The governor *rejected* the prisoner's plea for pardon. —*rejection, n.* rejections.

re·joice (ri-JOISS) *v.* rejoices, rejoiced, rejoicing. Feel glad, or feel joyful.—We will *rejoice* when the baby is well again.

re·lapse (ri-LAPSS) *v.* relapses, relapsed, relapsing. Slip back into a former, and usually worse, condition or habit.—The sick man *relapsed* into unconsciousness after having been conscious for two hours.

re·late (ri-LAYT) *v.* relates, related, relating. 1. Tell.—Grandfather *related* the story of his first fishing trip. 2. Have a relation (to).—Shoes *relate* to feet. 3. Connect, or show the relations between.—The teacher asked each of us to write a composition *relating* the French and American revolutions.

re·lat·ed (ri-LAY-tid) *adj.* 1. Belonging to the same family.—Brothers are *related*. They belong to the same family. 2. Connected.—Several *related* events led to John's lateness.

re·la·tion (ri-LAY-shən) *n.* relations. 1. A telling.—The captain's *relation* of the storm at sea was thrilling.

2. Connection.—The *relation* between bread and meat is that they are foods. 3. Members of a family.—Parents, sisters, and brothers are some of one's *relations*. 4. (Often used in the plural) Dealing; condition of friendliness; day-to-day association. —My *relations* with Alice are not very good just now. We are not very friendly.—The Secretary of State conducts our foreign *relations*. He looks after the United States' association with other countries.

re·la·tion·ship (ri-LAY-shən-ship) *n.* relationships. 1. The state of being related; connection.—The doctor explained the *relationship* between germs and disease. 2. Family tie.—What is your *relationship* to Sally? I am her sister.

rel·a·tive (REL-ə-tiv) *n.* relatives. Person who is related to another; one who belongs to the same family.—Father, mother, aunts, uncles, brothers, sisters, and the like are *relatives*. They belong to one family. —*adj.;* relatively, *adv.* 1. Related.—Keep your comments *relative* to what we discussed. 2. Compared; comparative. — We discussed the *relative* advantages of the two plans. 3. Depending for its meaning on a standard. —Tom told Father that he was old. Father said, "That's *relative*. Grandfather thinks that I am young."

re·lax (ri-LAKS) *v.* relaxes, relaxed, relaxing. 1. Become loose or less tense.—When you sleep, your muscles *relax*. 2. Make less rigid or strict.—During hot weather, the rules in school are *relaxed*. We can do things that we can't do at other times.

re·lay (REE-lay) *n.* relays. 1. A fresh replacement.—A *relay* of fire fighters relieved those who had been fighting the fire all night. 2. A race in which a runner carries something, runs a certain distance, and hands the thing he is carrying to another runner, who takes up the race at that point. Several sets of runners take part in the race.

—(REE-lay *or* ri-LAY) *v.* relays, relayed, relaying. Pass on from one to another.—The message was *relayed* to the general by radio, telephone, and messenger.

re·lease (ri-LEESS) *n. releases.* 1. Freedom. —The prisoner was given his *release.*
2. A statement for publication.—The school issued a news *release* about the students who had won scholarships.
—*v. releases, released, releasing.* Let go.—The woman *released* the child's hand, and he fell. —Bob took off the dog's collar and *released* him.

re·li·a·ble (ri-LY-ə-bəl) *adj.; reliably, adv.; reliability, n.* Trustworthy or dependable.—Mary is *reliable* about getting her work done on time.

rel·ic (REL-ik) *n. relics.* Things left from times long past.—Arrowheads and stone hammers are Indian *relics.*

re·lief (ri-LEEF) *n.* 1. Help; comfort; easing or removing difficulty.—Medicine brings *relief* to the sick. It helps to make them well.— The Red Cross brings *relief* to victims of floods.
2. Freedom from a task.—The sailor kept a lookout until six o'clock and then got *relief.* Another man took his place.
3. A design that stands up higher than the surface from which it is cut.

re·lieve (ri-LEEV) *v. relieves, relieved, relieving.* 1. Comfort, ease, or help.—Medicine will *relieve* the patient's pain.
2. Free from a task.—A new baseball pitcher *relieved* Bob. He freed Bob by taking his place.
3. Change the sameness of.—The whiteness of the tablecloth and dishes on the table was *relieved* by a blue bowl of yellow roses.

re·li·gion (ri-LIJ-ən) *n. religions; religious, adj.; religiously, adv.* A belief in or worship of God or gods. *Religion* is any faith or method of worship.

re·luc·tance (ri-LUK-tənss) *n.; reluctant, adj.; reluctantly, adv.* Hesitation or slowness in doing something because of not wanting to do it, but having to; unwillingness.—The father punished his son with *reluctance.*

re·ly (ri-LY) *v. relies, relied, relying.* Trust or depend.—Mother can *rely* upon Bob to take good care of Sally.
—*reliance, n.*

re·main (ri-MAYN) *v. remains, remained, remaining.* 1. Stay.—The children came, but they could not *remain* for lunch.
2. Be left over.—Only two pencils *remained* in the box when we had each taken one from it.
3. Stay (the same).—Some metals *remain* bright all the time. They never tarnish.

re·main·der (ri-MAYN-der) *n. remainders.* 1. The part that is left.—I ate part of the apple pie and Father ate the *remainder.*
2. A number found by subtracting.—If you take 4 apples from 6 apples, the *remainder* is 2 apples.

re·mark (ri-MAHRK) *n. remarks.* A statement, or something said.—The teacher made a few *remarks* about the lesson.
—*v. remarks, remarked, remarking.* Say or notice.—Sally *remarked* that Father was growing fat, but said nothing about it. Mother *remarked* to Father that he was gaining weight. She said it out loud.

re·mark·a·ble (ri-MAHR-kə-bəl) *adj.; remarkably, adv.* Worth noticing, or wonderful. —The child's manners are *remarkable* for her age.

rem·e·dy (REM-ə-dee) *n. remedies.* A relief or cure.—Medicine is a *remedy* for sickness.
—*v. remedies, remedied, remedying.* Correct, or make right.—We will *remedy* the mistake at once. We will correct it.

re·mem·ber (ri-MEM-ber) *v. remembers, remembered, remembering.* 1. Recall, or bring back to mind.—Mother can *remember* things that happened when she was a little girl.
2. Keep in mind.—*Remember* that you are invited to come. Do not forget it.
3. Show that (someone) is thought of.—The children always *remember* Mother on her birthday. They show that they love her by giving her a gift.
4. Pass greetings on.—*Remember* me to all my friends. Mention my name and give them my regards, or best wishes.

re·mem·brance (ri-MEM-brənss) *n. remembrances.* 1. Gift, keepsake, or something to remember one by.—Mary gave me a little *remembrance* for my birthday. She gave me a locket with her picture in it.
2. Memory. — They held in loving *remembrance* their grandfather who had died.

re·mind (ri-MYND) *v.* reminds, reminded, reminding. Cause to recall or remember.— *Remind* me to take an umbrella.—Mary sometimes *reminds* me of Mother.
—*reminder, n.* reminders.

rem·nant (REM-nənt) *n.* remnants. 1. A piece of cloth that is left over from a larger piece. — Mother made a doll dress from a *remnant*.
2. Leftover.—We ate the *remnants* of Sunday's dinner for our lunch on Tuesday.

re·mod·el (ree-MAHD-l) *v.* remodels, remodeled or remodelled, remodeling or remodelling. Make over. — We plan to *remodel* our barn and make it into a guest house.

re·morse (ri-MORSS) *n.; remorseful, adj.; remorsefully, adv.* Regret or sorrow for something one has done.—The child felt *remorse*. He was sorry he had stolen the pencils.

re·mote (ri-MOHT) *adj.* remoter, remotest; remotely, adv. 1. Far-off.—The explorers had visited *remote* corners of the world.—To people in South America, Russia is a *remote* country.
2. Long past; long ago.—In *remote* times people lived in caves.
3. Vague or slight.—Bob has a *remote* idea that he wants to be an engineer.

re·move (ri-MOOV) *v.* removes, removed, removing. 1. Take off.—Mary *removed* her rubbers before going into the house.
2. Take away.—*Remove* the broom from the doorway before someone trips on it.
3. Put out of.—Dishonest persons are often *removed* from their jobs.
4. End.—The medicine *removed* his pain.
5. Take out.—*Remove* the gum from your mouth.

ren·ais·sance (ren-ə-SAHNSS or REN-ə-sahnss) *n.* 1. New birth; revival.—There seems to be a *renaissance* of interest in poems by Longfellow. Many people seem to be reading his poems again.
2. (Spelled with a capital "R.") The period in Europe, from the fourteenth through the sixteenth centuries, marked by a great revival of interest and achievement in art, literature, science, and learning.

re·new (ri-NOO or -NYOO) *v.* renews, renewed, renewing. 1. Start again; continue.— I shall *renew* my subscription to the magazine.—Mary *renewed* her efforts after the teacher praised her work.
2. Make like new again.—Father *renewed* the finish on the chair by varnishing it.
—*renewal, n.* renewals.

ren·o·vate (REN-ə-vayt) *v.* renovates, renovated, renovating. Clean, repair, or make like new again.—The old house will have to be *renovated* before the family moves in.
—*renovation, n.* renovations.

rent (RENT) *n.* rents. 1. Money paid regularly for the use of a building or property.— Father pays the *rent* on the first of the month.
2. A tear; a torn place.—Bob got a *rent* in his sleeve when he caught it on a nail.
—*v.* rents, rented, renting. 1. Use a building or property for which one makes regular payments.—We *rent* our house from a real-estate company.
2. Allow a building or property to be used in return for regular payment.—Last year we *rented* our summer cottage to the Browns.

re·or·gan·ize (ree-OR-gə-nyz) *v.* reorganizes, reorganized, reorganizing. 1. Arrange differently, or according to a new plan.—Our principal *reorganized* the classes this term. He changed the hours, some of the subjects, and the method of teaching.
2. Form or get together again.—The football team will *reorganize* this fall.
—*reorganization, n.* reorganizations.

re·paid (ri-PAYD) *v.* One form of the verb *repay*.—The money you lent me will be *repaid* by the first of the month.

re·pair (ri-PAIR) *n.* repairs. 1. Necessary work on something; mending or fixing; replacement of parts.—What *repairs* will have to be made on the house before it can be lived in?
2. Condition.—If you keep your shoes in good *repair*, they will wear longer. Have them mended as soon at they need it.
—*v.* repairs, repaired, repairing. 1. Fix; mend; put back in working order.—The mechanic *repaired* the radio.
2. Make right.—Jack tried to *repair* the damage his thoughtless words had done.

re·pay (ri-PAY) *v.* repays, repaid, repaying. Pay back.—I will *repay* the money you lent me as soon as I receive my wages.

re·peal (ri-PEEL) *v.* repeals, repealed, repealing. Officially do away with or withdraw; set aside.—The unpopular law was *repealed*.

re·peat (ri-PEET) *v.* repeats, repeated, repeating. 1. Say again.—I did not quite understand. Please *repeat* what you said.
2. Do again.—Yesterday you burned your finger; be careful not to *repeat* the accident.
3. Say from memory.—Can you *repeat* the words of "The Star-Spangled Banner"?

re·pent (ri-PENT) *v. repents, repented, repenting*. Regret, or be sorry for.—If you do wrong, you are sure to *repent* it.

rep·e·ti·tion (rep-ə-TISH-ən) *n.* The act of repeating; doing or saying again. — We learn many skills through *repetition*. We learn many skills by doing them over and over again until we have mastered them. — Bob was warned that a *repetition* of his rude behavior would result in his dismissal.

re·place (ri-PLAYSS) *v. replaces, replaced, replacing*. 1. Put in place again.—*Replace* the dishes in the cupboard after you dry them. 2. Substitute another for.—Mother *replaced* the broken mirror. She bought a new one. 3. Follow; fill the position of.—The pitcher was *replaced* by a younger boy.
—*replacement, n. replacements*.

re·plen·ish (ri-PLEN-ish) *v. replenishes, replenished, replenishing*. Fill again with supplies.—Mother *replenished* the empty cupboards. She stocked them with food.

rep·li·ca (REP-lə-kə) *n. replicas*. A copy or reproduction, especially of a work of art.—Father bought a small *replica* of the famous statue for his den.

re·ply (ri-PLY) *n. replies*. An answer.—It is wiser to make no *reply* to angry words.
—*v. replies, replied, replying*. Respond; answer.—Grandmother *replies* to our letters at once.

re·port (ri-PORT) *n. reports*. 1. A story or account.—The children gave a *report* of their trip to the zoo.
2. A statement.—Each month our teacher sends home a *report* that tells of our record in school. Jack had an "A" in arithmetic on his *report*.
3. News or rumor.—We heard a *report* that school would start earlier this year.
4. A sound or an explosive noise.—The *report* of the gun startled Sally.
—*v. reports, reported, reporting*. 1. Present oneself, or go in person.—The boys *reported* for baseball practice at four o'clock.
2. Tell; give the information.—Mary *reported* that enough money had been collected by the class to buy two new books.
3. Write up in a newspaper.—Mr. Bob Smith *reports* sports news for the "Daily Sentinel."
4. Make a charge against.—If you don't stay in the playground I shall have to *report* you to the principal.

re·port·er (ri-POR-ter) *n. reporters*. A person whose job is to gather news to be printed in a newspaper.—*Reporters* hurried to the scene of the accident.

EXTINCT REPTILES

pterodactyl

triceratops

tyrannosaurus

ichthyosaurus

stegosaurus

brontosaurus

re·pose (ri-POHZ) *n.* 1. Rest; relaxation.—Mother needs some *repose* every day, because she works so hard.
2. Peace; calm.—The minister has an air of *repose* about him.
—*v. reposes, reposed, reposing*. Rest.—Baby *reposed* on Father's lap.

rep·re·sent (rep-ri-ZENT) *v. represents, represented, representing*. 1. Mean or show.—The picture Mary drew *represented* the story of Little Red Riding Hood.
2. Act the part of; pretend to be.—Two boys *represented* knights in the play. — The spy *represented* himself as an American citizen.
3. Stand for.—A red cross on a background of white *represents* the Red Cross.
4. Act for.—The Congressman we elect from this area *represents* us in Congress.

rep·re·sent·a·tive (rep-ri-ZEN-tə-tiv) *n. representatives*. 1. Someone chosen by a group to speak and act for it.—The class chose Dick as their *representative*.
2. (Sometimes spelled with a capital "R.") A member of the House of Representatives of the United States or of one of the states.

rep·ri·mand (REP-rə-mand) *v. reprimands, reprimanded, reprimanding*. Blame, especially in a formal manner; reprove sternly.—The officer was *reprimanded* for neglecting his duty.

REPTILES

crocodile
iguana
Gila monster
horned lizard
snapping turtle
box turtle
king snake
eastern fence swift
coral snake
python
cobra
garter snake
rattlesnake

re·print (REE-print) *n. reprints.* Something printed again, usually after a lapse of time.—This book is a paperbound *reprint* of one originally issued in a hard cover.
—(ree-PRINT) *v. reprints, reprinted, reprinting.* Print again.—When all the copies of the book were sold, the publisher *reprinted* it.

re·proach (ri-PROHCH) *n. reproaches.* A blaming.—The teacher's *reproach* made us sorry that we had not done our homework.
—*v. reproaches, reproached, reproaching.* Put blame on.—The teacher *reproached* us for not doing our homework.

re·pro·duce (ree-prə-DOOSS *or* -DYOOSS) *v. reproduces, reproduced, reproducing.* 1. Produce again.—A phonograph, a tape recorder, and a radio all *reproduce* sound.
2. Make a duplicate or copy of.—Carbon paper is placed between sheets of paper to *reproduce* on the bottom sheet exactly what is written on the top sheet.
3. Bring forth offspring; bear young.
—*reproduction, n. reproductions.*

re·prove (ri-PROOV) *v. reproves, reproved, reproving.* Scold.—Father *reproved* Mary for being late.

rep·tile (REP-tyl) *n. reptiles.* A cold-blooded, animal that crawls or moves on short legs. Snakes, lizards, alligators, and turtles are *reptiles. Reptiles* have backbones.

re·pub·lic (ri-PUB-lik) *n. republics.* A nation in which the people elect or choose their rulers or representatives.—The United States is a *republic.*

re·pulse (ri-PULSS) *n. repulses.* A holding off or beating back.—The *repulse* of the outlaws was made possible by many cowboys.
—*v. repulses, repulsed, repulsing.* 1. Turn down or refuse.—The unhappy man *repulsed* all offers of friendship.
2. Beat or drive back.—The trainer *repulsed* the angry lions.

rep·u·ta·tion (rep-yə-TAY-shən) *n. reputations.* What people think and say about a person's behavior, character, or work.—Our doctor has an excellent *reputation.*

re·quest (ri-KWEST) *n. requests.* 1. A thing one asks for.—All Bob's *requests* were granted at Christmas. He was given everything he had asked for.
2. An asking (for something).—The teacher hasn't yet answered my *request* to see her.
—*v. requests, requested, requesting.* Ask.—The teacher *requested* us to work quietly.

re·quire (ri-KWYR) *v. requires, required, requiring.* 1. Have to have.—Baby *requires* much sleep.
2. Demand.—The teacher *requires* us to be on time for class.
—*requirement, n. requirements.*

res·cue (RESS-kyoo) *n. rescues.* Saving.—The *rescue* of the pilots lost at sea was difficult.

—*v. rescues, rescued, rescuing.* Save or set free from danger.—The sailors *rescued* the man from the sinking ship.

res·cu·er (RESS-kyoo-er) *n. rescuers.* A person who rescues or saves someone from harm or danger. — The man who fell overboard thanked his *rescuers.* He thanked the men who had saved him from the sea.

re·search (ri-SERCH *or* REE-serch) *n. researches.* Careful study and investigation; the search for knowledge, especially new knowledge.—Scientists are constantly doing *research.*

re·sem·blance (ri-ZEM-blənss) *n. resemblances.* A like or similar appearance.—There is a strong *resemblance* between Mother and Ann. They look very much alike.

re·sem·ble (ri-ZEM-bəl) *v. resembles, resembled, resembling.* Look somewhat like.— Our dog is so big he *resembles* a horse.

re·sent (ri-ZENT) *v. resents, resented, resenting.* Feel angry and hurt at.—Bob *resents* being called a coward.
—*resentment, n. resentments.*

re·sent·ful (ri-ZENT-fuhl) *adj.; resentfully, adv.* Showing anger and ill feeling.—Bob is *resentful* because someone called him a coward.

res·er·va·tion (rez-er-VAY-shən) *n. reservations.* 1. Anything that is held back for a special use or purpose.—Bob has a *reservation* for the ball game. A ticket for a seat is being held for him.
2. A restriction or limit.—The teacher recommended Tom without *reservations.*

re·serve (ri-ZERV) *n. reserves.* 1. Care not to be too friendly; restraint in speech or manner.—Mary answers the questions of strangers with *reserve.*
2. Extra supply for a time of need. — The teacher keeps a *reserve* of pencils in her drawer.

—*v. reserves, reserved, reserving.* Set aside or hold.—Father said he would *reserve* a day to take us to the park.

res·er·voir (REZ-er-vor *or* -vwahr) *n. reservoirs.* A huge tank, pool, or lake where water is kept for use when needed.

re·set (ree-SET) *v. resets, reset, resetting.* Place in a new setting, or set again. — The pearls were *reset* in a modern-style necklace.

re·side (ri-ZYD) *v. resides, resided, residing.* Live or have one's home.—Grandmother *resides* in the country.—We *reside* in town.

res·i·dence (REZ-ə-dənss) *n. residences.* A house, or place where one lives. — Alan's *residence* is on Wycoff Street.

—*Take up residence* means make one's home; go to live.—We have *taken up residence* on a farm.

res·i·dent (REZ-ə-dənt) *n. residents.* Someone who lives or makes his home in a particular place.—The *residents* of the town built a new playground for the children.

re·sign (ri-ZYN) *v. resigns, resigned, resigning.* 1. Give up.—Father *resigned* his position for a better one.
2. Make up one's mind to; submit.—Mary has *resigned* herself to spending the day at home, since it is raining too hard to go out. She knows that she must stay home.

res·ig·na·tion (rez-ig-NAY-shən) *n. resignations.* 1. The act of giving up a job or position. — John's *resignation* from the student government made a new election necessary.
2. A statement that one is resigning.—John made his *resignation* in writing.
3. Quiet patience, or quiet giving in.—Father receives bad news with *resignation.* He doesn't complain.

res·in (REZ-ən) *n.* A sticky sap that flows from such trees as the pine.—*Resin* is used in varnish and in medicines.

re·sist (ri-ZIST) *v.* resists, resisted, resisting. Fight or hold out against.—The thief did not *resist* the policeman who arrested him.—The child was not strong enough to *resist* the disease.

re·sist·ance (ri-ZISS-tənss) *n.* resistances. 1. Opposing action or power.—The outlaws put up no *resistance* when they saw they were outnumbered. 2. Strength to fight off.—The child has little *resistance*, so she catches cold easily.

res·o·lu·tion (rez-ə-LOO-shən *or* rez-ə-LYOO-shən) *n.* resolutions. 1. A decision, or something one decides to do.—Mary made a New Year's *resolution* to do better work in school. 2. A statement that something should be done. — The mayor proposed a *resolution* stating that the parks of the city should be made larger and pleasanter for the people. 3. Determination. — The President approached his new responsibilities with *resolution*.

re·solve (ri-ZAHLV) *n.* Determination; resolution.—He approached the difficult task with a *resolve* to do it well. —*v.* resolves, resolved, resolving. 1. Decide or determine.—Bob *resolved* to eat less candy. 2. Decide by a vote.—The class *resolved* that paper in the schoolyard should be picked up by the children each afternoon. 3. Solve.—The children *resolved* the problem of litter in the schoolyard by cleaning it up each afternoon.

re·sort (ri-ZORT) *n.* resorts. 1. A place to go, especially for recreation.—In summer many people go to *resorts* for vacations.

2. What a person gets help from.—Begging was the poor old man's last *resort*. —*v.* resorts, resorted, resorting. 1. Turn for help.—The old man *resorted* to begging in order to obtain food. 2. Turn to or make use of, when other means have failed.—When every other effort failed to keep the dog from running away, Bob finally *resorted* to tying him up.

re·source (ri-SORSS *or* REE-sorss) *n.* resources. 1. A supply of anything to be used when needed. — Our country has great *resources* of cotton, metal, timber, and other natural products. 2. Ability to meet difficult situations.—Here is a job that will test your mental *resources*.

re·spect (ri-SPEKT) *n.* respects. 1. Admiration and honor. — The children have great *respect* for their teacher. 2. Care; consideration.—The children show *respect* for their books. They take care of them. 3. A way.—In what *respect* do you disagree with Mary? In what way do you disagree with her opinion? —*v.* respects, respected, respecting. 1. Show or feel admiration for. — The children *respect* their teacher. 2. Take care of.—The children *respect* their books.

re·spect·ful (ri-SPEKT-fuhl) *adj.; respectfully, adv.* Showing that one thinks highly of a person or thing.—Jack disagreed with the teacher's idea in a *respectful* way. He told her very politely how he thought differently.—We should handle the flag *respectfully*. We should treat it with honor.

res·pi·ra·tion (ress-pə-RAY-shən) *n.* The inhaling and exhaling of air; breathing. — *Respiration* is difficult at high altitudes because the air contains less oxygen.

res·pi·ra·tor (RESS-pə-ray-ter) *n.* respirators. A device or apparatus used to help someone to breathe.—An oxygen or gas mask is a *respirator*.

re·spir·a·to·ry (RESS-pə-rə-tor-ee) *adj.* Having to do with breathing. — Bronchitis and pneumonia are *respiratory* diseases.

res·pite (RESS-pit) *n.* respites. A time off for rest; a relief.—We had a short *respite* between classes.—We are having a *respite* from cold weather. It is warm now.

re·spond (ri-SPAHND) *v.* responds, responded, responding. 1. Answer.—Sally did not *respond* to Mother's call because she did not hear her. 2. Show effect, or react.—Some children *respond* to medicine more quickly than others. Medicine acts more quickly on some than on others.

re·sponse (ri-SPAHNSS) *n. responses.* 1. An answer.—Father is waiting for a *response* to his letter.
2. A reaction.—The child shows no *response* to the medicine.

re·spon·si·bil·i·ty (ri-spahn-sə-BIL-ə-tee) *n. responsibilities.* 1. Anything one is expected to do or attend to.—Mother's *responsibilities* are keeping the house clean, cooking, caring for the children, and helping us when we come to her.
2. Ability to carry through on obligations; trustworthiness.—John does not have much sense of *responsibility.* He just can't be depended on.

re·spon·si·ble (ri-SPAHN-sə-bəl) *adj.; responsibly, adv.* 1. Reliable.—Bob is a *responsible* person. You can always depend upon him.
2. Answerable or accountable.—The driver of the car was held *responsible* for the accident. He had to answer for it.
3. Involving important tasks.—A teacher has a very *responsible* position.

rest (REST) *n. rests.* 1. Relaxation; freedom from work or trouble. — Father must have *rest* so that he can play in the golf tournament.
2. Stillness; absence of motion. — The ball whizzed through the air and came to *rest* on the grass.
3. A pause, or sign showing a pause.—A *rest* in music is a slight pause, a short time when no note is sounded.
4. Something to lean on.—Most automobiles have arm*rests* on the doors.

5. The remainder, or all that is left.—Mary ate all the ice cream that she wanted, and Bob ate the *rest.*
—*v. rests, rested, resting.* 1. Be still or free from work or action.—Grandfather let his horses *rest* for a time so that they would not get too tired.
2. Get over being tired.—Stop and *rest* when you are out of breath.
3. Remain.—The kitten's eyes *rested* on the mouse across the kitchen. She kept looking at the mouse.
4. Lie.—The broom *rests* against the wall.—The book *rests* upon the table.
—*Rest with* means depend upon.—The prisoner's freedom *rests with* the court.

res·tau·rant (RESS-tə-rənt) *n. restaurants.* A public place where food is served.—We stopped at a *restaurant* and ordered dinner.

rest·ful (REST-fuhl) *adj.; restfully, adv.* 1. Giving relaxation and rest.—The man had a *restful* night. It freed him from being tired.
2. Peaceful or calm; quiet.—We found a *restful* place in the hills to stay.

rest·less (REST-ləss) *adj.; restlessly, adv.* 1. Not able to keep calm or quiet.—Children in school are often *restless* in warm weather.
2. Without rest or sleep.—Father had a *restless* night because of his bad sunburn.

re·store (ri-STOR) *v. restores, restored, restoring.* 1. Renew or repair. — Bald-headed men often want to *restore* their hair. They try to grow hair again.—When the patient's health is *restored,* he will leave the hospital.
2. Put back.—The boy *restored* the stolen pen because he had a guilty conscience.

re·strain (ri-STRAYN) *v. restrains, restrained, restraining.* Hold in check or keep back.—It was hard for the rider to *restrain* the nervous horse.—The children could not *restrain* their laughter at the clown.
—*restraint, n. restraints.*

re·strict (ri-STRIKT) *v. restricts, restricted, restricting.* Keep within bounds; limit.—The hospital *restricts* the number of visitors each patient may receive.
—*restriction, n. restrictions.*

re·sult (ri-ZULT) *n. results.* A thing which happens because of something else that has happened before.—Good marks in school are a *result* of hard work.
—*v. results, resulted, resulting.* 1. Cause.—Carelessness often *results* in accidents.
2. Happen because of something.—Accidents often *result* from carelessness.

re·sume (ri-ZOOM *or* -ZYOOM) *v. resumes, resumed, resuming.* 1. Begin again; continue after a pause.—The orchestra *resumed* the concert after a brief intermission.
2. Take or occupy again.—The ballplayers are *resuming* their positions on the field.—*Resume* your seats, please.

Res·ur·rec·tion (rez-ə-REK-shən) *n.* The rising of Jesus Christ from the dead.

re·tail (REE-tayl) *adj.* Having to do with selling things in small amounts. — *Retail* stores sell goods to people who buy for their own use.

re·tain (ri-TAYN) *v. retains, retained, retaining.* 1. Hold or keep.—Some cloth does not *retain* its color when hung outdoors in the sunshine. It fades.
2. Remember. — Some children *retain* what they learn longer than others.
3. Hire for a fee.—After the accident, Father *retained* a lawyer to defend him in court.

re·tal·i·ate (ri-TAL-ee-ayt) *v. retaliates, retaliated, retaliating.* Get even, usually by paying back in a similar way.—When John pulled Mary's hair, she *retaliated* by stepping on his toes.
—*retaliation, n. retaliations.*

re·tard (ri-TAHRD) *v. retards, retarded, retarding.* Prevent progress; make (something) slow.—The boulder in the middle of the road *retarded* the flow of traffic.—Lack of sunshine *retards* the growth of many plants.

ret·i·na (RET-ə-nə) *n. retinas.* The membrane at the rear of the eyeball that receives the images seen by the eye.

re·tire (ri-TYR) *v. retires, retired, retiring.*
1. Go to bed.—We *retire* at eight o'clock.
2. Stop working forever.—Grandfather has *retired* because he is getting old.
3. Withdraw; go away.—Father *retired* from the party because he had to get up early the next morning.
—*retirement, n. retirements.*

re·treat (ri-TREET) *n. retreats.* 1. A moving or falling back.—The beaten wolf made a quick *retreat* into the forest.
2. A place of quiet; a refuge.—Father calls the den his *retreat.* He can work there without being disturbed.
—*v. retreats, retreated, retreating.* Move or fall back.—The outlaw band was caught in the canyon and could not *retreat.*

re·trieve (ri-TREEV) *v. retrieves, retrieved, retrieving.* 1. Get back again; regain; recover.—Jack *retrieved* the ball he had dropped in the lake.
2. Find and bring back. — The hound *retrieved* the wild duck shot by the hunter.
3. Repair; make good.—Ed *retrieved* his mistake in calling Mrs. Smith "Mrs. Jones" by introducing her correctly to his friends.

re·turn (ri-TERN) *n. returns.* 1. A report.—We sat up late to see the election *returns* on television.
2. A payment back; something received in exchange for something else.—Bob's *return* for hard study was an "A" in arithmetic.—The *returns,* or amount of money made, from the puppet show were twenty dollars.
3. Coming or going back.—We welcome the *return* of the robins in spring.
—*v. returns, returned, returning.* 1. Come back.—Father will *return* after work.
2. Go back.—Mother had to *return* to the house for her key.
3. Give or send back.—*Return* your aunt's umbrella the next time you go to see her.
4. Put back.—*Return* the book to the shelf when you are through with it.
5. Pay back.—Lend me a nickel, and I will *return* it soon.
—*adj.* Used for going and coming back.—Father bought a *return* ticket to Chicago.

re·un·ion (ree-YOON-yən) *n. reunions.* Gathering or coming together again.—The students plan to hold a *reunion* each year after they graduate. They all plan to get together once each year.

re·veal (ri-VEEL) *v. reveals, revealed, revealing.* 1. Make known.—At last the truth was *revealed* to us.
2. Indicate, display, or show.—Mary's shaky voice *revealed* her nervousness.

rev·eil·le (REV-ə-lee) *n.* A military or naval signal sounded in the early morning on a bugle or drum to rouse sleeping soldiers or sailors for their duties.

re·venge (ri-VENJ) *n.* Harm or injury done to another in return for harm or injury.—When the angry man hit the mule, the mule's *revenge* was to kick the man.
—*v. revenges, revenged, revenging.* To harm or to hurt in return.—The mule *revenged* itself by kicking the man who hit it.

rev·e·nue (REV-ə-noo *or* -nyoo) *n. revenues.* Income, or money coming in.—Most of the government's *revenue* comes from taxes.

rev·er·ence (REV-rənss) *n.* Solemn respect and love.—We bow our heads in *reverence* for the soldiers who died.

Rev·er·end (REV-er-ənd) *adj.* The title of a minister or preacher of a church.—The *Reverend* Frank Smith is our minister.

re·verse (ri-VERSS) *n. reverses* and *adj.* 1. A misfortune.—During the flood, many stores and shops met with *reverses.* Their business changed from good to bad.
2. The opposite or backward direction.—To back a car out of a garage, move it in *reverse.*
3. The other side.—What is on the *reverse* of the newspaper page you want to clip?
—*v. reverses, reversed, reversing.* Turn or change to the opposite direction, position, or the like. — At first Father's answer was "No," but he *reversed* his decision. He changed it to "Yes."—The runner *reversed* his direction and ran the other way.

re·vers·i·ble (ri-VER-sə-bəl) *adj.* Able to be changed or used in an opposite manner or direction.—Mary has a *reversible* coat. She can wear it with either side out. — Father's decision proved to be *reversible.* He said that John could go after all.

re·view (ri-VYOO) *n. reviews.* 1. A going over again.—We had a *review* in spelling.
2. A report about a book, play, concert, etc.—The newspaper gave a *review* of the new book. It told what the story was about, and revealed its good and bad points.
3. An inspection.—The officer made a *review* of the troops. He looked them over to see whether they were well trained.
—*v. reviews, reviewed, reviewing.* 1. Go over again.—We did not know our lesson well, so we had to *review* it.—The judge *reviewed* the case. He examined carefully all the stories about the accident.
2. Give a report of a book, play, concert, etc.—Our teacher asked us to *review* the book.
3. Inspect.—The general *reviewed* the troops.

re·vise (ri-VYZ) *v. revises, revised, revising.* Correct, or change to improve.—After writing our stories, we had to *revise* them.
—*revision, n. revisions.*

re·vive (ri-VYV) *v. revives, revived, reviving.*
1. Bring back again.—Old movies are often *revived* on television.
2. Restore to consciousness, life, or activity; refresh.—The doctor *revived* the woman who had fainted.—A cold shower *revived* the tired athlete.
—*revival, n. revivals.*

re·volt (ri-VOHLT) *n. revolts.* Fighting against those in control.—All the prisoners joined the *revolt* against the guards.
—*v. revolts, revolted, revolting.* Fight against the government, or those in lawful control.—The prisoners *revolted* against their guards.

rev·o·lu·tion (rev-ə-LOO-shən *or* rev-əl-YOO-shən) *n. revolutions; revolutionary, adj.*
1. The complete changing of the government or rulers by people who are against the government. — In the American *Revolution,* the Americans freed themselves from England and became a separate country, with a government they made for themselves.
2. A sudden, complete change.—The use of the automobile has made a great *revolution* in people's lives. They can do things they never could do before.
3. A complete turning around of something.—The children in the circle made three *revolutions* to the right.

re·volve (ri-VAHLV) *v. revolves, revolved, revolving.* Roll or go around.—The hands on a clock *revolve.*—A merry-go-round *revolves,* too.

re·volv·er (ri-VAHL-ver) *n. revolvers.* A short, repeating gun which can be held in one hand and has a cylinder to hold the cartridges.

re·ward (ri-WORD) *n. rewards.* A payment or prize given for some special act. — The teacher gave a *reward* of five dollars for the return of her lost ring.
—*v. rewards, rewarded, rewarding.* Recognize by giving a prize or payment.—The policeman's bravery was *rewarded* with a medal.

rheu·ma·tism (ROO-mə-tiz-əm) *n.* A disease of a person's joints or muscles. *Rheumatism* causes pain, stiffness, and swelling.

rhi·noc·er·os (ry-NAHSS-er-əss) *n. rhinoceroses.* A large four-legged animal with a very thick, gray skin and with one or two horns that stand up on its snout. *Rhinoceroses* live in Asia and Africa.

rhi·zome (RY-zohm) *n. rhizomes.* An underground plant stem that grows sideways. It takes root on its lower side, and sends up shoots from its top side. *Rhizomes* look 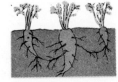 different from real roots because they have buds and scaly leaves. Certain types of turnips and herbs have *rhizomes.*

Rhode Is·land (rohd Y-lənd) *n.* A manufacturing state on the east coast of the United States. It was the first colony in the U. S. to have complete religious  freedom. *Rhode Island* is the smallest of the states.

rhu·barb (ROO-bahrb) *n.* A plant with very large green leaves that grow on large stalks, or stems. The long juicy stems are stewed and used for sauce, and as a filling for pies.

rhyme or **rime** (RYM) *n. rhymes* or *rimes.* A verse or poem in which the last words of each line sound alike.—This is a *rhyme:*
 "Jack and Jill
  Went up the hill."
—*v. rhymes, rhymed, rhyming.* End with the same sound.—The words "snow" and "show" *rhyme.* — Can you name two words that *rhyme?*

rhythm (RITH-əm) *n. rhythms.* The regular beat of sound or movement.—It is easy to dance to music because of its *rhythm.* The dance steps have the same regular beat as the music.

rib (RIB) *n. ribs.* 1. One of a group of bones that fasten to the spine, or backbone, and curve around to the front of the body over the chest. *Ribs*  form a "box" to protect the lungs and the heart. People and many kinds of animals have *ribs.*
2. Anything like a person's ribs in shape or use.—The *ribs* of an umbrella are the thin metal "spokes," or rods, to which the cloth is fastened.

rib·bon (RIB-ən) *n. ribbons.* A strip or narrow band of cloth.—Ruth wears bows of *ribbon* on her braids.

rice (RYSS) *n.* A grass whose seeds are used for food. *Rice* grows in a warm climate.

rich (RICH) *adj. richer, richest; richly, adv.; richness, n.* 1. Wealthy, or having much money, land, or the like. — The *rich* family lives in a big house with beautiful grounds.
2. Able to produce much.—A *rich* soil is soil that has plenty of food to make plants grow.
3. Having plenty. — Our country is *rich* in copper ore. It has a great supply of it.
4. Expensive or valuable.—Things that cost much, and are of the best quality, are *rich.*— The queen wore a *rich* velvet gown.
5. Nourishing or satisfying to the appetite; having much sugar, butter, etc.—The cake Mother baked was too *rich.*—*Rich* soups are very nourishing.
6. Filled with deep, pleasing shades of color and sound.—Mother's party dress is of a *rich,* warm green color.—The story of Robinson Crusoe is filled with *rich* description.

rich·es (RICH-əz) *n. pl.* Money or valuable things.—*Riches* alone could not make King Midas happy.

rich·ly (RICH-lee) *adv.* Expensively or elegantly.—The queen was *richly* dressed in velvet embroidered with emeralds.

rick·ets (RIK-itss) *n. pl.* A disease that attacks poorly fed children. Children with *rickets* suffer a softening of the bones and often become crippled.

ric·o·chet (rik-ə-SHAY) *v. ricochets, ricocheted, ricocheting.* Move in a bouncing, skipping manner, as a bullet off a wall.—Bob threw a rock which *ricocheted* off the fence.

rid (RID) *v. rids, rid, ridding.* Clear or free.— The Pied Piper *rid* the city of rats.
—*Get rid of* means become free of.—We *got rid of* our old car.

rid·den (RID-n) *v.* One form of the verb *ride.*—After we had *ridden* in the car for two days, Mother was very tired.

rid·dle (RID-l) *n. riddles.* A puzzle.—This is a *riddle:* The more you take from it, the bigger it grows. What is it? Answer: A hole.
—*v. riddles, riddled, riddling.* Pierce many holes in.—Bullets *riddled* the target.

ride (RYD) *n. rides.* A trip or journey.—Last night we went for a *ride* in the car.
—*v. rides, rode, riding.* Sit on or in, and be carried along.—Jack likes to *ride* on his pony.
—We *ride* on a boat, on a train, and in a car.

rid·er (RYD-er) *n. riders.* A person who rides.
—When we ride in the car, Father is the driver, and we are the *riders.*—The wild horse threw his *rider.*

ridge (RIJ) *n. ridges.* 1. A raised line or edge where two slanting surfaces meet. — The long top part of the roof on a house is a *ridge.*

2. Any narrow, raised strip.—A heavy thread in a piece of cloth makes a *ridge.*

rid·i·cule (RID-ə-kyool) *v. ridicules, ridiculed, ridiculing.* Make fun of; mock.—Mother told the boys that it was unkind to *ridicule* the woman in the funny hat.

ri·dic·u·lous (rə-DIK-yə-ləss) *adj.; ridiculously, adv.; ridiculousness, n.* Very silly.—Men would look *ridiculous* wearing women's clothes.

ri·fle (RYF-əl) *n. rifles.* A long-barreled gun held with two hands, and with a spiral groove in the barrel. The spiral groove makes the bullet spin when it is fired, so it will go straight.

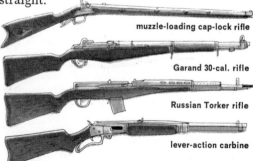

muzzle-loading cap-lock rifle

Garand 30-cal. rifle

Russian Torker rifle

lever-action carbine

right (RYT) *n. rights.* A privilege; a lawful claim.—In the United States it is a person's *right* to go to the church he chooses.
—*v. rights, righted, righting.* 1. Correct.—Mary *righted* the misunderstanding between herself and Mother.
2. Set in the proper position. — The upset boat must be *righted* before it can be used.

—*adj.* 1. Good, proper, decent, or lawful.—*Right* is the opposite of wrong. Bad deeds are wrong. Good deeds are *right.*
2. On or toward the side opposite your left hand.—If you face south, your *right* shoulder will be pointing toward the west; your left shoulder will be pointing to the east.
3. Correct.—This clock gives the *right* time.
4. True. — John says that you have a new book. Is that *right*?
5. Intended to show, or to be worn outwards.—There is a wrong and a *right* side to this tablecloth.
6. Satisfactory. — Bob's teeth are all *right* since he had them cleaned.
7. Straight.—A *right* line is a straight line.
—*adv.* 1. Directly. — Mary looked *right* at the book and yet didn't see it.
2. Straight.—Go *right* ahead.
3. Exactly.—Tom put his toys *right* where they were supposed to go.
—*Right now* means immediately.

right·eous (RY-chəss) *adj.; righteously, adv.; righteousness, n.* Acting properly; good.—That woman is a very *righteous* person. She does the things that are good and right.

right-hand (RYT-HAND) *adj.* At or toward the hand that is on the right.—Put your book on the *right-hand* side of your desk.

right-hand·ed (RYT-han-dəd) *adj.* Mary is *right-handed.* She writes with and uses her right hand more easily and more often than her left hand.

right·ly (RYT-lee) *adv.* 1. Exactly or correctly.—I cannot *rightly* say how far it is to the city.
2. Honestly or in fairness.—Mother cannot *rightly* give more to Jack than she gives to Mary.

rig·id (RIJ-id) *adj.; rigidly, adv.* 1. Stiff and hard to bend.—Iron bars are *rigid.*
2. Unchanging, or allowing no exceptions; strict.—In some schools the rules are very *rigid.*

rill (RIL) *n. rills.* A little stream or river.—The boys went wading in the *rill.*

rim (RIM) *n. rims.* A border or edge.—The *rims* on Mother's eyeglasses are gold.—The *rim* of a tumbler is the top edge.

rime or **rhyme** (RYM) *n. rimes* or *rhymes.* This is a *rime,* because the ends of the lines sound alike:

> "Jack and Jill
>   Went up the hill."

rind (RYND) *n. rinds.* The outer skin on such things as oranges, melons, squash, cucumbers, and bacon. —We eat the fruit but throw away the *rind.*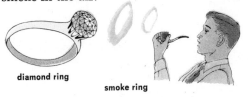

ring (RING) *n. rings.* 1. A circle. — When Father smokes his pipe, he makes *rings* of smoke in the air.

diamond ring

smoke ring

2. A round band worn on the finger.—Mother wears a wedding *ring.*
3. Any round band.—The farmer put a *ring* in the pig's nose to keep him from digging up the ground with his nose.
4. A band or group.—A group of people who work together for bad purposes is a *ring.*—A *ring* of thieves stole the gold.
5. Sound of or like a bell.—We heard three short *rings* and knew it was Bob at the door.—The *ring* of Mary's laugh could be heard from the garden.

—*v. rings, rang, ringing.* 1. Make a sound of or like a bell.—Mary dropped the cover of the saucepan, and we could hear it *ring* as it hit the floor.
2. Make (a bell) sound.—*Ring* the doorbell, please.
3. Be filled (with sound).—The theater *rings* with laughter every time the comedian comes onto the stage.

ring·let (RING-lət) *n. ringlets.* A small, tight curl.—After a rain, Baby's hair curls in *ringlets* all over her head.

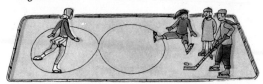

rink (RINGK) *n. rinks.* A floor, or sheet of ice, marked off or fenced in for roller skating, or ice skating.

rinse (RINSS) *v. rinses, rinsed, rinsing.* Pour water over, or dip in water, especially to wash away the soap.—Mary washed the dishes in soapsuds, and then *rinsed* them with very hot water.—Clothes that have been washed in soapy water are *rinsed* by moving them in and out of clear water again and again.

ri·ot (RY-ət) *n. riots.* Noisy quarreling and fighting by a large number of people, especially in a public place.

rip (RIP) *n. rips.* A tear or opening.—Bob had a *rip* in his coat sleeve where the threads of the seam had come out.
—*v. rips, ripped, ripping.* 1. Tear; pull apart by force.—Mother *ripped* off the bandage on her arm.—Mother *ripped* up Mary's old coat to make a coat for the baby. She cut or pulled out the threads from the seams.

rip cord (RIP kord) *rip cords.* The cord which, when pulled, opens a parachute.—The paratrooper pulled the *rip cord* to open his parachute.

ripe (RYP) *adj. riper, ripest.* Completely grown and ready to be picked for eating.—Grandfather told Bob to pick only the *ripe* cherries off the tree.

rip·en (RYP-ən) *v. ripens, ripened, ripening.* Become ripe or ready to eat.—Tomatoes *ripen* in the sun more quickly than they do in the shade.

rip·ple (RIP-əl) *n. ripples.* A tiny wave.— There isn't a *ripple* on the lake today.—When the frog jumped into the water, little *ripples* formed on the surface.
—*v. ripples, rippled, rippling.* Make little waves on.—The breeze *rippled* the lake.

rise (RYZ) *n. rises.* 1. An increase.—The *rise* in the price of milk made it hard for the large family to buy milk for their six children.
2. A slope or slant.—The steep *rise* of the roof makes it difficult to climb.
—*v. rises, rose, rising.* 1. Get up or stand up.—*Rise* before you speak in class.
2. Go or move up.—A balloon *rises* because it is lighter than air.
3. Increase. — The temperature sometimes *rises* during the daytime. The air grows warmer.
4. Slant upward. — We have made a rock garden in our backyard where the bank *rises* sharply.

risk (RISK) *n. risks.* Chance or danger.— There is no *risk* of falling if you hold on to the ladder.

—*v. risks, risked, risking.* 1. Take the chance of.—Do not *risk* crossing the street in front of a moving car.
2. Put in danger of loss or harm.—The man *risked* his life to save the child.

risk·y (RISS-kee) *adj. riskier, riskiest; riskily, adv.; riskiness, n.* Dangerous; involving chance. — It is *risky* to get too tired while swimming.

rite (RYT) *n. rites.* A solemn act or special service usually carried out according to a set form or pattern.—Marriage *rites* in our church are carried out in the same way each time a man and a woman are married.

ri·val (RY-vəl) *n. rivals.* One of two or more persons who are trying to get something only one can have.—Mary and Ruth were *rivals* in the final spelling bee. Each of them wanted to be the winner.

—*v. rivals, rivaled, rivaling.* Be a rival to.—The girls *rivaled* each other in the spelling bee.

ri·val·ry (RY-vəl-ree) *n. rivalries.* Competition between rivals.—There is *rivalry* between the boys to see who will get the higher mark.

riv·er (RIV-er) *n. rivers.* Large brook or stream.—Boats steam up and down the *river*.

riv·et (RIV-it) *n. rivets.* A metal bolt with a rounded head and without threads. A *rivet* is put through matching holes in the pieces to be fastened together, and then the small end is flattened with an automatic hammer to make another head so that the *rivet* will not come out.

—*v. rivets, riveted, riveting.* Fasten with one or more rivets. — The workmen *riveted* the heavy steel beams together.

roach (ROHCH) *n. roaches.* A cockroach; an insect with a hard shell sometimes found in kitchens, bathrooms, and other damp places. —*Roaches* come out at night when it is dark.

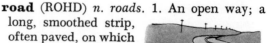

road (ROHD) *n. roads.* 1. An open way; a long, smoothed strip, often paved, on which people, cars, animals, and other things travel. *Roads* lead from one place to another. 2. A way.—Kindness is a *road* to happiness.

road·side (ROHD-syd) *n. roadsides.* Land at the side of a road.—The *roadside* was covered with weeds.

—*adj.* Located at the side of a road.—We buy vegetables at a *roadside* market, a market at the side of a road.

roam (ROHM) *v. roams, roamed, roaming.* Wander about.—On Sundays we like to *roam* through the woods.

roar (ROR) *n. roars.* A loud, deep sound or noise.—We heard the *roar* of the guns.

—*v. roars, roared, roaring.* Make a deep, loud sound.—The lions at the zoo *roar*.

roast (ROHST) *n. roasts.* A piece of meat to be cooked in the oven.—We ate the entire *roast* for dinner.

—*v. roasts, roasted, roasting.* Bake or cook in an oven or over live coals on an open fire.— Mother *roasted* the beef in the oven.

rob (RAHB) *v. robs, robbed, robbing.* Steal from, or force one to hand over.—The bandits *robbed* the man of his wallet and then fled.

rob·ber (RAHB-er) *n. robbers.* A person who robs or steals.—The highway *robbers* held up travelers who passed by.

rob·ber·y (RAHB-er-ee) *n. robberies.* The act of robbing or stealing. — The bank *robbery* took place at night.

robe (ROHB) *n. robes.* 1. A long, loose gown worn over other clothing. — Father has a new bath*robe*.— Men in certain offices, such as judges and ministers, wear *robes*.
2. A covering to put over the feet, legs, and lap when one sits outdoors.—We have a lap *robe* in our car.

rob·in (RAHB-in) *n. robins.* A bird of the thrush family. It has a reddish breast and is sometimes called a redbreast. — *Robins* have a cheerful song.

ro·bot (ROH-but *or* -baht) *n. robots.* 1. A machine, made to look like a man, that can walk around and do certain other things a man can do.
2. A person who acts like a machine.

ro·bust (roh-BUST *or* ROH-bust) *adj.* Strong, healthy, and sound; sturdy.—The champion is tall and *robust.*

rock (RAHK) *n. rocks.* 1. The solid material of the earth's crust, made up of minerals.— The bottom of this lake is solid *rock.*
2. A large mass of stone.—The mountain is a huge *rock.*
3. A large stone.—The boys threw *rocks* into the lake and watched them splash.
—*v. rocks, rocked, rocking.* Move to and fro and from side to side.—The boat *rocked* dangerously during the storm.—Sally *rocked* her doll to sleep in its cradle.

rock·er (RAHK-er) *n. rockers.* 1. A curved piece of wood on which the legs of a piece of furniture are set.
2. A rocking chair, or chair that moves back and forth on rockers.

rock·et (RAHK-it) *n. rockets* and *adj.* 1. A type of engine; a method of propulsion. When the fuel inside a *rocket* is lit and explodes, the explosion knocks against the walls of the *rocket* and pushes it forward. When liquid fuel is used, it is sprayed with oxygen into a combustion chamber and ignited. When solid fuel is used, the fire just eats away at the fuel.
2. A missile that uses rocket propulsion. *Rockets* are used as signals, fireworks, and weapons. Recently they have been used to send satellites into orbit.

rock·ing chair (RAHK-ing chair) *rocking chairs.* A chair on rockers. — Grandmother sits in her *rocking chair* and rocks Baby to sleep.

rock salt (RAHK sawlt). Common salt found in large, rocklike, solid masses. When pure, it is colorless and transparent. When impure, it is often yellow, red, or brown, and not transparent.

rock·y (RAHK-ee) *adj. rockier, rockiest.* Made up of rocks or covered with rocks.—The coast is very *rocky* here.

ROCKETS

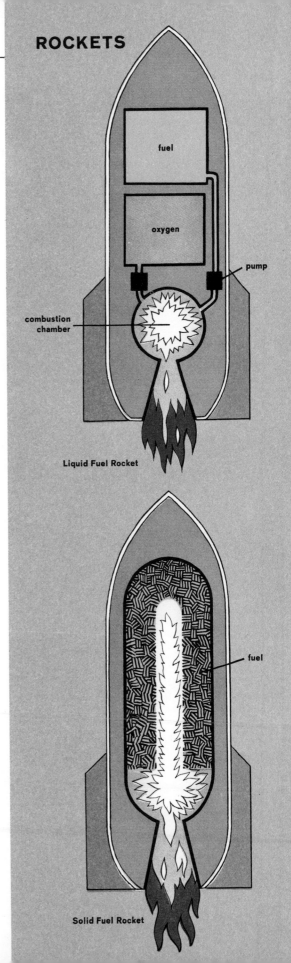

fuel

oxygen

pump

combustion chamber

Liquid Fuel Rocket

fuel

Solid Fuel Rocket

rod (RAHD) *n. rods.* 1. A straight, slender piece of wood or metal.—The doors of a prison cell are made of iron bars or *rods.*
2. A stick used to whip, or punish, a person or an animal.
3. A pole for fishing.—Father has a new fishing *rod.*

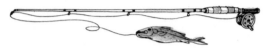

4. A measure of length equal to 16½ feet.— Ribbon is measured by the yard. Land is measured by the foot and by the *rod.*

rode (ROHD) *v.* One form of the verb *ride.*— Yesterday I *rode* my bicycle.

ro·dent (ROH-dənt) *n. rodents.* An animal, such as a rat or squirrel, that has long, sharp teeth which it uses to gnaw or bite things away little by little.—Rabbits and mice are *rodents.*

chipmunk
squirrel
rat
beaver

ro·de·o (ROH-dee-oh *or* roh-DAY-oh) *n. rodeos.* 1. A cowboy show in which men rope cattle and ride bulls and wild horses.—Bob and Father went to a *rodeo.*

2. In the West, a roundup, or a gathering together of many cattle by riding around them and driving them in.

rogue (ROHG) *n. rogues.* 1. A dishonest, tricky person; a rascal. — A *rogue* cheated Father by selling him worthless goods.
2. A mischief maker.—Sally is a little *rogue.* She likes to play tricks on people.

role (ROHL) *n. roles.* 1. A character or part in a show or movie played by an actor or actress. — Tim had the leading *role* in the school play. He played the part of the king.
2. Any part played in life.—Every night at suppertime, Mother plays the *role* of a cook.

roll (ROHL) *n. rolls.* 1. A continuous rumbling sound.—The prisoners heard the *roll* of the drums and the tramping of feet.—We saw a flash of lightning and heard a *roll* of thunder.
2. A list of names.—Mary checked the *roll* to see if all the children were in school.
3. Anything wound around something else, such as a *roll* of cloth, paper towels, wrapping paper, or the like.
4. Anything wound about itself. — The children made a *roll* of the clay in art class.
5. A kind of bread shaped into buns or small pieces before it is baked.—We have cinnamon *rolls* for breakfast every Sunday morning.

—*v. rolls, rolled, rolling.* 1. Turn over and over and move ahead.—The bowling ball *rolled* down the alley.
2. Wind up, or turn over and over.—The children *rolled* a snowball.—Grandmother *rolled* the yarn into a ball.—The children *rolled* up their papers and put a rubber band around them to take them home.
3. Push along on wheels or rollers.—Sally *rolled* the crippled man's wheel chair out onto the porch.
4. Flatten out with a rolling pin.—Mother *rolled* the cookie dough a quarter of an inch thick, and Mary cut out the cookies.
5. Swing from side to side.—During the storm the ship *rolled.*
6. Move continuously in a rolling, curved fashion.—The waves *rolled* in to shore.
7. Trill.—Some people *roll* their "r's" when they speak. They make their tongues vibrate against the roof of their mouth when they pronounce the letter "r."
8. Pile. — Our team *rolled* up a big score against the Rangers.

roll call (ROHL kawl) *roll calls.* A calling of names to see if anyone is absent.—After *roll call*, the teacher read us a story.

roll·er (ROHL-er) *n. rollers.* Anything that rolls, or moves along by turning over and over.—The small wheels on the legs of beds, tables, and chairs are *rollers.* — The wringer on the washing machine has two *rollers.*

roll·er skate (ROHL-er skayt) *roller skates.* A skate with rollers, or wheels, instead of a runner or blade. —*v. roller skate, roller skated, roller skating.* Skate or glide on roller skates. – Children *roller skate* on the sidewalk.

roll·ing pin (ROHL-ing pin) *rolling pins.* A roller of wood or other material with a handle at each end. It is used to roll pie crust, to crush bread into crumbs, to roll cookie dough, and the like.

ro·mance (roh-MANSS *or* ROH-manss) *n. romances.* A poem or a story about heroes, adventure, or love.—Many people call any love story a *romance.*

Ro·man nu·mer·als (ROH-mən NOO- *or* NYOO-mer-əlz). Numbers such as I, V, X, L, C, D, and M are *Roman numerals.* I=1; V=5; X=10; L=50; C=100; D=500; and M=1,000. *Roman numerals* are often used on clocks instead of Arabic numerals.

romp (RAHMP) *n. romps.* Rough-and-tumble play.—The boys had their *romp* today. —*v. romps, romped, romping.* Play roughly and noisily.—Jack and his dog *romp* in the yard.

roof (ROOF *or* RUHF) *n. roofs.* 1. The top covering of a building.—Our *roof* is made of green shingles.
2. Anything that is similar to a roof in position or use, such as the top of a car.

room (ROOM) *n. rooms.* 1. One of the inside divisions or parts of a building. *Rooms* are separated by walls and connected by doors. —We sleep in a bed*room.*
2. Space.—There wasn't *room* for one more thing in Mother's pocketbook.
3. Opportunity or chance.—There is *room* for advancement in Uncle Ned's business. A young man can go far.
—*v. rooms, roomed, rooming.* Live in a room in someone else's house.—Our teacher *rooms* at Mrs. Jones's house.

roost (ROOST) *n. roosts.* A perch, bar, branch, or anything else on which birds sit, stand, or rest while they sleep. The stick across a bird cage is a *roost.* —*v. roosts, roosted, roosting.* Sit on a roost.—The canary *roosts* on his swing to sleep.

roost·er (ROOST-er) *n. roosters.* A male chicken. The mother chicken is a hen; the father chicken is a *rooster.*—The farmer's *roosters* crow early in the morning.

root (ROOT *or* RUHT) *n. roots.* 1. A part of a plant, bush, or tree that grows downward into the earth. *Roots* hold plants in place and feed them moisture and food from the soil. We eat some *roots,* such as turnips, beets, carrots, and radishes.
2. A part that is like the root of a plant.— Teeth have *roots* to hold them securely in place.
3. A beginning or source.—Spending all his allowance for candy was the *root* of Sam's troubles.
—*v. roots, rooted, rooting.* 1. Plant, set, or fix deeply.—The tree is well *rooted.*—It is hard to break a deeply *rooted* habit.—Bill's dislike of school is *rooted* in his lack of willingness to study.
2. Dig, pull, or remove.—The dogs *rooted* the fox out from his hiding place.—The farmer put rings in the pigs' noses so that they would not *root* up the earth.

rope (ROHP) *n. ropes.* 1. A strong, heavy cord made by twisting together several smaller cords.
2. Any large twisted strand or braid. – The children made a *rope* of dandelions to wear around their necks and heads.
—*v. ropes, roped, roping.* 1. Separate, tie off, or divide with a rope.—A part of the street was *roped* off so that the children could play there.
2. Lasso or capture by throwing a rope around. – The cowboy *roped* the runaway horse.
3. Bind or tie with a rope.—The farmer *roped* the goat to the stake.

ro·sa·ry (ROH-zə-ree) *n. rosaries.* 1. A string of beads used to keep count in saying a number or series of prayers.
2. A group of prayers recited with this string of beads.

rose (ROHZ) *n. roses.* 1. A fragrant flower that grows on a bush. It has a prickly stem. *Roses* are red, yellow, pink, or white.
2. A deep pinkish color.
—*v.* One form of the verb *rise.*— The sun *rose* bright and hot.

ros·in (RAHZ-in) *n.* A hard brownish substance made from turpentine. *Rosin* is used on a violin bow to keep it from slipping while one plays the violin.

ros·y (ROH-zee) *adj. rosier, rosiest.* 1. Deep pink or reddish.—Baby has *rosy* cheeks.
2. Cheerful; full of promise of good things.— The days ahead of us look *rosy.*

rot (RAHT) *v. rots, rotted, rotting.* Decay; become soft and spoiled. — The potatoes remained in the wet ground so long that they *rotted.*

ro·ta·ry (ROH-tə-ree) *adj.* Rotating; turning round, as a wheel turns on its axle.—An egg beater has *rotary* parts.

ro·tate (ROH-tayt) *v. rotates, rotated, rotating.* 1. Turn around about a center or axis. —The earth *rotates* on its axis.—The wheels of a moving cart *rotate.*
2. Arrange one after the other; take in turn. —The farmer *rotates* his crops. One year he plants corn in a field, the next year he plants wheat in that field, and so on.
—*rotation, n. rotations.*

ro·tor (ROH-ter) *n. rotors.* 1. The part of a tool, machine, or device that rotates. — The blade of an electric fan is a *rotor.*
2. The arrangement of rotating blades by means of which a helicopter flies.—The workmen put a new *rotor* on the Police Department's new helicopter.

rot·ten (RAHT-n) *adj. rottener, rottenest.* 1. Decayed; soft and spoiled. — The tomatoes that were not kept in the refrigerator are *rotten.*
2. In bad condition; weak; not sound.—The boards in the front steps are *rotten,* so be careful.

ro·tun·da (roh-TUN-də) *n. rotundas.* A large round room or building, especially one with a dome.—There is a *rotunda* in the Capitol in Washington, D. C.

rouge (ROOZH) *n.* A pink or red powder or cream for coloring the skin.—Mother wears *rouge* on her cheeks.
—*v. rouges, rouged, rouging.* Put rouge on.— Mother *rouges* her cheeks.

rough (RUF) *adj. rougher, roughest; roughly, adv.; roughness, n.* 1. Uneven; irregular; not smooth or level.—Plowed ground is *rough.*— Sandpaper is *rough.*
2. Stormy; not quiet or still.—The sailors found the sea *rough.*
3. Wild and active.—Boys seem to like *rough* play. Many boys enjoy *rough* games.
4. Difficult, or filled with hard work.—Grandfather had a *rough* life when he was a boy.
5. Unpolished; not finished.—Diamonds are polished when you buy them in rings, but they are *rough* when they come from the mines.
6. Tangled; coarse.—The dog has *rough* fur.
7. Rude or ill-mannered.—The man met our offers of help with *rough* refusals.
8. Crude; not detailed or accurate. — Bob made a *rough* drawing of the model airplane he wants to build.
—*v. roughs, roughed, roughing.* 1. Rumple or tangle.—Father *roughed* up the baby's hair.
2. Make a rough outline, shape, or model of. —At first the children *roughed* out the vases they were making; then they made them smooth and true to form.
—*Rough it* means to live without the comforts of home.—The boys *roughed it* when they were camping.

rough·age (RUF-ij) *n.* Any rough or coarse material, especially certain foods that aid digestion, such as lettuce, celery, carrots, and bran. — The fragile glasses were packed in boxes filled with *roughage* to keep them from breaking. The *roughage* included strips of paper, wood shavings, and straw.

rough·en (RUF-ən) *v. roughens, roughened, roughening.* Make rough or coarse. — Cold weather *roughens* one's hands. Creams make them smooth again.

round (ROWND) *n. rounds.* 1. A regular route. — A policeman makes his *rounds* each day.
2. A dance which moves in a circle. — The Maypole dance is a *round.*
3. A number of duties, sports, pleasures, or other happenings coming one right after the other.—On our vacation we had a *round* of parties.
4. A part or period into which a fight or a game is divided.—The heavyweight champion knocked out his opponent in the third *round.*

5. Something which many people join in doing at the same time.—There was a *round* of boos when the batter struck out.

6. A song sung by a number of people beginning at different times.—Children think it is fun to sing *rounds*.

—*v.* rounds, rounded, rounding. 1. Go around.—The speeding car *rounded* the corner on two wheels.

2. Make or become circular.—Jack *rounded* the wheels of his model airplane.

—*adj.* Shaped like a ball, a circle, a wheel, or a water pipe.—Anything *round* and smooth will roll.

—*Round out* means complete. — Bob *rounded out* his story with one more paragraph.

round·a·bout (ROWND-ə-bowt) *adj.* Not straight or direct.—Because the road was being repaired, we went a *roundabout* way to the farm.

round·house (ROWND-howss) *n.* round-houses. A round building to house railroad engines. It is built around a turning platform; the engines run onto the platform and the platform turns. In this way the engines are turned around.

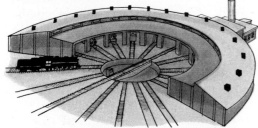

round-shoul·dered (ROWND-shohl-derd) *adj.* Having shoulders that lean forward.—The tall, thin girl is *round-shouldered*. She does not stand up straight.

round·up (ROWND-up) *n.* roundups. 1. Bringing cattle together.—The cowboys took part in the *roundup*. They brought together a large number of cattle by forming a circle around them and driving them into one herd.

2. Any gathering together of people by the efforts of others.—The police were praised for their *roundup* of gangsters in the town.

rouse (ROWZ) *v.* rouses, roused, rousing. 1. Disturb, wake up, or excite.—You may *rouse* the sleeping baby if you make too much noise.

2. Stir up or make angry.—The kidnaping *roused* the people of the town.

route (ROOT *or* ROWT) *n.* routes. A way of travel; a road or path.—What *route* did you take to the city?

—*v.* routes, routed, routing. Send along a way or road. — The policeman *routed* the cars around the washed-out bridge. He told them how to go by another way.

rou·tine (roo-TEEN) *n.* routines. A regular plan or way of doing things that is followed every time.—Mother gets her work done early because she follows a *routine*.

rove (ROHV) *v.* roves, roved, roving. Roam or wander.—The children like to *rove* in the woods.

row (ROH) *n.* rows. A line.—We sat in the first *row* of seats.—The wind destroyed a *row* of trees.

—*v.* rows, rowed, rowing. Move (a boat) with oars.—Bob *rowed* the boat to the spot where we fished.

row (ROW) *n.* rows. Noisy fight or quarrel.—The boys had a *row* over who would get the biggest piece of pie.

row·boat (ROH-boht) *n.* rowboats. A small boat moved by rowing.—The fishermen rented a *rowboat*.

roy·al (ROI-əl) *adj.; royally, adv.* Having to do with, or fit for, kings and queens.—The king and queen and their family live in the *royal* palace.—We were given a *royal* welcome.

roy·al·ty (ROI-əl-tee) *n.* royalties. 1. Kings, queens, and members of their families.—The feast was prepared for *royalty*.

2. Money paid to an inventor, author, or composer as his share of money made from the sale of his work. — Persons who write books often receive *royalties*.

rub (RUB) *v. rubs, rubbed, rubbing.* 1. Press against or together, and move back and forth. —Father's hands were so cold that he had to *rub* them together to get them warm.
2. Clean or polish by rubbing.—The maid *rubbed* the pots and pans with a cloth and scouring powder.
3. Erase.—*Rub* out the pencil marks with an eraser.

rub·ber (RUB-er) *n. rubbers.* A stretchy material made from the thick sap or juice of many plants that grow in certain warm countries; something made of this material. —Erasers, tires for cars, galoshes, water hoses, hot-water bottles, balls, and many other things are made of *rubber.*—Wear your *rubbers* when it rains.

balloons
eraser
ball
hot-water bottle
boots
tire
rubber tree
garden hose

rub·bish (RUB-ish) *n.* Things to be thrown out; worthless things.—The children cleaned out the basement and put all the *rubbish* in the alley.

ru·by (ROO-bee) *n. rubies.* A deep-red precious stone.—Grandmother has a ring set with a large *ruby.*
—*adj.* Of a deep-red color.—The beautiful Snow White had coal-black hair, snow-white skin, and *ruby* lips.

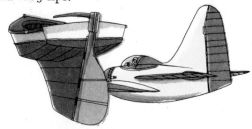

rud·der (RUD-er) *n. rudders.* A flat piece of wood or metal on the back of a boat, used for steering. Airplanes have *rudders,* too.

rude (ROOD) *adj. ruder, rudest; rudely, adv.; rudeness, n.* 1. Not polite; not courteous. — The boy was *rude;* he interrupted while his mother was talking.
2. Rough. — The boys made a *rude* boat of some old boards and a log.

ruf·fi·an (RUF-ee-ən) *n. ruffians.* A cruel, rough person.—The *ruffians* seized the salesman and beat him.

ruf·fle (RUF-əl) *n. ruffles.* A narrow piece of cloth or lace gathered at one edge and used as a trimming. — Mary's dress has *ruffles* around the hem and around the sleeves.
—*v. ruffles, ruffled, ruffling.* 1. Gather or make tiny pleats in cloth. —Mother *ruffled* the curtain borders on the sewing machine.

2. Puff out; cause to become rough or rear up.—The rooster *ruffles* his feathers when you go near him.
3. Disturb . or vex. — Jack's teasing *ruffled* Mary. It made her angry.

rug (RUG) *n. rugs.* 1. A large carpet or other floor covering. *Rugs* are made of wool, cotton, rags, reeds, and grass.—Mother wants a new living-room *rug.*
2. A blanketlike robe. — Grandmother puts her *rug* over her lap when she rides with Father in the car.

rug·ged (RUG-id) *adj.; ruggedly, adv.; ruggedness, n.* 1. Uneven; rough.—The mountain country in the West is very *rugged.*
2. Rough and very simple.—Camping out is too *rugged* for Mother.
3. Strong and hardy.—Father likes to tell us how *rugged* he was when he was a boy.

ru·in (ROO-in) *n. ruins.* 1. Partly destroyed remains.—The country was in *ruins* after the storm. Buildings, trees, and other things were destroyed or damaged.—The *ruins* of some ancient buildings are still standing.
2. Useless or worthless condition. — The farmer's machines are in *ruin* from being left out in the rain so often.
3. Something which causes destruction or downfall. — Laziness and drink were the man's *ruin.*
4. Downfall or destruction. — War brought *ruin* to the country.
—*v. ruins, ruined, ruining.* Spoil or destroy.— The hailstorm *ruined* the fruit in the orchard

rule (ROOL) *n. rules.* 1. A direction telling what may and what may not be done.–The children know the *rules* of the game.
2. A flat stick, marked with evenly spaced lines, used for measuring and for drawing straight lines; a ruler.–Bob used a *rule* to measure the border on his paper and to guide his pencil in drawing the border.
3. Usual custom.–It is the *rule* to plant gardens in the spring.
–*v. rules, ruled, ruling.* 1. Mark with straight lines.–We *ruled* the paper for ten spelling words.
2. Control or govern.–The king *rules* over his country.
3. Decide.–The children *ruled* that the rules of the game should be followed carefully.

rul·er (ROOL-er) *n. rulers.* 1. A person who governs or controls.–A king is a *ruler*.
2. A flat stick marked off in inches, half inches, and so on. A *ruler* is used to measure with and to guide one's pencil in making straight lines.

rul·ing (ROOL-ing) *n. rulings.* A judgment given by a judge or court.–It is the judge's *ruling* that the man be fined.

rum (RUM) *n. rums.* A drink containing alcohol and made from sugar cane. *Rum* is sometimes used as a flavoring in cake.

rum·ba (RUM- *or* ROOM-bə) *n. rumbas.* A dance originating among the Negroes of Cuba; an American version of the dance. The music played for the *rumba* is called by the same name.

rum·ble (RUM-bəl) *n. rumbles.* A low, heavy, rolling sound.–During the night we heard the *rumble* of thunder.
–*v. rumbles, rumbled, rumbling.* Make a low, heavy, rolling sound.–Father's old car *rumbled* as it went down the road.

rum·mage (RUM-ij) *v. rummages, rummaged, rummaging.* Look for something by moving things about haphazardly.–Father *rummaged* through the tool chest for a few nails.

ru·mor (ROO-mer) *n. rumors.* A report or story told as news without knowledge of whether it is true.–There is a *rumor* going about that the teacher is getting married.
–*v. rumors, rumored, rumoring.* Tell or spread news without knowing if it is true.–It is *rumored* that the king is sick.

rum·ple (RUM-pəl) *v. rumples, rumpled, rumpling.* 1. Wrinkle. – The baby *rumpled* the bedspread when he played on the bed.
2. Muss or tangle.–The wind *rumpled* the baby's curls.

run (RUN) *n. runs.* 1. A swift trip on foot.–Bob and his dog went for a *run* in the field.
2. A trip.–The engineer has made his last *run* on the train. He is retiring today.
3. A place where a thread has pulled out of some material; a row of raveled stitches.–Mother caught her stocking on a splinter and got a *run* in it.
4. A series of happenings.–The ball team had a *run* of bad luck.
5. A score in baseball.–The team needed two *runs* to win the game.
6. A sudden great demand. – When coffee was scarce, there was a great *run* on the stores for it.
7. A spreading.–There is a *run* of measles in the school now.
–*v. runs, ran, running.* 1. Move so fast that, at a moment in each step, all or both the legs are off the ground at the same time.–When Jack whistles, his dog *runs* to him.
2. Go or move.–The motor of the car *runs* fast and smoothly.
3. Flow.–Water *runs* from the faucet.
4. Reach or stretch out.–Our yard *runs* from the house to the corner.
5. Operate or make go.–Mary can *run* the sewing machine.
6. Thrust or push.–Do not *run* your finger into your eye.
7. Be a candidate or try to get elected. – Father would not *run* for mayor even if he were asked.
8. Become. – The sick child's temperature *ran* higher every hour.
9. Average; be usually.–The fish in this lake *run* about ten inches long.

run·a·way (RUN-ə-way) *n. runaways.* A person or animal that runs away.–A fleeing robber is a *runaway*.
–*adj.* Running out of control.–A car moving without a driver is a *runaway* car.

rung (RUNG) *n. rungs.* A round bar, usually of wood, used as a crosspiece on a ladder or between the legs of a chair or as a wheel spoke. –The painter stood on the top *rung* of the ladder.
–*v.* One form of the verb *ring.*– The bell had already *rung* when we got to school.

run·ner (RUN-er) *n. runners.* 1. A smooth, narrow strip on which something slides.—Sleds, ice skates, and drawers in cabinets move on *runners.*

2. Small stems that stretch along the ground and form roots from which new plants grow.—Strawberry plants have *runners.*

3. A person who runs, races, or carries messages.—An Indian *runner* stopped at the trading post with a message. — There were five *runners* in the 100-yard dash.

4. A narrow strip.—Mother put a clean *runner* of white lace on the table.—A long strip of carpet is a *runner.*

run·ning (RUN-ing) *n.* Operating.—Mother attends to the *running* of the house.—Father attends to the *running* of the car; he always drives it.

—*v.* One form of the verb *run.*—The dog is *running* after the cat.

—*adj.* 1. Flowing.—We have *running* water in the bathroom.

2. One after another, in a row.—It has rained for six days *running.*

runt (RUNT) *n. runts.* A person or animal that doesn't grow to be as large as others of the same kind.—Our dog is just a *runt,* but he can run faster than most big dogs.

run·way (RUN-way) *n. runways.* 1. A track or roadway on which something runs, slides, or moves.—The new ship slid down the *runway* into the water.—Airplanes take off from *runways.*

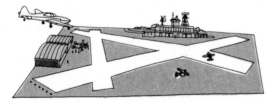

2. A path that is beaten down by animals in going to and from their feeding or drinking places.

rup·ture (RUP-cher) *v. ruptures, ruptured, rupturing.* Break; split; burst. — John *ruptured* the tiny blood vessels in his nose and had a nosebleed.

ru·ral (RUHR-əl) *adj.; rurally, adv.* Having to do with the country; living in the country.—*Rural* life is life in the country.

rush (RUSH) *n. rushes.* 1. A time of great hurrying and crowding.—We came home on the subway during the evening *rush.*

2. A sudden movement. — A *rush* of wind blew the door open.

3. A hollow reed or stem that grows in marshy or wet places.—Indians made baskets of *rushes.*

—*v. rushes, rushed, rushing.* 1. Go fast or in a hurry.—The fire truck *rushed* to the burning building.—The water *rushed* over the rocks.

2. Hurry.—Do not *rush* through your meals.

3. Attack or charge.—The football players *rushed* the players on the other team.

rust (RUST) *n.* 1. A rough, orange-brown crust that forms on iron and steel. — Unpainted iron or steel tools left out in the air or in a wet place are soon covered with *rust.*

2. A plant disease that makes spots on leaves and stems.—The wheat crop was spoiled by *rust.*

—*v. rusts, rusted, rusting.* Become covered with rust.—Your bicycle will *rust* if you leave it out all night.

rus·tic (RUSS-tik) *adj.* Rural; having to do with the country; simple and rough.—Grandfather lives in a *rustic* cottage.

rus·tle (RUSS-əl) *n.* A crackling noise.—We can hear the *rustle* of the leaves on the oak trees in autumn.

—*v. rustles, rustled, rustling.* 1. Make a crackling or whispering sound.—Mother's taffeta dress *rustles* as she walks.

2. Steal (cattle or other livestock).—A band of thieves *rustled* cattle from the ranches in the foothills.

rus·tler (RUSS-ler) *n. rustlers.* A person who steals cattle or other livestock.—The *rustler* was caught by the cowboy.

rust·y (RUST-ee) *adj. rustier, rustiest.* 1. Covered with rust.—The old saw is *rusty.*

2. Out of practice.—The musician is *rusty* because he hasn't practiced.

rut (RUT) *n. ruts.* 1. A groove or track such as one worn in the ground by the wheels of cars. — The *rut* in the road is filled with water.

2. Habit, or unchanging ways of doing things.—People who do the same work in the same way day after day may get into a *rut.*

ruth·less (ROOTH-ləss) *adj.; ruthlessly, adv.; ruthlessness, n.* Cruel and heartless; without pity or mercy.—The *ruthless* landlord put the poor family out on the street.

rye (RY) *n. and adj.* A grain.—Farmers grow *rye.*—*Rye* is made into flour which is used in making *rye* bread.

S s

S, s (ESS) *n. S's, s's.* The nineteenth letter of the alphabet.

Sab·bath (SAB-əth) *n. Sabbaths.* Day of rest and worship.—Sunday, the first day of the week, is the Christian *Sabbath.* — Saturday, the seventh and last day of the week, is the Jewish *Sabbath.*

sa·ber (SAY-ber) *n. sabers.* A sword with a heavy, curved blade.—Soldiers on horseback use *sabers.*

sab·o·tage (SAB-ə-tahzh) *n.* Damage or destruction of property, such as machinery and tools, especially by enemy agents during wartime, or by employees during a labor dispute.—The man who had blown up the bridge was charged with *sabotage.*

sac·cha·rin (SAK-ə-rin) *n.* An artificial sweetener; a substitute for sugar. *Saccharin* is often used by persons who are not allowed to use sugar because of illness, or who are trying to lose weight.

sack (SAK) *n. sacks.* A large bag, usually one made of burlap or other coarse material.—

burlap sack   string sack   paper sack   cotton sack

Sacks are used to hold potatoes, onions, wheat, and the like.

sa·cred (SAY-krid) *adj.; sacredness, n.* Holy; worthy of worship and deep respect. Things having to do with God or religion are *sacred.* —We sing *sacred* songs in Sunday school.— The name of God is *sacred.*

sac·ri·fice (SAK-rə-fyss) *n. sacrifices.* 1. Something offered to a god as a religious act. —In the Bible, Abraham killed a ram as a *sacrifice* to God.
2. A loss.—Bob sold his bicycle at a *sacrifice.*
—*v. sacrifices, sacrificed, sacrificing.* Give up.— Many soldiers have *sacrificed* their lives for our freedom.

sad (SAD) *adj. sadder, saddest; sadly, adv.; sadness, n.* 1. Having a feeling of sorrow or unhappiness.—Children are *sad* when they lose or break a toy, or when their pet dies.
2. Causing sorrow or unhappiness. — The train wreck was a *sad* accident.

sad·den (SAD-n) *v. saddens, saddened, saddening.* Make unhappy.—The loss of his dog *saddened* Jim.

sad·dle (SAD-l) *n. saddles.* A seat, usually of leather, for a person riding on a horse, bicycle, tricycle, motorcycle, or the like.— Tom sits up straight in the *saddle* on his new horse.
—*v. saddles, saddled, saddling.* 1. Put a saddle on.—The farmer *saddled* the pony for his little boy.
2. Load or burden.—The farmer *saddled* his hired man with many chores.

sad·ness (SAD-nəss) *n.* Sorrow or grief.— Much *sadness* was caused by the death of the family pet.

sa·fa·ri (sə-FAHR-ee) *n. safaris.* 1. An expedition or journey, especially for hunting.— The hunters are planning a *safari* in Africa.
2. The caravan of persons, animals, and equipment on such an expedition. — The *safari* camped near a river for the night.

safe (SAYF) *n. safes.* A steel cabinet with a lock, for keeping valuable things. — The grocer keeps his money in a *safe.*
—*adj. safer, safest; safely, adv.* Free from danger.—It is *safe* to cross the street when the light is green.—The lost child has turned up *safe* and sound at a neighbor's house.

safe·ty (SAYF-tee) *n.* Freedom from danger. —The porch has a railing around it so that the baby can play there in *safety.*
—*adj.* Giving or making sure of safety.—Father uses a *safety* razor. It is designed to protect him from cutting his skin. — Mother uses *safety* pins in dressing the baby.

safe·ty belt (SAYF-tee belt) *safety belts.* A specially designed belt fixed to each seat in an airplane. The *safety belt* is used to hold a passenger or crew member securely  in his seat during take-offs, landings, and bad flying weather. *Safety belts* are also used in cars.

sag (SAG) *v. sags, sagged, sagging.* Droop or hang unevenly.—The curtain *sags* in the middle. — The tennis net is not stretched tight enough. It *sags.*

sage (SAYJ) *n.* A plant whose dried leaves are used as flavoring. — We put *sage* in chicken dressing to flavor it.

sage·brush (SAYJ-brush) *n.* A silvery-gray shrublike plant found in the western United States. *Sagebrush* grows in dry or partly dry regions. It sometimes reaches a height of twelve feet.

said (SED) *v.* One form of the verb *say.*—I *said,* "It is a nice day."

sail (SAYL) *n. sails.* 1. A large piece of heavy cloth raised over a boat so that the wind blows on it and moves the boat along.
2. A trip on a sailboat.—We went for a *sail* with Ed.
—*v. sails, sailed, sailing.* 1. Start a voyage.—The steamer *sailed* Monday.
2. Move along (of a ship).—The ship *sailed* slowly down the river.
3. Soar or move smoothly and swiftly.—The arrow *sailed* right over the top of the target. —The airplane *sailed* over the city.
4. Direct and operate (a ship or boat).—The captain and sailors *sailed* the ship.

sail·boat (SAYL-boht) *n. sailboats.* A boat moved by the wind blowing against its sails.—We went for a sail on Ed's new *sail-boat.*

sail·or (SAY-ler) *n. sailors.* A man who sails, or works on, a boat or ship.—There were only three *sailors* in the crew of the small ship.

saint (SAYNT) *n. saints.* A holy person worthy of worship.

Saint Ber·nard (SAYNT ber-NAHRD) *Saint Bernards.* A very large, tan-and-white breed of dog. *Saint Bernard* dogs are very intelligent.

sake (SAYK) *n. sakes.* Account; cause; benefit of.—I hope the baby sleeps this afternoon, for Mother's *sake.* It will give Mother a chance to rest.—The patriots gave their lives for the *sake* of freedom.

sal·ad (SAL-əd) *n. salads.* Raw vegetables or fruits, usually served with oil and vinegar, or some other dressing.—We eat cabbage *salad,* potato *salad,* and apple and walnut *salad.* Cold eggs, meats, or fish mixed with vegetables and a dressing are *salads,* too.

sal·a·man·der (SAL-ə-man-der) *n. salamanders.* Any of various small amphibians that look very much like lizards but do not have claws or scaly skin. *Salamanders* live either on moist land or in the water.

sal·a·ry (SAL-ə-ree) *n. salaries.* Money paid to a person at regular times for work done.— Fathers gets his *salary* weekly.

sale (SAYL) *n. sales.* 1. A selling of something, or an exchanging of something for money.—Bob made ten dollars on the *sale* of his bicycle.
2. A selling at prices lower than usual.—The store had a *sale* of shoes.
3. Amount of goods sold.—The Christmas *sales* were very large.

sales·man (SAYLZ-mən) *n. salesmen.* A man who is paid to sell things.—Father is a *salesman.* He sells automobiles.

sales·wom·an (SAYLZ-wuhm-ən) *n. saleswomen.* A woman who is paid to sell things. —The *saleswoman* sold me two books.

sa·li·va (sə-LY-və) *n.* The liquid that forms in the mouth and keeps it moist.—The sight of meat makes *saliva* run from the dog's mouth.

salm·on (SAM-ən) *n. sing.* and *pl.* A kind of large fish whose pink flesh is good to eat.—*Salmon* is canned for food.
—*adj.* Yellowish-pink.—Mary's hair ribbon is a *salmon* color.

sa·loon (sə-LOON) *n. saloons.* A place where wine, beer, and other alcoholic drinks are sold and served.—The man went into a *saloon* to get a glass of beer.

salt (SAWLT) *n. salts* and *adj.* 1. A grainy white substance found in the earth and in sea water. *Salt* is used to give flavor to foods and also to preserve them, or keep them from spoiling. — Mother seasoned the vegetables with a little *salt*.
2. An old and experienced sailor. A sailor is called a *salt* because he sails the *salt* water of the sea.—The old *salt* knew many good stories.
—*v. salts, salted, salting.* 1. Put salt on or in.—Sue *salts* the water when she boils corn.
2. Provide salt for. — The farmer *salts* his cattle.

salt·cel·lar (SAWLT-sel-er) *n. saltcellars.* A small dish or other container to hold salt.—You lift the salt from a *saltcellar* with a small spoon, or shake it through a cap with little holes in it.

salt·y (SAWL-tee) *adj. saltier, saltiest.* Having much salt.—The vegetables were too *salty*.

sal·u·ta·tion (sal-yə-TAY-shən) *n. salutations.* 1. A greeting.—Shaking hands, tipping the hat, saying good morning, and saluting are all *salutations*.
2. The beginning of a letter, which addresses the person to whom one is writing.—"Dear Mother" is a *salutation*.

sa·lute (sə-LOOT) *n. salutes.* A formal greeting between officers and men in the armed forces, exchanged by raising the right hand to the forehead.—A bow or handshake is also a *salute*.
—*v. salutes, saluted, saluting.* To make a salute, or formal greeting.—The soldier *salutes* his officers. He shows respect and honor for his officers by raising his right hand to his head as if touching his hat.—Mary *saluted* the audience with a bow.

sal·vage (SAL-vij) *n. salvages.* 1. Things saved from damage.—There were several machines among the *salvage* from the burned factory. There were several machines that were not burned.
2. Money paid for saving a ship and its cargo.—The men received $10,000 in *salvage* for saving the sinking ship.
—*v. salvages, salvaged, salvaging.* Save from damage. — When the factory burned down, the men *salvaged* everything they could.

salve (SAV) *n. salves.* A kind of soft, creamy substance used as a medicine on sores, burns, and the like.—Mother rubbed *salve* on Bob's sore finger.

same (SAYM) *adj.; sameness, n.* 1. The very one; not another.—Mary wore the *same* dress to school that she wore Sunday. She did not wear a different one.
2. Just like.—Sally's pocketbook is the *same* as Mary's. It is the *same* color and the *same* style. Both are red and close with zippers.

sam·ple (SAM-pəl) *n. samples.* 1. A small part that shows what the rest is like.—This is a *sample* of my handwriting.
2. One of a number of like things used to show what all the rest are like.—This book is a *sample* copy. There are many others just like it.
—*v. samples, sampled, sampling.* Try or test.—Won't you *sample* these new cookies.

sanc·tu·ar·y (SANGK-choo-air-ee) *n. sanctuaries.* 1. A holy place.—Churches, temples, and shrines are *sanctuaries*.
2. The holiest section of a church or temple. The *sanctuary* is usually near the altar.
3. A place of refuge; a safe and protected area.—The rich old lady is having a *sanctuary* built for stray cats.
4. Protection; safety; refuge. — The fugitive sought *sanctuary* in a foreign country.

sand (SAND) *n. sands.* A large number of tiny bits of stone, often found along the shores of oceans, lakes, and rivers.—Children like to play in the white *sand* on the beach.
—*v. sands, sanded, sanding.* Scrape, polish, or smooth with sand or sandpaper. — Father *sanded* the floor before he varnished it.

san·dal (SAN-dl) *n. sandals.* 1. A shoe that is just a sole with a strap or straps to fasten it onto the foot. – Children wear *sandals* in warm weather.
2. A kind of light, open, fancy slipper.—Mother wears *sandals* when she dances.

sand·bag (SAND-bag) *n. sandbags.* A bag filled with sand. *Sandbags* are used to dam flood waters, provide balloon and boat ballast, serve as defensive barriers, and to do other jobs for which bulk is necessary.

sand bar (SAND bahr) *sand bars.* A narrow ridge of sand sometimes found in coastal waters, rivers, or across the mouth of a bay. *Sand bars* are formed by the action of tides and water currents.

sand·pa·per (SAND-pay-per) *n.* A heavy paper coated on one side with a layer of sand. *Sandpaper* is used to smooth rough surfaces.

sand·pip·er (SAND-py-per) *n. sandpipers.* A rather small wading bird with long legs and a long bill.—We saw a flock of *sandpipers* at the beach.

sand·stone (SAND-stohn) *n.* A type of rock made largely of sand and held together by a natural cement, such as clay.

sand·wich (SAND- *or* SAN-wich) *n. sandwiches.* Two or more slices of bread with cheese, eggs, lettuce, jam, or other food between them. — *Sandwiches* are good to take on picnics.
—*v. sandwiches, sandwiched, sandwiching.* Squeeze (someone or something) between two other persons or things. —The little house was *sandwiched* in between two tall buildings.

sane (SAYN) *adj. saner, sanest; sanely, adv.; sanity, n.* Having good sense and a healthy mind.

sang (SANG) *v.* One form of the verb *sing.*—The children *sang* "The Star-Spangled Banner " and other songs yesterday.

san·i·tar·i·um (san-ə-TAIR-ee-əm) *n. sanitariums.* A resort or hotel in a healthful place where people go to rest or to get well after sickness.

san·i·tar·y (SAN-ə-tair-ee) *adj.* Clean and healthful.—Everything in the hospital is very *sanitary.* It is kept free from germs and all kinds of dirt.

San·ta Claus (SAN-tə klawz). The one who brings gifts to children on Christmas.— *Santa Claus* has a long white beard and a red suit.

sap (SAP) *n. saps.* A juice that flows through trees and other plants and helps them live and grow.—The *sap* of some maple trees is made into maple sugar and maple syrup.

sap·ling (SAP-ling) *n. saplings.* A young, slender tree.

sap·phire (SAF-yr) *n. sapphires.* A very costly, hard, bright blue gem.— Mother has a ring set with a *sapphire.*
—*adj.* Bright blue.—The fairy has golden hair and *sapphire* eyes.

sar·casm (SAHR-kaz-əm) *n.; sarcastic, adj.; sarcastically, adv.* Harsh, biting remarks.—The man's *sarcasm* hurt his friend's feelings.

sar·dine (sahr-DEEN) *n. sardines.* A tiny fish canned in oil, mustard, or tomato sauce. *Sardines* are good to eat.

sa·ri (SAH-ree) *n. saris.* A long, thin dress worn mostly by the women of India. A *sari* usually is made of one long piece of cotton or silk. It is worn wrapped around and draped on the body.

sash (SASH) *n. sashes.* 1. A long wide band of cloth or ribbon worn around the waist or hips or over the shoulder. — The dancer wore a *sash.*
2. The part of a window that opens.

sas·sa·fras (SASS-ə-frass) *n. and adj.* A tree whose roots are used as flavoring and in medicine. — The roots of the *sassafras* are often used to make *sassafras* tea.

sat (SAT) *v.* One form of the verb *sit.*—Bob *sat* in his seat and read a book all morning.

satch·el (SACH-əl) *n. satchels.* A small bag with a handle.—When we went to Grandmother's, we put our clothes in a *satchel.*

sat·el·lite (SAT-ə-lyt) *n. satellites.* 1. A heavenly body revolving around a larger heavenly body; an artificial or man-made "moon."—The planet Saturn has nine known *satellites.* The earth has one, the moon.—A number of artificial *satellites* have been placed in orbit around the earth by means of rockets fired into space. These *satellites* carry instruments and cameras which collect important information, not only about space, but about our atmosphere and the earth's surface, as well.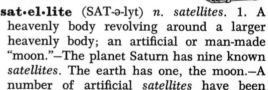
2. A country influenced or dominated by a larger neighboring country.
3. Someone attending or depending upon an important or powerful person.—The powerful lord's *satellites* swarmed about him.

sat·is·fac·tion (sat-iss-FAK-shən) *n. satisfactions*. 1. A feeling of being satisfied or contented.–Father's new car gives him much *satisfaction*.
2. Something which causes a contented feeling.–Keeping up to date on one's school work is a *satisfaction*.

sat·is·fac·to·ry (sat-iss-FAK-tə-ree) *adj.; satisfactorily, adv.* Good enough or sufficient to satisfy or please.–Jack asked the teacher if his paper were *satisfactory*.

sat·is·fy (SAT-iss-fy) *v. satisfies, satisfied, satisfying.* 1. Please.–Baby is perfectly *satisfied* with her old toys.
2. Make one feel sure; convince.–Mary *satisfied* Father that the clock was slow. She proved to him that it was slow.
3. End (a need) by filling it.–Bob *satisfied* his thirst by having a drink of water.

sat·u·rate (SACH-ə-rayt) *v. saturates, saturated, saturating.* Soak or fill completely.–The blotter was *saturated* with spilled ink.

Sat·ur·day (SAT-er-dee) *n. Saturdays.* The day after Friday. *Saturday* is the seventh day of the week.–We have no school on *Saturday·*

Sat·urn (SAT-ern) *n.* 1. The ancient Roman god of seed sowing.
2. The sixth planet away from our sun. *Saturn* is the second largest planet in our solar system.

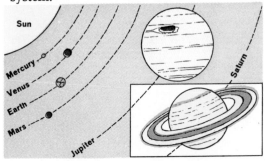

sauce (SAWSS) *n. sauces.* 1. A liquid put over food to make it tastier.–Father likes tomato *sauce* on meat loaf.
2. Stewed fruit.–Mother put lemon rind in the apple*sauce* to give it flavor.

sauce·pan (SAWSS-pan) *n. saucepans.* A metal pan with a handle, used for cooking. – Mary cooked the fudge in a *saucepan*.

sau·cer (SAWSS-er) *n. saucers.* A dish used to set a cup in.–Do not leave your spoon in your cocoa cup after stirring the sugar; lay it in the *saucer*.

sau·sage (SAW-sij) *n. sausages.* Beef, pork, or other meat prepared by grinding up and seasoning. Usually it is stuffed into a long, thin casing, like a tube.–*Sausage* is good to eat with pancakes.

sav·age (SAV-ij) *n. savages.* A person who is not civilized; one who lives a wild, simple, rough life in ignorance and superstition.–The cave men of long ago were *savages*.
–*adj.* 1. Wild or untamed.–Animals of the jungle are *savage* animals.
2. Cruel or vicious; bloodthirsty.–The *savage* king ordered the death of all his prisoners.

save (SAYV) *v. saves, saved, saving.* 1. Rescue or free from danger.–The fireman *saved* the child from the burning house.
2. Set aside; keep without using; keep for later use.–Father *saves* some money each month for our college education.
3. Lessen.–A washing machine *saves* work.
4. Prevent; avoid.–"A stitch in time *saves* nine."
5. Treat with care, or protect.–*Save* your eyes by reading only in a good light.
–*prep.* Except.–The fisherman used up all his wishes *save* one.

sav·ior (SAYV-yer) *n. saviors.* 1. One who saves.–When the man rescued Sally's kitten from the tree, Sally called him her *savior*.
2. (Spelled *Saviour* in the Bible) Jesus Christ.

saw (SAW) *n. saws.* A tool for cutting wood, metal, and the like. *Saws* are made of thin steel with sharp teeth along one edge for cutting. Some *saws* are run by electricity; some are used by hand.

–*v. saws, sawed, sawing.* 1. Cut with a saw.–Bob *sawed* the sticks for his kite out of an old crate.
2. One form of the verb *see*.–Mary *saw* the accident last week.

saw·dust (SAW-dust) *n.* The tiny bits of wood made in sawing wood.–Sally found that her doll was stuffed with *sawdust*.

saw·horse (SAW-horss) *n. sawhorses.* A rack or frame upon which a piece of wood is placed or held while being sawed.

saw·mill (SAW-mil) *n. sawmills.* A mill or factory with machines for cutting logs into lumber or wood.

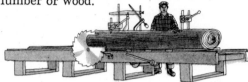

sax·o·phone (SAK-sə-fohn) *n. saxophones.* A brass musical instrument with a reed mouthpiece. You play the *saxophone* by blowing into the mouthpiece and pressing down on the keys.

say (SAY) *v. says, said, saying.* Speak words, or write words.—We *say* "Good morning" to our teacher when she comes into the room. —My book *says* that elephants live to be over one hundred years old.

say·ing (SAY-ing) *n. sayings.* A proverb, or wise words that have been handed down to us from the past. This is an old *saying:*
"Early to bed and early to rise
Makes a man healthy, wealthy, and wise."

scab (SKAB) *n. scabs.* A thin crust that forms over a sore or wound. The *scab* drops off when the sore is all healed.

scab·bard (SKAB-erd) *n. scabbards.* A case

to cover the blade of a sword.—The knight drew his sword from the *scabbard*.

scaf·fold (SKAF-əld) *n. scaffolds.* A platform for men to stand on when they build or paint houses, or do other work in high places. Some *scaffolds* can be raised or lowered to the place where the workmen want to work.

scald (SKAWLD) *v. scalds, scalded, scalding.* 1. Burn with steam or hot water.—Baby *scalded* her finger when she tried to pick a carrot out of the hot soup.
2. Clean with boiling water. — *Scald* the baby's bottle before you fill it.
3. Heat until nearly boiling.—In making this pudding, you *scald* the milk and then add the sugar, eggs, and flavoring.

scale (SKAYL) *n. scales.* 1. Small, thin, horny piece something like one's fingernail.—Some fish are almost covered with *scales*.

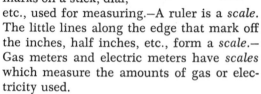

2. Small, thin flakes of skin. — Mary's back was covered with little *scales* from her sunburn.
3. A device for weighing things. — Bob stood on the *scale* while the nurse weighed him.
4. A regular series of marks on a stick, dial, etc., used for measuring.—A ruler is a *scale*. The little lines along the edge that mark off the inches, half inches, etc., form a *scale*.— Gas meters and electric meters have *scales* which measure the amounts of gas or electricity used.
5. A series of tones in music arranged in the order of their pitch. —Mary had to practice *scales* when she took music lessons.

6. Small distance between places on a map or drawing compared with the real distance between the same places.—The map is drawn to *scale*. Each inch on the map stands for fifty miles of country.
—*v. scales, scaled, scaling.* 1. Scrape the scales off.—We *scale* fish before we cook them.
2. Climb.—The men *scaled* the cliff. They climbed the side of the mountain with the aid of ropes.

scal·lop (SKAHL- *or* SKAL-əp) *n. scallops.* 1. A shellfish that is good to eat. Notice the shape of its shell in the picture.

2. One of a series of curves, like the curves on a scallop's shell. — Mother embroidered *scallops* on the end of the towel.
—*v. scallops, scalloped, scalloping.* 1. Cut a pattern of repeated curves in.—Mother *scallops* the edges of many of Baby's dresses.
2. Bake in a special way with milk and crumbs.—Mother is *scalloping* the potatoes for dinner tonight.

scalp (SKALP) *n. scalps.* The skin on one's head that is covered by the hair.
—*v. scalps, scalped, scalping.* Cut off the scalp of.—Some Indians used to *scalp* the people they killed.

scam·per (SKAM-per) *v. scampers, scampered, scampering.* Run hastily.—The frightened rabbit *scampered* off when he saw us.

scan (SKAN) *v. scans, scanned, scanning.* 1. Examine closely and carefully.—The searching party *scanned* every inch of the area.
2. Look through quickly.—Some persons like to *scan* a book before buying it.
3. Examine or analyze poetry, especially with respect to its meter. — The teacher is *scanning* the poem for the class.
4. Skim over thoroughly in a set pattern.—The searchlights *scanned* the sky.

scan·dal (SKAN-dl) *n. scandals; scandalous, adj.; scandalously, adv.* 1. Disgrace or shame caused by bad actions or deeds; the action or deed itself. — The boy's bad behavior is a *scandal.*
2. Exciting and harmful gossip or talk about someone.—The discovery of bribery in the city government was the cause of a great deal of *scandal.*

scar (SKAHR) *n. scars.* 1. A lasting mark left on the body after a sore, burn, or wound has healed. — The squirrel's bite left a *scar* on Jack's wrist.
2. A mark or dent that spoils the looks of something.—The table top has many *scars* from long use.
—*v. scars, scarred, scarring.* The squirrel's bite *scarred* Jack's wrist.

scarce (SKAIRSS) *adj. scarcer, scarcest.* Hard to get; not plentiful; rare.—Butter is often *scarce* in time of war.

scar·ci·ty (SKAIR-sə-tee) *n. scarcities.* Not a big enough supply.—There is a *scarcity* of meat here. There isn't enough.

scare (SKAIR) *n. scares.* A fright.—We had a big *scare* when the house caught fire. We were afraid.
—*v. scares, scared, scaring.* Make afraid.—The noise *scared* the baby. It frightened her.

scare·crow (SKAIR-kroh) *n. scarecrows.* A figure dressed to look like a man, used to scare off crows and other birds. — The farmer put a *scarecrow* in the middle of the cornfield.

scarf (SKAHRF) *n. scarves* or *scarfs.* 1. A long woven or knitted strip of cloth worn around the neck and shoulders or over the head. — Mother knitted a *scarf* for her nephew.
2. A strip of cloth used as a cover for furniture.—Mary put a clean lace *scarf* on her dresser.

scar·let (SKAHR-lət) *n. and adj.* A brilliant red.—We saw the *scarlet* of the bird's feathers.

scat·ter (SKAT-er) *v. scatters, scattered, scattering.* 1. Toss or sprinkle in all directions.—The boys *scattered* food for the birds.
2. Break up and go in different directions.—The crowd *scattered* when it started to rain.
3. Drive away in all directions.—The sudden thunderstorm *scattered* the people.

scav·en·ger (SKAV-in-jer) *n. scavengers.* Any animal that feeds or lives on decaying or dead matter.—Buzzards are *scavengers.*

scene (SEEN) *n. scenes.* 1. Time and place of a story.—The *scene* of this play is summertime in the mountains.
2. A painted screen or curtain serving as background for a play.—The *scene* is a beautiful mountaintop covered with pines.
3. A division of a play.—The star of the play appears for the first time in the second *scene.*
4. A view, or thing to look at.—You can see beautiful *scenes* from the top of that hill.

5. An action which causes people to stare.—The man with the dog made a *scene* on the corner. He yelled at the dog and beat him, so that people stared.

scen·er·y (SEEN-er-ee) *n.* 1. Painted scenes for an entertainment on the stage.—The children painted their own *scenery* for their play.

2. Things to look at seen all together.—The *scenery* in the mountains is beautiful.

scent (SENT) *n. scents.* 1. An odor, fragrance, or smell.–The *scent* of fried bacon and coffee makes one hungry.
2. A trail, or a means of tracking down.–The police were thrown off the *scent* of the robber because he had changed cars.
–v. scents, scented, scenting. 1. Smell; notice or follow by smelling.–The dog *scented* a squirrel.
2. Give a fragrant odor to.–Roses *scented* the whole room.

scep·ter (SEP-ter) *n. scepters.* A long, fancy rod or staff carried by a ruler of a country as a sign of his power.

sched·ule (SKEJ-uhl) *n. schedules.* A list or plan of the order and time for things to happen.–The teacher wrote our *schedule* for the day on the board.
–v. schedules, scheduled, scheduling. Plan or arrange in a schedule.–*Schedule* your work so that we can leave early.

scheme (SKEEM) *n. schemes.* 1. A secret plan or plot.–The criminals have a *scheme* to get out of jail.
2. A planned arrangement.–Mother has a nice color *scheme* in her bedroom. She has used colors that look well together.
–v. schemes, schemed, scheming. Plan secretly.–The prisoners *schemed* to escape.

schol·ar (SKAHL-er) *n. scholars.* 1. A student or pupil.–We have six hundred *scholars* in our school.
2. One who has studied thoroughly and learned a great deal.–Mr. Smith is a *scholar* in history.

schol·ar·ship (SKAHL-er-ship) *n. scholarships.* 1. Learning.–The teacher praised the bright boy for his fine *scholarship.*
2. An award, often a sum of money, given to a worthy student to help pay for additional education.–Tom received a university *scholarship* because of his brilliant school record.

school (SKOOL) *n. schools.* 1. A place for teaching and learning.–Children learn how to read in *school.*–A medical *school* is a place for teaching and learning about medicine.
2. The pupils who go to a school.–Our *school* will have a picnic on Saturday.
3. A large gathering of fish which swim together.–We saw a *school* of fish.

school·house (SKOOL-howss) *n. schoolhouses.* The building where school is held.–Our *schoolhouse* is made of white brick.–Grandfather went to school in a one-room *schoolhouse.*

schoon·er (SKOO-ner) *n. schooners.* A sailing ship with two or more masts and sails.

sci·ence (SY-ənss) *n. sciences.* 1. A way of learning about things by a planned method of seeing how things work and act, and by experimenting and testing.
2. An orderly collection of all the known facts and laws about any one kind of thing.–Botany is the *science* of plants.–Zoology is the *science* of animal life.–Mathematics is the *science* of numbers and amounts.

sci·en·tif·ic (sy-ən-TIF-ik) *adj.; scientifically, adv.* Having to do with science; like science.–John likes the *scientific* subjects in school best. His teachers all say that he has a *scientific* mind.

sci·en·tist (SY-ən-tist) *n. scientists.* A person who is learned or skilled in some science.–Charles Darwin was a great *scientist.*

scis·sors (SIZ-erz) *n. pl.* A cutting tool with two handles and two sharp blades fastened together so that the sharp blades move against each other when the handles are brought together. — Sally uses *scissors* to cut out her paper dolls.

scold (SKOHLD) *v. scolds, scolded, scolding.* Find fault with in an angry way.–The teacher *scolded* her class for being disorderly during the fire drill.

scoop (SKOOP) *n. scoops.* 1. A tool like a

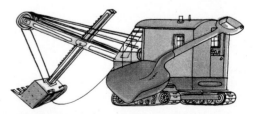

shovel, but deeper.–The man who brought the coal shoveled it with a *scoop.*

2. A big bucketlike holder which picks up sand, dirt, etc.—The men used a steam shovel with a large *scoop* to lift the sand.

3. A small shovel-shaped ladle with a short handle.—The clerk puts candy and peanuts into bags with a *scoop*.

4. As much as a scoop will hold.—She put a *scoop* of peanuts into the bag.

—*v. scoops, scooped, scooping.* 1. Pick up with a scoop.—Mother *scooped* up the spilled flour. 2. Hollow or dig out.—Father *scooped* a hole in the ground to plant seeds.

scoot (SKOOT) *v. scoots, scooted, scooting.* Dart quickly.—The child *scooted* across the street.

scope (SKOHP) *n.* 1. The extent of one's mental ability.—The difficult book was beyond the *scope* of the young child. 2. Range; extent.—What is the *scope* of that field? How large is that field?—The king's power had great *scope*.

scorch (SKORCH) *v. scorches, scorched, scorching.* 1. Burn slightly.—The iron was so hot that Mother *scorched* a towel while ironing it. 2. Make dry and withered.—The hot sun has *scorched* the grass.

score (SKOR) *n. scores.* 1. The record of points made in a game.—The *score* was 5 to 1. 2. Twenty.—Four*score* years ago, Grandfather was born. Grandfather is eighty.

—*v. scores, scored, scoring.* 1. Mark. — The teacher *scored* our spelling papers. 2. Win points for the score. — Jack *scored* twice during the game. 3. Keep a record of points. — Bob was appointed to *score* the baseball game.

scorn (SKORN) *n. scorns.* Contempt; feeling of shame for.—The children looked with *scorn* at the boy who copied from someone else on the examination.

—*v. scorns, scorned, scorning.* Look down on or despise.—The children *scorned* the boy who copied.

scor·pi·on (SKOR-pee-ən) *n. scorpions.* A small, backboneless animal with a long and narrow tail that has a poisonous sting at the tip of it.

scoun·drel (SKOWN-drəl) *n. scoundrels.* A wicked person; a rascal; a villain.—The police arrested the *scoundrel* who broke the school windows.

scour (SKOWR) *v. scours, scoured, scouring.* 1. Clean; scrub the grease and dirt off. — Mother *scours* the pots and pans with steel-wool soap pads. 2. Search. — The Boy Scouts *scoured* the stores for a tent.

scout (SKOWT) *n. scouts.* 1. (Usually spelled with a capital "S.") A boy or girl who belongs to the Boy *Scouts* or the Girl *Scouts*.—Bill and Ann are *Scouts*.

2. A person who goes out looking for news of the enemy, or for other information.—Daniel Boone was a famous Indian *scout*.

—*v. scouts, scouted, scouting.* Examine; search. —The children *scouted* the town for Jack's lost dog.

scowl (SKOWL) *n. scowls.* A frown; an angry look.—Bill read his bad report card with a *scowl*.

—*v. scowls, scowled, scowling.* — Baby *scowls* when she can't have her own way.

scram·ble (SKRAM-bəl) *n. scrambles.* A hasty crowding and struggling.—There was a *scramble* for the pennies.

—*v. scrambles, scrambled, scrambling.* 1. Push, struggle, or crowd. — The children *scrambled* for the pennies. 2. Climb, crawl, or walk on hands and knees. —The Boy Scouts *scrambled* up the hillside. 3. Mix together.—Ned *scrambled* the clues to the puzzle.

scrap (SKRAP) *n. scraps.* 1. A small bit; a small piece. — The children picked up the *scraps* of paper. 2. Bits of leftover food. — We fed the *scraps* to the chickens.

—*v. scraps, scrapped, scrapping.* 1. Discard, or throw away as useless.—Jack *scrapped* the work he had done wrong and started again. 2. Quarrel or fight.—The children *scrapped* over who should be first.

scrap·book (SKRAP-buhk) *n. scrapbooks.* A book with blank pages for pasting in different kinds of clippings.—Mary made a *scrapbook* for the sick children.

scrape (SKRAYP) *n. scrapes.* 1. A harsh, grating sound.—We heard the *scrape* of the wheels of the milk wagon on the pavement. 2. Bill is always in a *scrape.* He is always in trouble because he has done something he should not have done.

—v. scrapes, scraped, scraping. 1. Scratch things off. — A painter *scrapes* loose paint from the house before he puts on new paint. 2. Rub.—Baby *scraped* the skin off her knee when she fell on the sidewalk. 3. Drag.—The children *scraped* their feet on the sidewalk. 4. Get together with difficulty. — The girls *scraped* together enough money to buy their mother a gift.

scratch (SKRACH) *n. scratches.* 1. Mark made by digging or scraping with anything sharp or rough.—There was a red *scratch* on Sally's arm from the kitten's claws. 2. The sound made by scraping or rubbing with something rough.—A *scratch* at the door reminded us that the dog wanted to come in.

—v. scratches, scratched, scratching. 1. Dig into with a sharp point.—The kitten *scratched* Sally when Sally tried to put her doll's dress on him. 2. Make a mark by digging or scraping with anything sharp or rough. — The carpenter *scratched* a line on the board with a nail. 3. Cut slightly.—Mother *scratched* her finger on a pin. 4. Rub with the fingers.—When Mary's nose itches, she *scratches* it. 5. Mark out or draw a line through.—Bob *scratched* out one word in his story that was not spelled right, and wrote it over. 6. Write poorly.—Father *scratches* his signature when he is in a hurry.

scrawl (SKRAWL) *n. scrawls.* Careless handwriting.—Father signs his name in a *scrawl* when he is in a hurry.

—v. scrawls, scrawled, scrawling. Scribble; write poorly. — The teacher told us not to *scrawl,* but to write neatly.

scraw·ny (SKRAW-nee) *adj. scrawnier, scrawniest.* Thin; skinny.—A *scrawny* little kitten came up to Father to be petted.

scream (SKREEM) *n. screams.* A loud, sharp outcry. — We ran to the window when we heard a *scream* in the street.

—v. screams, screamed, screaming. Cry out loudly and sharply. — People often *scream* when they are in pain, terror, or great grief.— The girl *screamed* when she saw the flames.

screech (SKREECH) *n. screeches.* A shrill, harsh cry or noise.—The car stopped with a *screech* of the brakes.

—v. screeches, screeched, screeching. Cry out or sound loudly in a shrill, harsh way.—The children *screeched* with mirth when the clown fell down on his face.

screech owl (SKREECH owl) *screech owls.* A kind of owl that has a cry like a scream, instead of a hoot.

screen (SKREEN) *n. screens* and *adj.* 1. Anything that is used to hide, cover, or protect a thing, or for sifting.—A *screen* door or a window *screen* is a frame covered with a wire netting to keep out flies, mosquitoes, and other insects.—A frame covered with a coarse

wire mesh used to sift sand, coal, and other materials is also a *screen.*—Another kind of *screen* is a frame, usually folding, that is used to cover a doorway, protect against drafts, set off part of a room, etc.—A smoke *screen* is a lot of smoke made to hide something that is going on from the enemy, like the movements of troops or ships.

2. A white or silver curtain on which motion pictures are shown. — Mary squealed with delight when her favorite actor appeared on the *screen.*

—v. screens, screened, screening. Cover with a screen.—Father *screened* in the front porch for the summer.

screw (SKROO) *n. screws.* A nail with a ridge or "thread" twisting around it from the point to the head. *Screws* are twisted or turned into wood instead of being hammered like nails.

—v. screws, screwed, screwing. 1. Fasten together with screws.—The sides of the box were *screwed* together. 2. Turn; twist.—Mother *screwed* the cover of the fruit jar down tight.

scrib·ble (SKRIB-əl) *v. scribbles, scribbled, scribbling.* Write poorly and carelessly.—Bob *scribbled* a hasty note to Mother.

scribe (SKRYB) *n. scribes.* 1. A person, especially in olden times, who earned his living by writing or by copying writings. Before the printing press was invented, there were many *scribes*.
2. In the Bible, a scholar or teacher of the Jewish law.

scrim·mage (SKRIM-ij) *n. scrimmages.* 1. A rough-and-tumble fight. — The teacher stopped the *scrimmage* on the playground and sent the fighting boys back to study hall.
2. In a football game, the action that takes place while the ball is in play.—Tom sprained his ankle during the *scrimmage*.

script (SKRIPT) *n. scripts.* 1. Handwriting; also, a kind of printing that looks like handwriting.

All men are created equal

2. A copy of a play.—The actor forgot his part in the play and had to look at the *script* before he could go on.

scrip·ture (SKRIP-cher) *n. scriptures.* 1. (Spelled with a capital "S.") The Old and the New Testaments.—The minister read from the *Scriptures*.
2. Any sacred writing.—The *scripture* of the Moslems is called the Koran.

scroll (SKROHL) *n. scrolls.* 1. A roll of paper or other writing material.—In olden times much writing was done on *scrolls* of parchment. *Scrolls* were rolled at both ends. The reader rolled the parchment from one roll to the other instead of turning the pages as we do.
2. A design drawn to look like a partly-rolled streamer of paper. — The first page of the book of fairy tales was decorated with *scrolls*.

scrub (SKRUB) *n. scrubs.* Washing, or rubbing.—Jack gave his dog a good *scrub* after it had fallen in the puddle.
—*v. scrubs, scrubbed, scrubbing.* Clean by rubbing hard.—Mother *scrubbed* the floor with soapy water and a brush.

sculp·tor (SKULP-ter) *n. sculptors.* A person who carves or molds statues or other figures of stone, wood, plaster, and other materials.

sculp·ture (SKULP-cher) *n. sculptures.* The art of carving or molding statues and other figures from stone, wood, or other materials; the work so produced.—Many fine pieces of *sculpture* can be seen in an art museum.

scum (SKUM) *n.* A thin coating that forms on the top of liquids.—*Scum* often collects on shallow, still water.

scur·ry (SKER-ee) *n. scurries.* Lively running or patter.—We heard the *scurry* of Sally's feet as she tried to catch the kitten.
—*v. scurries, scurried, scurrying.* Hurry or scamper.—When the bell rang, the children *scurried* into the room.

scur·vy (SKER-vee) *n.* A disease caused by a lack of vitamin C in the diet. A person with *scurvy* usually suffers from bleeding gums, weakness, and spots on the skin. Sailors on long voyages often used to get *scurvy* because they rarely ate fruits and vegetables containing vitamin C.

scythe (SYTH) *n. scythes.* A farm tool used for cutting weeds, grain, and long grasses by hand. A *scythe* has a long handle and a long, curved blade.

sea (SEE) *n. seas.* 1. The ocean; a very large body of salt water that covers more of the earth's surface than land does.—The old salt had sailed the seven *seas*.
2. Large bodies of salt water smaller than oceans are called *seas*.—The island of Sicily is in the Mediterranean *Sea*.

3. A body of water that is rough from heavy waves. — The fishermen could not fish because of a high *sea*.

sea·coast (SEE-kohst) *n. seacoasts.* Land along the ocean or sea.—New York City is located on the eastern *seacoast* of the United States; San Francisco is on the western *seacoast*.

sea·far·ing (SEE-fair-ing) *n. and adj.* Working, traveling, or living on the sea or ocean.—The retired sailor misses his days of *seafaring*.

sea gull (SEE gul) *sea gulls.* A large, graceful sea bird with mostly white feathers. *Sea gulls* often follow ships and eat bits of food that are thrown from the ship. They also eat fish.

sea horse (SEE horss) *sea horses.* A fish with a head that looks like a horse's head, and a tail that curls up. The body is covered with thin bony plates. The *sea horse* is found in most warm and temperate seas around the world.

seal (SEEL) *n. seals.* 1. A sea animal that lives near the coast, especially in cold waters.

2. The fur of certain seals.—Coats and coat collars are often made of *seal.*
3. A stamping device with a raised symbol or design used for stamping letters, official papers, and the like.—Mary has a *seal* with her initials on it to close letters. She puts a little melted red wax on the envelope and then presses her *seal* against the wax. The *seal* presses her initials into the wax.

—*v. seals, sealed, sealing.* 1. Close tightly.—Mother *sealed* the fruit jars with paraffin.
2. Mark with a seal.—The lawyer *sealed* the will.
3. Settle or make final.—The boys shook hands to *seal* the bargain.

sea lev·el (SEE lev-əl). The surface of the sea. *Sea level* is measured from a point halfway between the average high and low tide. *Sea level* is used as the starting point in measuring altitude.

seam (SEEM) *n. seams.* A fold or line where two pieces of material join.—The *seam* of Father's coat ripped.

sea·man (SEE-mən) *n. seamen.* A sailor.

sea·port (SEE-port) *n. seaports.* A port or harbor where ships that sail the seas load and unload cargoes and passengers.

sear (SIR) *v. sears, seared, searing.* 1. Burn the surface of.—The hot stove *seared* Father's finger.
2. Cook or brown the outside of.—Mother *seared* the meat quickly in a pan with a little water in it.

search (SERCH) *n. searches.* An effort made to find something.—After a long *search* for his keys, Father found them in his pocket.
—*v. searches, searched, searching.* 1. Look for; try to find.—The children all *searched* for the lost purse.
2. Look through; examine. — Bob *searched* the book for the picture of the flame-snorting dragon.

search·light (SERCH-lyt) *n. searchlights.* A very strong, turning light that can throw a powerful ray of light in any direction. — A *searchlight* can be seen for many miles.

sea·shore (SEE-shor) *n. seashores.* The land along the ocean or sea.—We often go to the *seashore* for our summer vacation, so we can spend our days on the beach.

sea·sick (SEE-sik) *adj.* Sick at the stomach because of the rolling movement of a boat.—Even old sailors sometimes get *seasick* during bad storms at sea.

sea·side (SEE-syd) *n.* Seashore, or the land along the sea or ocean.—Sally likes to cover up Father with sand when we go to the *seaside.*

sea·son (SEE-zən) *n. seasons.* 1. One of the four parts into which the year is divided. Spring, summer, autumn, and winter are the four *seasons.*
2. A special time of the year in which a particular thing happens.—The planting *season* is the time of year for planting.
3. The time of year when something can be found, or is at its best.—Fresh strawberries taste best in *season.*
—*v. seasons, seasoned, seasoning.* 1. Flavor.—Mother *seasoned* the soup with onions and celery salt.
2. Treat or prepare for use.—Lumber to be made into furniture should first be *seasoned,* or dried thoroughly.

sea·son·ing (SEE-zən-ing) *n. seasonings.* Flavoring; something added in a small quantity to improve the taste. Salt, pepper, spices, onions, and the like are *seasonings.*

seat (SEET) *n. seats.* 1. A place in which to sit, or a thing to sit on. Chairs, benches, stools, and the like are *seats.*—The usher at the theater took us to our *seats.*

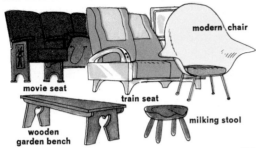

movie seat

modern chair

train seat

wooden garden bench

milking stool

2. The part of anything that you sit on.—We have leather *seats* on our dining chairs.—Father wore a hole in the *seat* of his everyday trousers.

3. Main location or headquarters.—Detroit is the county *seat* of Wayne County. It is the principal city of that county, the city where county government is carried on.—Washington, D.C., is the *seat* of the Federal Government.

—*v. seats, seated, seating.* 1. Show to a seat or place in a seat.—The usher *seated* us in the fourth row.

2. Have enough seats for.—This room *seats* forty pupils.

sea·weed (SEE-weed) *n. seaweeds.* A kind of plant that grows in the sea.—Slippery strings of *seaweed* sometimes catch around your feet when you go swimming.

se·cede (si-SEED) *v. secedes, seceded, seceding.* Withdraw formally from a union of states, an organization, a religious or political body, etc.—The discontented group threatened to *secede* from the association.

sec·ond (SEK-ənd) *n. seconds.* 1. One of the 60 equal parts into which a minute is divided.—If you count slowly to 60, it will take you about 1 minute, or 60 *seconds.*

2. A person chosen to help a prize fighter or duelist.—The tired boxer's *second* kept urging him on.

—*adj.* 1. Directly following the first.—Sunday is the first day of the week. Monday, the day following Sunday, is the *second* day of the week.

2. One next after the first, in rank or value.—Jack won first prize, and Bob won *second* prize.

3. Like the first.—The ballplayer wanted to be a *second* Joe DiMaggio.

4. Below the first in rank or quality.—This cloth is *second* quality.

—*v. seconds, seconded, seconding.* Speak in agreement or support of.—In the class meeting, Mary made a motion to start a club, and Ruth *seconded* it.

sec·ond·hand (SEK-ənd-HAND) *adj.* Not new; used before.—We bought a *secondhand* piano.—This store sells *secondhand* goods. It buys goods from people who have been using them, and resells them to others.

se·cret (SEE-krit) *n. secrets.* Something that people are kept from knowing.—What we have for Mother's birthday is a *secret.*

—*adj.; secretly, adv.* Hidden; not known.—The man disappeared through a *secret* door.

sec·re·tar·y (SEK-rə-tair-ee) *n. secretaries.* 1. A person who writes letters, makes records, and takes care of many office duties for a person, a business, or a club.—Bob is the *secretary* for his class.

2. A kind of old-fashioned writing desk.

se·crete (si-KREET) *v. secretes, secreted, secreting.* 1. Produce and discharge, as a gland making and giving off a substance in the body.—A gland in the mouth *secretes* saliva.

2. Hide carefully; conceal.—The thief *secreted* the stolen money in a large vase.

sec·tion (SEK-shən) *n. sections.* 1. A part of anything; one of the pieces into which a thing is divided or cut. —Grapefruit and oranges are divided inside into *sections* by thin walls, or membranes.—Our class is divided into two *sections.*

2. A region.—Miners live in the mining *sections* of the country.

se·cure (si-KYUHR) *v. secures, secured, securing.* Get or obtain.—We hope to *secure* enough money to buy the new books.

—*adj.* 1. Tightly fastened.—The lock is not *secure.*

2. Free from danger or fear.—The cat had a *secure* feeling that she was safe from the dog when she was up the tree.

se·dan (sə-DAN) *n. sedans.* 1. A closed car with two seats, one in front and one in back. —Our automobile is a *sedan.*

2. (Also called a "sedan chair.") An enclosed chair carried by servants.—Long ago queens rode in *sedans.*

sed·a·tive (SED-ə-tiv) *n. sedatives.* A soothing medicine used to relieve pain and nervous excitement.—The doctor gave the sick woman a *sedative* to help her sleep.

sed·i·ment (SED-ə-mənt) *n.* The material in a liquid that settles to the bottom.—The material sometimes found at the bottom of a cup of coffee is *sediment.*

sed·i·men·ta·ry rock (sed-ə-MEN-tə-ree rahk) *sedimentary rocks.* Rock, usually in layers, made up of rock fragments and sometimes plant and animal remains that have been cemented together by heat and pressure. *Sedimentary rock* is usually formed at the bottom of a body of water, but may also form windblown sand. Shale, sandstone, and limestone are common *sedimentary rocks.*

see (SEE) *v. sees, saw, seeing.* 1. Have the power of sight.—We hear with our ears, and *see* with our eyes.
2. Notice with the eyes.—Did you *see* the dog that just passed?
3. Make certain.—*See* that the door is locked before you go to bed.
4. Go with.—Mother will *see* you to the door.
5. Visit.—We went to *see* Grandfather last week.
6. Understand.—We *saw* how to do the problem after our teacher explained it.
7. Find out.—*See* if someone is at the door.
8. Experience or live through.—That poor family has *seen* better days.

seed (SEED) *n. seeds.* The part of a plant from which another plant will grow.—Fruits have *seeds* in them.—Trees, vegetables, and flowers all grow from *seeds.*—Some *seeds* are carried by the wind.
—*v. seeds, seeded, seeding.* 1. Sow seeds in.—Last week Bob helped Grandmother *seed* her garden.
2. Take the seeds from.—Mother *seeds* grapes before making grape jelly.
3. Produce or have seeds.—Radishes and lettuce *seed* earlier in the summer than some other vegetables.

seed·ling (SEED-ling) *n. seedlings.* A young tree or plant that has grown from a seed.

seek (SEEK) *v. seeks, sought, seeking.* 1. Look for; hunt; try to find.—We are *seeking* a house to live in.
2. Try.—The old man *seeks* to give happiness to his friends.

seem (SEEM) *v. seems, seemed, seeming.* Appear to be.—The old man *seemed* very unhappy.—The child *seemed* hungry.

seen (SEEN) *v.* One form of the verb *see.*—I have *seen* the moving picture you are speaking of.

seep (SEEP) *v. seeps, seeped, seeping.* Leak slowly or ooze.—The milk *seeped* through the crack in the bottle.

see·saw (SEE-saw) *n. seesaws.* 1. A game in which a person rides on each end of a heavy board that rests on something near the middle to balance it. First one end of the board goes up in the air and then the other.
2. Something balanced near the middle so that the ends go up and down, first one and then the other.
—*v. seesaws, seesawed, seesawing.* Teeter or rock as a board balanced in the middle does.

seg·ment (SEG-mənt) *n. segments.* Any piece, section, or part of a divided or naturally separated whole.—The circle is divided into many *segments.*—Please give me a few *segments* of the tangerine.

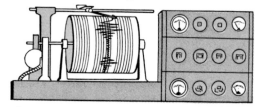

seis·mo·graph (SYZ- *or* SYSS-mə-graf) *n. seismographs.* An instrument for measuring and recording earthquakes. — The *seismograph* in California recorded an earthquake in Japan.

seize (SEEZ) *v. seizes, seized, seizing.* 1. Suddenly or violently take hold of; grab.—The frightened man *seized* a club and threw it at the wolf that was snarling at him.
2. Capture or take over.—The posse *seized* the outlaws' guns.
—*seizure, n. seizures.*

sel·dom (SEL-dəm) *adv.* Rarely, or not often.
—We *seldom* see the boys, because they live too far away.

se·lect (sə-LEKT) *v. selects, selected, selecting.* Choose or pick out.—Mary likes to *select* her own dresses.
—*selection, n. selections.*

self (SELF) *n. selves.* One's own being. My*self* is I. Your*self* is you. *Self* is used with many words, as: *self*-control, meaning control of one's behavior; *self*-direction, meaning directing and guiding one's own work or actions.—Father him*self* sometimes makes mistakes in spelling.—You owe it to your*self* to do the best work you know how.

self·ish (SEL-fish) *adj.; selfishly, adv.; selfishness, n.* Too interested in oneself; without thought for others.—Bill is too *selfish* to help the class raise money to give the janitor a present.

self-re·spect (self-rə-SPEKT) *n.; self-respecting, adj.* Concern with maintaining one's own decency, honesty, and goodness.—We have *self-respect* if we are not ashamed of our own actions.

sell (SEL) *v. sells, sold, selling.* 1. Exchange for money.—The farmer *sells* chickens. He exchanges chickens for money.
2. Be exchanged.—Oranges *sell* at the corner store for sixty cents a dozen.

selves (SELVZ) *n. pl.* A form of the word *self.* Him*self* refers to one *self*, or to one boy or man alone. Them*selves* means many persons.—Mary and Sally wanted to go to town all alone, all by them*selves.*

sem·a·phore (SEM-ə-for) *n. semaphores.* 1. A system of sending signals in which the position of certain objects, such as lights or flags, gives a message.
2. An apparatus for sending such a system of signals.

sem·i·co·lon (SEM-ə-koh-lən) *n. semicolons.* A punctuation mark made by a dot with a comma under it [;]. It stands between two main parts of a sentence.—The weather was very cold; the roads were covered with ice.

sen·ate (SEN-ət) *n. senates.* 1. A group of persons elected to make the laws. Most states in the United States have *senates* to make the laws.
2. (Spelled with a capital "S.") One of two bodies of elected people making up the Congress of the United States, or one of the houses of a state legislature. The United States has a *Senate* and a House of Representatives to make laws for the country.

sen·a·tor (SEN-ət-er) *n. senators; senatorial, adj.* 1. A person elected to be a member of a senate.
2. (Spelled with a capital "S.") Title of a member of the U. S. Senate.

send (SEND) *v. sends, sent, sending.* Cause a person or thing to go or be taken from one place to another.—I will *send* your sweater to you.—Please *send* Bob home.

sen·ior (SEEN-yer) *n. seniors.* 1. An older person.—I am your *senior* by ten years. I am ten years older.
2. A person of the highest class in a college or high school.—Ed is a *senior* in college.
—*adj.* 1. The older (of two people with the same name).—Bob's father's name is Robert Smith, *Senior.* Bob's name is Robert Smith, Junior.
2. Older or higher in rank or length of service.—Mr. Miller is the *senior* member of the Miller and Black Lumber Co.—The *senior* class in high school gave a play.

sen·sa·tion (sen-SAY-shən) *n. sensations.* 1. A feeling.—Riding the merry-go-round gives Mary a dizzy *sensation.* — Standing near a radiator gives you a *sensation* of heat.
2. Great excitement.—When the lion got loose, it caused a big *sensation.*

sense (SENSS) *n. senses.* 1. Feeling.—The man who stole the money had a *sense* of guilt.
2. A quality of the body which makes us aware of things around us. The five *senses* which a person has are sight, hearing, smell, touch, and taste.
3. Judgment or intelligence.—The boy uses good *sense* in crossing the street. He knows when to cross it and when not to.
4. Meaning.—Mary couldn't get the *sense* of the sentence.
5. Idea or understanding.—The boy has a good *sense* of fairness in the games he plays.
6. (In the plural only) Mind or sanity.—A person who behaves in a strange, unreasonable way is out of his *senses.*
—*v. senses, sensed, sensing.* Feel or be aware of.—Mother *sensed* that the boy was upset.

sen·si·ble (SEN-sə-bəl) *adj.; sensibly, adv.* Wise or intelligent.—A *sensible* person is one who uses good sense or judgment.

sen·si·tive (SEN-sə-tiv) *adj.; sensitively, adv.; sensitiveness, n.* 1. Easily affected.— Mary's tooth is *sensitive* to heat. Hot tea makes it hurt.
2. Easily offended or hurt. — Johnny was *sensitive* when his two front teeth fell out. They soon grew back, and he got over it.

sent (SENT) *v.* One form of the verb *send.*— We *sent* flowers to the sick woman.

sen·tence (SEN-tənss) *n. sentences.* 1. A group of words that tells something or asks something. These are *sentences:* Mary has a new dress. Where did she get the dress?
2. A decision made by a judge as to what a person's punishment shall be for doing something not lawful.
—*v. sentences, sentenced, sentencing.* Pass official judgment on.—The judge *sentenced* the man to a year in prison.

sen·ti·nel (SEN-tə-nəl) *n. sentinels.* A guard; a sentry.—*Sentinels* were stationed at the palace gates.

sen·try (SEN-tree) *n. sentries.* A soldier who guards a place to keep away persons who have no right to be there.

se·pal (SEE-pəl) *n. sepals.* One of the leaflike parts of a flower that are found on the outside at the base of the petals. The *sepals* cover and protect the bud until it is ready to blossom; then they spread, and the flower opens.

sep·a·rate (SEP-ə-rət) *adj.* 1. Not joined or connected.—We live in *separate* houses. They are in different places, and you cannot go from one to the other without going outside.
2. Alone; just one.—A *separate* dish costs more than it would if you were to buy it as part of the whole set.
—(SEP-ə-rayt) *v. separates, separated, separating.* 1. Divide or put in different groups.— The teacher told Mary to *separate* the blue from the red crayons.
2. Keep apart or divide.—A large river *separates* the two towns.—The children were *separated* during the summer. They were no longer together.

sep·a·ra·tion (sep-ə-RAY-shən) *n. separations.* A parting or division.—The earthquake caused a *separation* of the ground.

sep·a·ra·tor (SEP-ə-ray-ter) *n. separators.* A machine which separates cream from milk. — The farmer uses a *separator* to separate the cream from the milk.

Sep·tem·ber (sep-TEM-ber) *n. Septembers.* The ninth month of the year. *September* has thirty days.

se·quel (SEE-kwəl) *n. sequels.* 1. Something that follows an earlier event; a result or consequence.—Hunger and disease were the *sequels* of the flood.
2. A new and complete story in continuation of a previous story.—The author wrote a *sequel* to his novel. He wrote another novel about the same characters.

se·quence (SEE-kwənss) *n. sequences.* 1. An order of succession, as the way one thing follows another.—The magazines are arranged in *sequence*, according to their dates.
2. A related and connected series of things or events. — A traffic signal was installed at the intersection after a *sequence* of accidents.

se·quoi·a (si-KWOI-ə) *n. sequoias.* A giant pine or redwood tree that grows in California. The *sequoias* are over 300 feet high and are said to be the oldest living things. Some are believed to be over 3,000 years old.

se·rene (sə-REEN) *adj.; serenely, adv.* 1. Fair and clear.—During the summer the skies are usually *serene*.
2. Quiet and calm.—The sick man spent a *serene* night. His sleep was not disturbed.

ser·geant (SAHR-jənt) *n. sergeants.* A non-commissioned officer in the army, air force, or marines. His rank is next above that of corporal, but below that of lieutenant.

se·ri·al (SIR-ee-əl) *n. serials* and *adj.* A story, movie, or radio play presented in parts.—Mother is reading a *serial* in a magazine.—Some people like to listen to the *serials* on television and radio.

se·ries (SIR-eez) *n. sing.* and *pl.* A number of like happenings one after the other, such as a *series* of baseball games, a *series* of articles about sewing, or a *series* of lessons in cooking.—Mother listened to a *series* of radio talks on how to can fruits and vegetables.

se·ri·ous (SIR-ee-əss) *adj.; seriously, adv.; seriousness, n.* 1. Dangerous or harmful.—The boy's injuries did not prove to be *serious* when they were examined.
2. Thoughtful or earnest.—The old man's face grew *serious* as he began his story.—Bob is a *serious* student.
3. Important; worthy of concern.—To Mary, becoming a movie actress is a *serious* problem.
4. Honest or in earnest.—Are you *serious* about quitting school?

ser·mon (SER-mən) *n. sermons.* 1. A religious talk.—Bob went to church and listened to the minister's *sermon.*
2. A very serious talk.—Father delivered a *sermon* to the children about getting their work done before they played.

ser·pent (SER-pənt) *n. serpents.* A snake, especially a large one.

se·rum (SIR-əm) *n. serums.* 1. The liquid part of the blood. When blood thickens, the *serum* separates from the clot, or the part that gets somewhat hard.
2. Liquid taken from the blood of an animal that has had a certain disease. When this liquid is injected into a person, it may keep the person from having the disease.

serv·ant (SER-vənt) *n. servants.* 1. A person hired by others to do personal or house work.—Many *servants* work for the rich man.
2. Persons whose lives are given to serving others.—Teachers are public *servants.* They serve their city and their country by teaching boys and girls.

serve (SERV) *v. serves, served, serving.* 1. Work, help, or do good for.—A store clerk *serves* the customers.—The mayor *serves* the people of the city.
2. Be used or useful.—Boy Scouts can make two stones *serve* as a fireplace.

3. Bring food to.—The waitress *served* us. She carried our food to our table.
4. Supply or furnish.—The bakery *serves* us with bread.
5. Spend or pass (time).—The sailor *served* three years in the navy.
6. To deal with.—Having his play period taken away *served* the boy right for being tardy.
7. We *served* a notice on the family to move. We sent them a written note asking them to move.
8. Put the ball in play in certain games.—It was Mary's turn to *serve* in the championship tennis game.

serv·ice (SER-vəss) *n. services.* 1. Help or aid.—May I be of *service* to you?
2. The work one does for another.—A nurse's *services* are needed when someone is very sick.
3. A religious meeting or ceremony.—We attend *services* every Sunday.
4. A set of silver, dishes, or tableware.—Mother has a *service* for eight people. She has enough dishes for eight people.
5. Serving.—The *service* at the restaurant is good. The food is served well and promptly.
6. A military organization, as the army, navy, or air force.—Many young men are in *service* now.
7. Government work. — Postmen are in Civil *Service.* They are hired by the Government.
—*v. services, serviced, servicing.* Repair.—A man *serviced* our electric iron. He put it in working order.

ses·a·me (SESS-ə-mee) *n.* An herb growing in tropical countries. An oil similar to that obtained from olives is pressed from seeds of *sesame.* Both oil and seeds are edible.

ses·sion (SESH-ən) *n. sessions.* 1. A meeting of a class, school, court, lawmaking body, or club.—The judge looked sternly at the lawyer who was late for the first court *session* of the day.
2. A number of meetings, one after the other, by a club, court, school, etc.—The school's morning *session* is from 9 o'clock to noon.
3. A time when an organization is active.—Our school has a summer *session* and a winter *session.*

set (SET) *n. sets.* A group of articles used together.—Father has a *set* of tools.—Mother has a *set* of dishes.

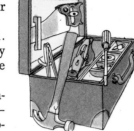

—*v. sets, set, setting.* 1. Put or place. — Mary *set* the basket on the table.

2. Put in proper condition or position.— The doctor *set* the broken bone.—Mary *set* the table for Mother.— Father *set* the alarm for five o'clock.—The men *set* the stage for the next scene of the play.

3. Put (into some condition).—The dog who was caught in the trap was *set* free.—The boys *set* the old Christmas tree on fire.

4. Get solid; take on a definite form.—Mother put the gelatin dessert in the icebox to *set*.

5. Go down (of the sun, moon, or stars).— The sun rises in the east and *sets* in the west.

6. Start or begin.—We *set* out on our trip at sunrise.

—*adj.* Established; fixed.—It is a *set* rule that we must get to school by nine o'clock.

set·ter (SET-er) *n. setters.* A hunting dog that is trained to stand very still with its tail straight out and its nose pointing toward the bird or other game which it smells.

set·tle (SET-l) *v. settles, settled, settling.* 1. Get quiet and comfortably placed and prepared.—The teacher told the children to *settle* down and study their spelling.—Bob *settled* himself in the big armchair to read his favorite book.

2. Make a permanent home, or go to live.— My uncle wants to *settle* in the country.—We *settled* in this community ten years ago.

3. Sink to the bottom.—Sand in water *settles* if the water is allowed to stand.

4. Pay.—Father *settled* the bill at the grocer's.

5. Come to rest; stop.—The golf ball rolled and then *settled* on the green.

6. Put in order; arrange.—Mother wants to *settle* her house before company comes.

7. Decide upon; agree upon.—The day for the picnic has not been *settled* upon yet.

8. End.—The teacher told the boys to *settle* their quarrel.

set·tle·ment (SET-l-mənt) *n. settlements.*

1. An agreeable ending.—After the *settlement* of the quarrel, the boys shook hands.—The two countries arranged a peaceful *settlement* of their dispute.

2. A new community or village.—A small *settlement* of French people may be found near the river.

3. A payment.—The store asked for a *settlement* of the bill.

4. A place or building in a community where help is given to the needy.

set·tler (SET-ler) *n. settlers.* One who makes his home in a new land.—The Pilgrims were among the early *settlers* in America.

sev·en (SEV-ən) *n. sevens* and *adj.* The number [7] coming after 6 and before 8.—Six and one make *seven*.

sev·en·teen (sev-ən-TEEN) *n. seventeens* and *adj.* The number [17] coming after 16 and before 18.—Ten and seven make *seventeen*.

sev·en·teenth (sev-ən-TEENTH) *n. seventeenths.* One of 17 equal parts.—If you divide anything into seventeen equal parts, each part is one *seventeenth*. It may be written 1/17.

—*adj.* Coming as number 17 in a series.—Tom is celebrating his *seventeenth* birthday.

sev·enth (SEV-ənth) *n. sevenths.* One of 7 equal parts.—If you divide anything into seven parts all the same size, each part is one *seventh*. It may be written 1/7.

—*adj.* Coming as number 7 in a series.—Billy has had six birthdays. His next one will be his *seventh*.

sev·en·ty (SEV-ən-tee) *n. seventies* and *adj.* The number [70] coming after 69 and before 71.—*Seventy* is ten more than sixty.

sev·er (SEV-er) *v. severs, severed, severing.*

1. Cut; divide; separate; part.—Jack had to *sever* the cord around the package in order to open it.

2. Cut off or break, as ties between nations.— The quarreling governments are about to *sever* relations.

sev·er·al (SEV-er-əl) *adj.* More than two, but not many.—*Several* flowers are in blossom.

se·vere (sə-VIR) *adj.; severely, adv.; severeness, n.* 1. Sharp; intense; great.—Mother had a *severe* pain in her tooth.—The poor man was shivering from the *severe* cold.
2. Hard; difficult.—Climbing the mountain was a *severe* test of the explorer's strength.
3. Strict; harsh.—Father sometimes tries to be *severe* with the children when they have disobeyed.
4. Very plain; without any trimming.—Mother's new evening dress is a *severe*, straight black gown.

sew (SOH) *v. sews, sewed, sewing.* Fasten

cloth together by putting thread through it with a needle; stitch. —Mother *sews* on the sewing machine. Mary *sews* by hand.—Mother *sewed* up the rip in Father's sleeve.

sew·age (SOO- *or* SYOO-ij) *n.* Waste liquids and solids that pass through sewers.—*Sewage* is often purified and then passed into rivers to be carried off by water currents.

sew·er (SOO- *or* SYOO-er) *n. sewers.* A drain, usually underground, made of large pipes or tiles, to carry waste away from homes.—Dishwater poured into the sink is carried away by the *sewer*.

sex (SEKS) *n. sexes.* 1. Either of the two classes or divisions of living things, male or female; males or females as a group.—The club has members of both *sexes*. Both boys and girls belong to the club.
2. The differences which make a person, plant, or animal either male or female.

sex·tant (SEKS-tənt) *n. sextants.* An instrument for measuring angles, distances, and altitudes. The *sextant* is used at sea to determine latitude and longitude by measuring the heights of heavenly bodies over the horizon.

shab·by (SHAB-ee) *adj. shabbier, shabbiest.*
1. Worn and faded.—The detective put on *shabby* clothes to disguise himself.
2. Mean; not generous.—The boy's feelings were hurt because of the *shabby* way the children treated him.

shack (SHAK) *n. shacks.* A small, poorly or roughly built house.—We went into the fisherman's *shack* when we were at the shore.

shad (SHAD) *n. sing.* and *pl.* A kind of fish used for food. *Shad* are found along the eastern coast of America.

shade (SHAYD) *n. shades.* 1. A shadow or partial darkness made by something blocking the light.—We ate our picnic lunch in the *shade* of the tree.

2. Something made to shut out light.—Window *shades* cover the windows of a house.—A lamp *shade* keeps the light out of your eyes.
3. A small degree.—Bob is just a *shade* taller than Bill.
4. A tone of a color.—Mother's green dress is a lovely soft *shade*.—The sky has several different *shades* of blue.
—*v. shades, shaded, shading.* 1. Shield or partly cover.—Father *shaded* his eyes from the sun with his hands.
2. Make darker in some places than in others.—The artist *shaded* the drawing of the vase to make it look round.

shad·ow (SHAD-oh) *n. shadows.* 1. A shaded spot made by a solid body which is blocking off a light.—The *shadow* cast by the tree is longer in the morning that it is at noon, when the sun is right above it.

2. A suggestion; slight bit.—There cannot be a *shadow* of a doubt of Jack's honesty.
—*v. shadows, shadowed, shadowing:* Follow closely.—The burglar didn't know he was being *shadowed* by the detective.

shaft (SHAFT) *n. shafts.* 1. A pole, long stick, handle, or the like.—The *shaft* of the spear

was wooden, but the point was steel.—A tall *shaft* on the building supported a radio aerial. 2. A long up-and-down tunnel or opening.—The miners went down a *shaft* to get into the mine.—The elevator runs in a *shaft*.

shag·gy (SHAG-ee) *adj. shaggier, shaggiest.* Covered with long, coarse, thick, woolly hair. —Jack likes *shaggy* dogs.

shake (SHAYK) *n. shakes.* A jerk, or a quick movement up and down or to and fro.—After a few *shakes,* the salt shaker was empty. —*v. shakes, shook, shaking.* 1. Jerk, or move up and down or to and fro quickly.—We *shake* salt out of a salt shaker.—We *shake* rugs to get the dust out of them.—The angry man *shook* his fist at the ruffian. 2. Clasp (hands).—The minister *shakes* hands with the people at the door after the service. 3. Tremble.—Mary *shook* with excitement.

shale (SHAYL) *n. shales.* A type of rock formed of thin, hardened layers of mud, clay, or silt.—*Shale* is used in making certain types of building bricks.

shall (SHAL) *v. should.* 1. Is, am, or are going to.—We *shall* see the movie tomorrow. 2. Expect or intend to.—I *shall* study my lessons before school. 3. Be required to.—He *shall* repay the money if it takes his last cent.

shal·low (SHAL-oh) *adj. shallower, shallowest.* Not deep.—Small children bathe where the water is *shallow*.

sham (SHAM) *adj.* Make-believe or pretended.—The boys had a *sham* battle.

shame (SHAYM) *n. shames.* 1. An uncomfortable feeling caused by having done something wrong or foolish.—The boy who was caught cheating felt much *shame*. 2. Disgrace or loss of respect.—The boy's bad behavior brought *shame* to the team. 3. A thing to be sorry about.—It is a *shame* that Mary didn't get to go to the play. —*v. shames, shamed, shaming.* Cause to feel shame.—We tried to *shame* the boy for not telling the truth. We tried to make him feel bad about it.

sham·poo (sham-POO) *n. shampoos.* 1. A hair-washing.—Mother went to the beauty parlor to get a *shampoo*. 2. Soap to wash the hair with.—Some *shampoo* is liquid and comes in bottles. —*v. shampoos, shampooed, shampooing.* Wash (hair).—Mary is *shampooing* her hair.

sham·rock (SHAM-rahk) *n. shamrocks.* A three-leaved plant that looks like a clover. It is the national emblem of Ireland.

shan·ty (SHAN-tee) *n. shanties.* A small house, or shack.—The fisherman lives in a *shanty* on the bank of the river.

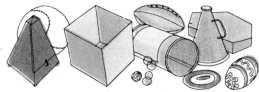

shape (SHAYP) *n. shapes.* 1. A form.—The *shape* of the ball is round.—The *shape* of the box is square.

2. A figure.—We saw the *shape* of a black cat on the fence in the moonlight. 3. Order; readiness.—Mother has everything in *shape* for us to start for school. —*v. shapes, shaped, shaping.* Mold; form.—Mary *shaped* a little bear out of clay.

share (SHAIR) *n. shares.* A part.—My *share* of the money is sixty cents.—Bob always does his *share* of the work in the garden. —*v. shares, shared, sharing.* Divide, or allow use or enjoyment of by others; have part in. —Sally *shares* her toys with the other children.

shark (SHAHRK) *n. sharks.* A large, fierce and dangerous fish that eats other fish.

sharp (SHAHRP) *n. sharps.* A tone in music that is a half step above or higher than a given note; the sign [♯] indicating this. —*adj. sharper, sharpest; sharply, adv.; sharpness, n.* 1. Made for cutting or piercing; not dull.—The knife is *sharp*.—The kitten's claws are *sharp*.

2. Not rounded; having a point or angle.—Mary knocked herself on the *sharp* corner of the table in the dark.—We came to a *sharp* curve in the road.

3. Biting; keen.—Vinegar has a *sharp* taste.—A *sharp* wind almost froze our faces.

4. Harsh; angry.—The teacher's *sharp* words hurt the boy's feelings.

5. Piercing.—Bob had a *sharp* pain in his stomach.

6. Quick; keen; alert.—The boy has a *sharp* mind. He is quick to solve a problem, quick to learn, quick to get a joke.—Birds have *sharp* eyes. They see well.

—*adv.* Exactly.—School starts at nine o'clock *sharp*.

sharp·en (SHAHR-pən) *v. sharpens, sharpened, sharpening.* Put a point on, or make an edge keener for cutting.—Mary *sharpened* her new pencil.—Father *sharpened* his razor this morning.

shat·ter (SHAT-er) *v. shatters, shattered, shattering.* 1. Break into many small pieces.—When the picture fell to the floor, the glass *shattered*.

2. Destroy.—The heavy snowfall *shattered* Mary's hopes for a sunny week end.

shave (SHAYV) *n. shaves.* A narrow escape.—The car almost hit the tree. It was a close *shave*.

—*v. shaves, shaved, shaving.* Cut hair off with a razor.—Father *shaves* his face every morning.

shav·ing (SHAY-ving) *n. shavings.* A thin

slice or strip cut off with a knife or a carpenter's plane.—The *shavings* of wood curled up when cut off.

shawl (SHAWL) *n. shawls.* A square or oblong piece of material worn over the head or shoulders. — Grandmother has a wool *shawl* with fringe on the ends.

she (SHEE) *pron.* A word that stands for a girl, woman, or female animal.—Grandmother said *she* would come to see us.—The cow's name is Bessie. *She* is red and white.

sheaf (SHEEF) *n. sheaves.* A bundle of flowers, grain, arrows, or the like.

shear (SHIR) *v. shears, sheared, shearing.* Cut off.—The farmer *shears* the sheep's wool with large scissors.

shears (SHIRZ) *n. pl.* Large scissors. — The farmer uses *shears* to cut the sheep's wool.

sheaves (SHEEVZ) *n. pl.* More than one *sheaf.*—The farmer tied the grain into *sheaves* after it was cut.

shed (SHED) *n. sheds.* A low, lightly built building.—The farmer keeps his tools in a *shed*.

—*v. sheds, shed, shedding.* 1. Let fall; pour out; drop.—The unhappy child *shed* tears.—The dog's hair is *shedding*.—This brush is *shedding* its bristles.

2. Give off or throw out.—The sun *sheds* light on the earth. The moon reflects light.

sheep (SHEEP) *n. sing.* and *pl.* An animal from which we get wool for clothes, flesh (mutton) to eat, and *sheep*skin for leather.

sheer (SHIR) *adj.; sheerly, adv.; sheerness, n.* 1. Thin enough to see partly through.—Mary has a pair of *sheer* silk stockings.—The living room curtains are *sheer*.

2. Complete.—Baby fell asleep in her highchair from *sheer* exhaustion.

3. Very steep; straight up and down, or almost so.—The north side of the mountain is a *sheer* cliff 3,000 feet high.

sheet (SHEET) *n. sheets.* 1. A piece of cloth big enough to cover a bed and tuck in at the sides and ends.—We sleep between two *sheets*.

2. A broad, thin piece of anything.—The teacher gave each of us a *sheet* of paper.—The ground and sidewalks were covered with a *sheet* of ice.

sheik (SHEEK) *n. sheiks.* An Arab chief or head man.—Some *sheiks* are extremely wealthy and powerful.

shelf (SHELF) *n. shelves.* A board or flat piece of metal fastened horizontally and used to set things on.—The cupboard has two *shelves* to set dishes on.

shell (SHEL) *n. shells.* 1. A hard outside covering, as on nuts, vegetables, animals, and eggs.—Walnuts, peas, turtles, ladybugs, oysters, and clams have *shells.*

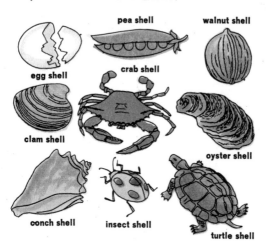

pea shell

walnut shell

egg shell

crab shell

clam shell

oyster shell

conch shell

insect shell

turtle shell

2. A crust of pastry shaped to hold a filling.—Mother made a *shell* for a lemon pie.
3. A case holding gunpowder to be fired in a gun.
4. A framework.—Only the *shell* of the house is built so far.
—*v. shells, shelled, shelling.* 1. Remove from a shell.—Mary *shelled* the peas. She took them out of the shells, or pods.
2. Fire shells at.—The soldiers *shelled* the enemy's lines until the enemy surrendered.

she'll (SHEE-əl). A short way of writing "she will."—*She'll* be here by three o'clock.

shel·lac (shə-LAK) *n. shellacs.* A clear varnishlike liquid used in finishing woods, furniture, etc.—Father put a coat of *shellac* on the bedroom floor.

shel·ter (SHEL-ter) *n. shelters.* 1. A covering that shields or protects.—An umbrella is a *shelter* from the rain.—A roof is a *shelter* from weather.
2. Protection.—We found *shelter* from the storm in the old shed.
—*v. shelters, sheltered, sheltering.* Protect or provide shelter for.—Grandfather didn't know he was *sheltering* thieves when he let the strangers sleep in the barn.

shelves (SHELVZ) *n. pl.* More than one *shelf.* —We have two cupboard *shelves* to set all the dishes on.

shep·herd (SHEP-erd) *n. shepherds.* A man who takes care of sheep.

shep·herd·ess (SHEP-er-dəss) *n. shepherdesses.* A woman who takes care of sheep.

sher·iff (SHAIR-əf) *n. sheriffs.* A man elected to enforce the law in a county.—The bank robbers were arrested by the *sheriff.*

she's (SHEEZ). A short way of writing "she is."—*She's* six years old today.

shield (SHEELD) *n. shields.* 1. Anything that protects or keeps one from harm.—The boy who stood in front of the baby to protect her from the flying stones was acting as a *shield.* 2. A large plate of metal or wood carried on the arm to protect one in battle.—The knights carried *shields.*
—*v. shields, shielded, shielding.* Protect.—Father would not *shield* the thief from the police.

shift (SHIFT) *n. shifts.* 1. A group of people who work during a certain time; also, the period of time they work.—Father now works on the day *shift.* Next month Father will work on the night *shift.*
2. A change of position.—There have been two *shifts* of the regular baseball players.
—*v. shifts, shifted, shifting.* 1. Change position.—The boy *shifted* in his seat.
2. Exchange positions of.—Mary had her slippers on the wrong feet, so she *shifted* them.

shift·less (SHIFT-ləss) *adj.; shiftlessly, adv.; shiftlessness, n.* Lazy or good-for-nothing.—Because the girl was so *shiftless,* she was not promoted.

shil·ling (SHIL-ing) *n. shillings.* An English coin. A *shilling* is worth about fourteen cents in American money.

shin (SHIN) *n. shins.* The front part of the leg below the knee.—Bob skinned his *shin* when he fell off the box.
—*v. shins, shinned, shinning.* Bob can *shin* a pole or tree. He pulls himself up by hugging the pole with his arms, then with his legs, while he reaches higher.

shine (SHYN) *n. shines.* 1. Clear or bright weather.—Rain or *shine,* the postman delivers the mail.
2. A polish.—Father gave his shoes a *shine.*
—*v. shines, shined* or *shone, shining.* 1. Send or give out light.—The sun *shines.*
2. Polish or make bright.—Mary *shined* the knives and forks for Mother.
3. Look bright; reflect light.—The furniture *shines* after Mother has waxed it.
4. Be noticeably smart or bright.—Bob *shines* in arithmetic.

shin·gle (SHING-gəl) *n. shingles.* 1. One of many thin pieces of wood, thicker at one end, that are used to cover roofs and sometimes outside walls. The thick end of one *shingle* laps over the thin end of another, to keep out water. *Shingles* made of fireproof materials are the same thickness from end to end. 2. A sign.—The new doctor has hung out his *shingle* over his office door.
—*v. shingles, shingled, shingling.* 1. Put shingles on.—Grandfather *shingled* his barn. 2. Cut (hair) quite short.—During the summer, Mary has her hair *shingled.*

shin·y (SHY-nee) *adj. shinier, shiniest.* Bright and glistening.

ship (SHIP) *n. ships.* 1. A large vessel that sails on the seas.—In olden times, *ships* were moved by wind blowing on the sails. 2. An airship.—Uncle Jim told about the time he was assigned to a new *ship* in the Air Force.
—*v. ships, shipped, shipping.* 1. Send.—We *shipped* the package by mail. 2. Go as a member of a ship's crew.—The sailor has *shipped* on the same vessel for many years.

ship·ment (SHIP-mənt) *n. shipments.* Goods sent at one time to a certain place.—We expect a *shipment* of coal today.

ship·wreck (SHIP-rek) *n. shipwrecks.* Destruction or loss of a ship.—A big windstorm at sea caused the *shipwreck.*

ship·yard (SHIP-yahrd) *n. shipyards.* Place where ships are built or repaired.

shirt (SHERT) *n. shirts.* 1. Cloth garment worn on the upper part of the body by boys. 2. Undergarment for the upper part of the body.

shiv·er (SHIV-er) *v. shivers, shivered, shivering.* Shake or quiver from cold, fright, or excitement.—The coatless boy *shivered.*

shoal (SHOHL) *n. shoals.* A place where the water is shallow, or a sand bar at such a place.—The boats were blown onto the *shoal.*

shock (SHAHK) *n. shocks.* 1. A sudden jar or blow.—The *shock* of the collision with the other car stunned Father for a few minutes. 2. Something very upsetting or disturbing.—When the man's house burned, it was a great *shock* to him. 3. The feeling caused by electricity passing through a person.—When Bob touched the broken electric wire, he got a *shock.*—An electric *shock* can be very dangerous.
—*v. shocks, shocked, shocking.* Upset, disturb, or offend.—The man's rage *shocked* us all.

shod (SHAHD) *v.* One form of the verb *shoe.* —A blacksmith *shod* the horses. He put shoes on them.

shoe (SHOO) *n. shoes.* 1. A covering for the feet.—Most *shoes* are made of leather. 2. A curved strip of iron nailed to the hoofs of certain animals, such as horses. It protects the hoof as a person's *shoe* protects his foot.
—*v. shoes, shod, shoeing.* Provide with shoes.— The blacksmith *shoes* horses. He fastens horseshoes to their hoofs.

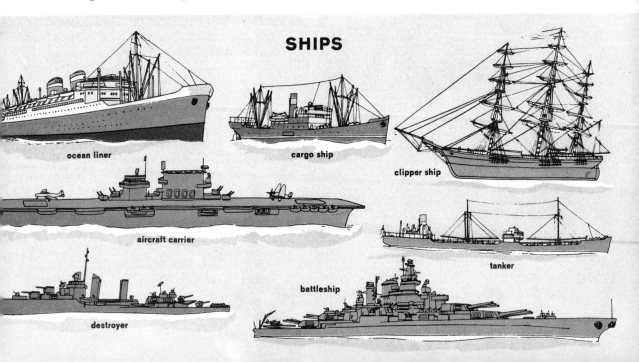

SHIPS

ocean liner

cargo ship

clipper ship

aircraft carrier

tanker

battleship

destroyer

shoe·mak·er (SHOO-mayk-er) *n. shoemakers.* A person who makes or repairs shoes. — When Bob's shoes needed repair, he took them to a *shoemaker.*

shone (SHOHN) *v.* One form of the verb *shine.*—Mary rubbed the big red apple until it *shone.*

shoo (SHOO) *n. shoos.* A sound made to scare away animals.—The farmer says *"Shoo!"* when he wants to chase the chickens away. *—v. shoos, shooed, shooing.* Scare away by shouting.—The farmer *shooed* the chickens from his porch.

shook (SHUHK) *v.* One form of the verb *shake.*—The boys *shook* the apple tree to make the apples fall.

shoot (SHOOT) *n. shoots.* A small branch.—The bush has many new *shoots,* now that spring has come. *—v. shoots, shot, shooting.* 1. Fire (a gun).—The hunter knew just when to *shoot.* 2. Hit with an arrow or bullet.—The hunter tried to *shoot* a squirrel. 3. Move very fast.—I saw the dog *shoot* through the door after the cat. 4. Send (a ball, arrow, or the like) swiftly and with force.—The pitcher *shoots* the ball over the plate past the batter.

shop (SHAHP) *n. shops.* 1. A small store.—Mother went to the hat *shop* to buy a new hat. 2. A place where things are made.—Father works in a machine *shop.* *—v. shops, shopped, shopping.* Look at and buy things in shops or stores.—We *shop* for groceries every Saturday.

shop·keep·er (SHAHP-kee-per) *n. shopkeepers.* A person who runs a shop.—The *shopkeeper* showed us several pocketbooks of leather.

shore (SHOR) *n. shores.* Land along the edge of an ocean, lake, or stream.—After the storm, we found many beautiful shells washed up on the *shore.*

shorn (SHORN) *v.* One form of the verb *shear.*—The farmer's sheep have been *shorn.*

short (SHORT) *adj. shorter, shortest.* 1. Not long; little in height or length.—The pencil has been sharpened so many times that it is very *short.*—A man is tall, and a little boy is *short.* — The children went for a *short* walk.

2. Having less than the right or needed amount.—We ran *short* of sugar when Mother canned the fruit.—My change from the grocer was five cents *short.* 3. So brief as to be almost rude.—Jack gave Mary a *short* answer when she asked him the same question for the third time. *—adv.* Suddenly.—Father put on the brakes and we stopped *short.*

short·age (SHOR-tij) *n. shortages.* An amount lacking; a needed quantity; a lack.—Many persons in the world suffer from *shortages* of food and clothing.

short·cake (SHORT-kayk) *n. shortcakes.* A dessert made of biscuit dough in layers with filling and with topping of strawberries or other fresh fruit, and often with whipped cream.

short·en (SHOR-tn) *v. shortens, shortened, shortening.* Make shorter, or less long.—The sleeves in Mary's new coat were too long, so Mother had to *shorten* them.

short·en·ing (SHORT-ning) *n.* Fat used in baking to make the dough crisp, rich, and crumbly.—Butter and lard are two kinds of *shortening.*

short·hand (SHORT-hand) *n.* A system of writing words quickly by using little marks like the ones in the picture. The marks stand for sounds, or for whole words, or for groups of words.

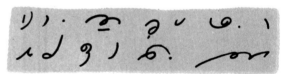

short·ly (SHORT-lee) *adv.* 1. In a short time; very soon.—We are going home *shortly,* for it is getting late. 2. Very briefly, so as to be almost rude.—Bill answered us *shortly* when we asked him where he got the bicycle he was riding.

short·stop (SHORT-stahp) *n. shortstops.* A baseball player who plays in the infield between second and third bases.—The *shortstop* threw the ball to the second baseman.

shot (SHAHT) *n. shots.* 1. The tiny balls of lead used in cartridges for shotguns.

2. The noise made when a gun is fired.—The farmer heard *shots* from the hunters' guns.

3. A marksman.—The men weren't very good *shots*, for no one hit the circle.

4. A throw, a strike, or a try at doing something.—When Father drove the golf ball a long way, he made a good *shot*.

—*v.* One form of the verb *shoot.*—The rocket *shot* through the air at 3000 miles per hour.—The hunter *shot* the rabbit.

should (SHUHD) *v.* 1. One form of the verb *shall.*

2. Ought to.—Tom *should* drink more milk.

3. Expect to.—I told her that I *should* receive the package in time to bring it to the party.

4. Would.—I *should* have been glad to help you if you had asked me, but you didn't.

shoul·der (SHOHL-der) *n. shoulders.* 1. The part of the body to which the arms of a person or the front legs of a four-footed animal are joined.—The girl carried her purse by a strap over her *shoulder*.

2. The part of a dress or coat that fits over a person's shoulders.—The *shoulder* seam on Bob's coat is ripped apart.

—*v. shoulders, shouldered, shouldering.* 1. Take upon oneself.—The teacher was not willing to *shoulder* the responsibility of taking the children along without their parents' consent.

2. Pick up and carry on one's shoulder. — Father *shouldered* Sally and marched down the hall with her.

shout (SHOWT) *n. shouts.* Yell or loud call.—We heard the *shout* of the newsboy.

—*v. shouts, shouted, shouting.* Yell, or call out loudly.—The teacher told the children to talk softly, not to *shout*.

shove (SHUV) *n. shoves.* A push.—Bill gave Jack a *shove*, and he fell off the diving board.

—*v. shoves, shoved, shoving.* Push.—The children *shoved* each other to get into the house.

shov·el (SHUV-əl) *n. shovels.* A tool used to lift and move snow, coal, dirt, or the like.—Father uses a *shovel* to put coal into the furnace.

—*v. shovels, shoveled* or *shovelled, shoveling* or *shovelling.* Lift up with a shovel and put somewhere else.—The boys *shoveled* the snow from the sidewalks.

show (SHOH) *n. shows.* 1. A display, or a place where things are taken to be looked at and admired.—We are going to a dog *show*. The finest dogs will get prizes.

2. An entertainment.—We went to the moving picture *show*.

—*v. shows, showed, showing.* 1. Allow to look at; allow or cause to be seen.—I will *show* you my stamp collection.—Mother *showed* pleasure at the compliment.

2. Be visible.—Mother's slip was longer than her dress, so it *showed*.

3. Teach by doing.—Our teacher *showed* us how to make a kite. She taught us by letting us watch her do it first.

4. Point out to.—The clerk *showed* us where to buy stockings.

show·case (SHOH-kayss) *n. showcases.* A

glass case where things are put so that they can be seen or looked at. — We saw the rings and watches in the *showcase* in the jeweler's window.

show·er (SHOW-er) *n. showers.* 1. A short rainstorm.—We had a *shower* this morning.

2. Anything that falls like a shower of rain. —A *shower* of paper came from the office windows.

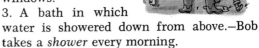

3. A bath in which water is showered down from above.—Bob takes a *shower* every morning.

—*v. showers, showered, showering.* Drop, or rain down.—The children *showered* rice upon the bride and groom.—It *showered* today.

shown (SHOHN) *v.* One form of the verb *show.*—The books were *shown* to the children.

shrank (SHRANGK) *v.* One form of the verb *shrink.* — Mary's dress *shrank* when it was washed.

shred (SHRED) *n. shreds.* 1. Narrow strip or rag.—The old flag was burned because it was worn into *shreds*.

2. Bit.—Not one *shred* of food was left after the picnic.

—*v. shreds, shredded, shredding.* Cut into small strips.—Mother *shredded* the cabbage.

shrewd (SHROOD) *adj.; shrewdly, adv.*
Sharp and clever; quick-witted, especially in
business dealings.–Mr. Greene is a *shrewd*
businessman.

shriek (SHREEK) *n. shrieks.* A scream; a
loud piercing sound like one made by a whistle, or a person who is afraid, hurt, or angry.
–*v. shrieks, shrieked, shrieking.* Make this
noise.–The police siren *shrieked* as it passed.

shrill (SHRIL) *v. shrills, shrilled, shrilling.*
Make a high piercing sound. – The birds
shrilled loudly. They called out in high, sharp
voices.
–*adj. shriller, shrillest; shrilly, adv.*–High and
piercing in tone.–Whistles and police sirens
make *shrill* sounds.

shrimp (SHRIMP) *n. shrimps.* 1. A kind of
small shellfish. – The meat of
shrimps is good to eat.
2. A little person (often used
scornfully). – Jack's feelings
were hurt when the big boys
called him a *shrimp*.

shrine (SHRYN) *n. shrines.* Any place or
thing that is sacred or holy or held in reverence.–The Lincoln Memorial is a *shrine* because it is loved and held as a sacred symbol
by Americans.

shrink (SHRINGK) *v. shrinks, shrank,
shrinking.* 1. Become or make smaller.–If
Baby's stockings *shrink* when they are
washed, she will not be able to wear them.
2. Draw back or away.–The horse is so afraid
that it *shrinks* every time it sees a whip.

shriv·el (SHRIV-əl) *v. shrivels, shriveled or
shrivelled, shriveling or shrivelling.* Dry up;
wrinkle; wither.–The apple was *shriveled*.

shrub (SHRUB) *n. shrubs.* A bush or low tree
with many stems that come from the ground

instead of from a trunk, as those of most
trees do.–*Shrubs* are used around houses
and in gardens.

shrub·ber·y (SHRUB-ə-ree) *n. shrubberies.*
A group of low bushes or shrubs.

shrug (SHRUG) *n. shrugs.* A raising of the
shoulders to show that one is not sure about
something, or does not care, or does not like
something.
–*v. shrugs, shrugged, shrugging.* Raise the
shoulders in a shrug. – When the teacher
asked Bill a question, he just *shrugged* his
shoulders.

shrunk (SHRUNGK) *v.* One form of the verb
shrink.–After Mother washed Mary's dress,
she found that it had *shrunk*.

shuck (SHUK) *n. shucks.* A husk or outer covering. The outer leaves or coverings on ears
of corn are *shucks*.

–*v. shucks, shucked, shucking.* Remove
shucks from. – The children like to *shuck*
corn for Mother.

shud·der (SHUD-er) *n. shudders.* A trem-
bling or shaking caused by fear, horror, disgust, or the like. – Mother gave a *shudder*
when Sally showed her the large black snake.
–*v. shudders, shuddered, shuddering.* Tremble with fear, horror, or disgust.–The ghost
story Jack told made us all *shudder*.

shuf·fle (SHUF-əl) *v. shuffles, shuffled,
shuffling.* 1. Walk, barely lifting the feet.–
The gardener was so tired that he just *shuffled* along.
2. Mix up (cards).–Bob likes to *shuffle* the
cards when we play card games.

shun (SHUN) *v. shuns, shunned, shunning.*
Keep away from or avoid. – Father *shuns*
driving during times when there is heavy
traffic.

shut (SHUT) *v. shuts, shut, shutting.* 1. Close.
–Please *shut* the door when you leave.
2. Keep out.–The window pane *shuts* out
the rain.–Do not *shut* the new boy out of
your games.
3. Imprison or close in.–Father *shut* the dog
in the garage for the night.
4. Close up.–We have *shut* up our seashore
cottage for the winter.
5. Turn (off).–Father forgot to *shut* off the
water while he fixed the faucet, and the
kitchen got flooded.
–*adj.* Closed.–The store seems to be *shut* for
there is no light inside.–Baby's eyes are *shut*;
she must be asleep.

shut·ter (SHUT-er) *n. shutters.* A cover for a window, usually on the out-side. *Shutters* generally are made of many slats fastened across a frame, and swing on hinges. – We live in a brown house with green *shutters.*

shut·tle (SHUT-l) *n. shuttles.* 1. A sliding thread holder that is used in weaving cloth. The *shuttle* holds the spool of thread that is thrown from side to side between the length-wise threads.
2. On a sewing machine, the part into which the bobbin or spool that holds the lower thread is put. The *shuttle* goes back and forth when you sew.
3. A train which travels regularly back and forth between two places.
–*v. shuttles, shuttled, shuttling.* Go back and forth regularly.–There is a subway train in New York City which *shuttles* between Grand Central Station and Times Square.

shy (SHY) *v. shies, shied, shying.* 1. Jump to one side; jump away from.–The horse *shied* when it heard the shrill whistle of the ex-press train.
2. Avoid; shrink (away).–Mary is apt to *shy* away from difficult tasks.
–*adj. shyer* or *shier, shyest* or *shiest.* 1. Bash-ful; uneasy in front of people, especially strangers.–George is very *shy.* He hides in his room whenever company comes.
2. Easily frightened. – Birds are very *shy.* They fly away if you come too near them.

shy·ness (SHY-nəss) *n.* Bashfulness.–The boy's *shyness* was caused by the fact that he had been brought up in the country and was not used to playing with other children.

sick (SIK) *adj. sicker, sickest.* 1. Not well; ill. –Grandmother is *sick* today. She has a bad cold. – When people have measles, or any other disease, they are *sick.*
2. Sick in the stomach.–Sally often gets *sick* from riding in the car.
3. Tired; bored.–Jack is *sick* of working on his model boat.
4. Miserable.–The girl is *sick* with longing to see her family.–Mother was *sick* with worry the night Jack was late coming home.

sick·le (SIK-əl) *n. sickles.* A farm tool with a sharp, curved blade set into a short handle; it is used for cut-ting grass.–The farmer cut the grass around the barn with a *sickle.*

sick·ness (SIK-nəss) *n. sicknesses.* Illness; bad health.–The man's *sickness* was serious.

side (SYD) *n. sides.* 1. Edge; outline.–Father put rails around the *sides* of the porch so that Baby could not fall off.
2. Not the front, back, top, or bottom, but one of the other two surfaces.–There are portholes in the *sides* of a ship.–The broken window is on the other *side* of the house.
3. A particular face or surface of anything.– Print your name and age and the date on the other *side* of your picture.
4. A section or part.–Father has to drive to the other *side* of town to get to work.
5. An opinion, position, or part in a game, argument, or fight.–Which *side* are you on in the discussion? Whom do you agree with?– Our *side* won the spelling bee.
–*v. sides, sided, siding.* Take the part of; stand up for.–Bob *sides* with Jack in a quarrel with the other boys; he is on Jack's side.

side show (SYD shoh) *side shows.* A small show, usually one of many accompanying a larger show.–There are many *side shows* at the circus.

side·walk (SYD-wawk) *n. sidewalks.* A path made of cement, stone, brick, or other material, at the side of a street or road, for the people on foot to walk on. – It is safer to roller skate on the *side-walk* than out in the street.

side·wise (SYD-wyz) *adj.* and *adv.* Toward the side, not toward the front or back.–Look *sidewise* before crossing the street.

si·es·ta (see-ESS-tə) *n. siestas.* A short nap or rest taken at midday or in the afternoon. People take *siestas* in Spain, Mexico, and other countries with hot climates.

sieve (SIV) *n. sieves.* A strainer; a kitchen tool that has a fine, screenlike bottom in it so that juice or very small pieces of anything will go through it, but not the larger pieces.–Mother rinses vegeta-bles by putting them in a *sieve* and running water over them.– She sifts flour through a *sieve* to get all the lumps out of it.

sift (SIFT) *v. sifts, sifted, sifting.* Strain, or put through a screened frame like a sieve, to separate smaller pieces from larger ones.– The workmen *sifted* the gravel.–Mother *sifts* the flour before baking.

sigh (SY) *n. sighs.* A sound made by breathing out a deep, long breath to show that one is tired, sad, or glad, or that something has happened or is over with.
—v. sighs, sighed, sighing. Make a sound in this way.—We heard Mary *sigh* as the lecture droned on.

sight (SYT) *n. sights.* 1. Power or ability to see.—People and animals have *sight.* They can see.—Father wears glasses to aid his *sight* when he reads.
2. Something to see.—The flower gardens are a beautiful *sight.*
3. Something seen.—The girl was very happy at the *sight* of her new doll.
4. Aim.—The man took *sight* at the target and then pulled the trigger on his gun.
5. A little piece of metal on the upper side of a gun barrel which helps in aiming at the target.
6. A glimpse; a short look at. — Mother caught *sight* of Bob hiding in the barn.
7. The distance that one can see.—The airplane is now out of *sight.*
—v. sights, sighted, sighting. See.—We *sighted* the tall buildings far ahead.

sign (SYN) *n. signs.* 1. A mark or movement used to stand for or mean something.—A red cross on a white background is the *sign* of the Red Cross.—The *sign* for adding is +; — is the *sign* for subtracting.—A nod of the head is a *sign* that one says "yes."
2. A board with lettering on it to advertise goods, name the owner of a shop or office, or tell anything else to people who see it.—Road *signs* say "Slow," "10 Miles to Detroit," etc.
3. A thing that tells that something exists, is about to happen, or has happened. — The first robin is a *sign* that spring will soon be here.
—v. signs, signed, signing. Write one's name on.—I *signed* the letter.

sig·nal (SIG-nəl) *n. signals.* A sign or indication to do something, or that something is about to happen, or has happened. — A green traffic light is the "go" *signal.* — The janitor gave the fire-drill *signal.* He rang the bell five times.

—v. signals, signaled or *signalled, signaling* or *signalling.* Tell by means of a signal.—The catcher *signaled* the pitcher to pitch a curve.

sig·na·ture (SIG-nə-cher) *n. signatures.* 1. One's own name, written by oneself. — The teacher put her *signature* on Bob's excuse to go home when he felt ill.

2. A sign written at the beginning of music to tell the time and the key in which the music is written.—The children looked at the *signature* before starting to sing the music.

sig·nif·i·cance (sig-NIF-ə-kənss) *n.* 1. A meaning. — The children did not know the *significance* of the bell's ringing at eleven o'clock.—Do you know the *significance* of the American eagle?
2. Importance.—Father got a letter of great *significance* to his business.

sig·nif·i·cant (sig-NIF-ə-kənt) *adj.; significantly, adv.* 1. Important.—The principal made a *significant* statement today. He said there would be no school tomorrow.
2. Carrying meaning; having meaning. — Father and Mother exchange many *significant* looks around Christmas time.

sig·ni·fy (SIG-nə-fy) *v. signifies, signified, signifying.* 1. Mean.—A red traffic light *signifies* danger.—This sign * next to a word usually *signifies* a note at the bottom of the page.
2. Make known; express.—If you are pleased with the music, *signify* it by clapping.

sign·post (SYN-pohst) *n. signposts.* A post with a sign or message fastened to it. — The sign on the *signpost* read, "No Hunting Allowed."

si·lence (SY-lənss) *n. silences.* A stillness, quietness, or absence of noise or sound.—The *silence* of the country is restful after the noise of the city.
—v. silences, silenced, silencing. Make quiet or make still.—Mother *silenced* Baby's crying by feeding her.

si·lent (SY-lənt) *adj.; silently, adv.* 1. Quiet; still; without sound.—The children were *silent* while their teacher read to them.—In *silent* reading we do not say the words out loud. We read to ourselves.
2. Not pronounced. — The "e" in the word "make" is *silent.* It is not pronounced.

sil·hou·ette (sil-ə-WET) *n. silhouettes.* 1. A picture showing only the outline of a form with the rest of the form filled in in black. A *silhouette* is usually painted on or fastened to a light surface so that it will show up easily.

2. Anything that the light strikes in such a way that all you can see is the dark form.—  At dusk the tall buildings of the city form a *silhouette* against the sky.

3. Outline.—Mary didn't like the *silhouette* of the skirt she tried on. It was straight and she likes her skirts to balloon out at the sides.

silk (SILK) *n. silks; silken, adj.* A kind of fine, shiny thread made by silkworms. These threads are woven into cloth which is also called *silk.*
—*adj.* Made of silk thread or cloth.—Grandmother wore *silk* stockings.

silk·worm (SILK-werm) *n. silkworms.* A caterpillar that makes a cocoon of silken threads from which silk is made. — *Silkworms* eat mulberry leaves.

sill (SIL) *n. sills.* A ledge or shelf across the bottom of the frame of a window, door, or building.—Mary set the plants on the window *sill,* where they would get the sun.—Today Mother scrubbed the door *sill.*—When the men tore down the house, they found that the *sills* were rotten.

sil·ly (SIL-ee) *adj. sillier, silliest.* Foolish; giddy. — The children were playing a *silly* game. It didn't make much sense but it was a lot of fun.

si·lo (SY-loh) *n. silos.* A tall, round, towerlike building made of wood, stone, cement, or brick. Sometimes a *silo* is a large hole in the ground.—The farmer puts green food or grain in a *silo* to keep it for his cows. Air cannot get to the grain in a *silo* and so the grain does not spoil.

silt (SILT) *n.* Bits of sand, earth, rock, etc., carried or deposited in water.—The sediment at the bottom of the river contains mud, clay, *silt,* and pebbles.

sil·ver (SIL-ver) *n.* 1. A kind of soft, whitish, valuable metal. — Some knives, forks, and spoons are made of *silver.*—*Silver* shines when it is polished.

—*adj.* 1. Made of silver.—I have a *silver* dollar.

2. Pale gray, bright and shiny.—Grandfather has *silver* hair.

sil·ver·ware (SIL-ver-wair) *n.* Knives, forks, spoons, and other tableware made out of silver.—Mary put the *silverware* on the table for Mother.

sim·i·lar (SIM-ə-ler) *adj.; similarly, adv.* Very much alike; about the same.—Mary did not buy the dress because it was too *similar* to the one she had.

sim·ple (SIM-pəl) *adj. simpler, simplest.* 1. Easy to understand.—This dictionary is very *simple.*

2. Plain; not fancy; not trimmed much. — Mary's new dress is quite *simple.*

3. Weak-minded; stupid. — The clown pretended to be *simple.*

sim·ple·ton (SIM-pəl-tn) *n. simpletons.* A very stupid or weak-minded person.—Simple Simon in the nursery rhyme is a *simpleton.*

sim·plic·i·ty (sim-PLISS-ə-tee) *n.* Plainness; quality of being simple, or of not being complicated.—The *simplicity* of the arithmetic problems made Jack smile. He thought they were too easy.

sim·ply (SIM-plee) *adv.* 1. Plainly. — The woman was dressed *simply.*

2. Just.—It is easy to find our house; you *simply* turn left at the next corner.

sin (SIN) *n. sins.* A wrong-doing; a bad act or deed.—It is a *sin* to kill, steal, or do any other evil thing.
—*v. sins, sinned, sinning.* To do something evil.

since (SINSS) *adv.* 1. From that time until now.—It started raining Sunday and it has rained ever *since.*

2. At some time between that time and now. —Yesterday Father said he could not go, but *since* then he has changed his mind.

3. Before now; ago. — The postman has passed our house long *since.*

—*conj.* Because; seeing that.—*Since* it is your birthday, you may stay up an hour later.

—*prep.* Ever after.—Bob has felt much better *since* last month when he got over his cold.

sin·cere (sin-SIR) *adj.; sincerely, adv.* Honest; not deceitful. – Grandmother is a very *sincere* person. She doesn't try to fool you.

sin·ew (SIN-yoo) *n. sinews; sinewy, adj.* A cord which fastens muscles to bones.–Bob strained the *sinews* in his ankle when he slipped.

sin·ful (SIN-fuhl) *adj.; sinfully, adv.; sinfulness, n.* Evil; wicked.–The man is *sinful*. He does evil, wicked deeds.

sing (SING) *v. sings, sang, singing.* 1. Make music with the voice.–The teacher plays the piano when the children *sing*.–Sometimes they hum and sometimes they *sing* the words. 2. Make a humming or whistling sound.– When the teakettle makes a humming sound, we say that it *sings*.–Birds *sing*, too.

singe (SINJ) *v. singes, singed, singeing.* Burn slightly.–When Mother got her fur coat too near the fire, she *singed* the fur.

sing·er (SING-er) *n. singers.* A person who makes music with his voice.

sin·gle (SING-gəl) *n. singles.* A hit in baseball which allows the batter to get to first base.–Bob's *single* drove in the winning run. –*v. singles, singled, singling.* 1. Pick.–The policeman *singled* out the boy who had saved the child from being struck by the car. 2. Hit a single in baseball.–Bob *singled* and the boy on third ran to home plate. –*adj.; singly, adv.* 1. One.–A *single* cookie was left on the plate. 2. Made for one only; having one.–We have a *single*-car garage. It holds only one car. 3. Not married.–My Uncle Alex is married, but my Uncle Paul is still *single*.

sin·gu·lar (SING-gyə-ler) *adj.; singularly, adv.* 1. Only one.–The word "boy" is *singular;* it means only one boy. If we mean more than one boy, we say "boys." 2. Strange; queer. – It is very *singular* that the cat was able to get into the house when all the doors were closed.

sink (SINGK) *n. sinks.* A basin with a pipe to drain off whatever is poured in. – Mary poured the water out of the glass into the kitchen *sink*. –*v. sinks, sank, sinking.* 1. Go down. – Boats sometimes *sink* to the bottom of the sea. 2. Fall slowly.–Tom was so weak from laughing that he *sank* to the floor.

sink·er (SINGK-er) *n. sinkers.* A small piece of lead put on the end of a fishing line to pull the hook deep into the water.

sin·ner (SIN-er) *n. sinners.* A person who does bad or wrong things.

si·nus (SY-nəss) *n. sinuses.* One of the air spaces in the front of the skull. The *sinuses* are lined with mucous membrane and connect with the passages of the nose. When the mucous membrane of the nose becomes inflamed, the *sinuses* are often affected the same way.

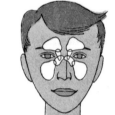

sip (SIP) *n. sips.* A small drink; a swallow.– Take a *sip* of this lemonade. –*v. sips, sipped, sipping.* Drink slowly in small amounts.–Do not drink ice water too fast. *Sip* it.

sir (SER) *n. sirs.* A title of honor or respect used in speaking to older men or officers of the army or navy.–Bob said to the policeman, "Will you help me, *sir*?"–Mary started her business letter with the words "Dear *Sir*."

si·ren (SY-rən) *n. sirens.* A kind of whistle which makes a loud noise by whirling around. –After the accident, we heard the sound of the *siren* on the ambulance.–The fire engine had a very loud *siren*.

sir·up or **syr·up** (SIR- *or* SER-əp) *n. sirups* or *syrups.* A liquid made of sugar or other sweet substance.–We eat *syrup* on pancakes and waffles.

sis·ter (SISS-ter) *n. sisters.* 1. A girl or woman born of the same parents as another person. –Mary is Bob's *sister*. Mary and Bob have the same father and mother. 2. A nun.–The *sister* was good to the child.

sis·ter-in-law (SISS-ter-in-law) *n. sisters-in-law.* The sister of one's wife or husband, or the wife of one's brother.–Your mother's sister is your father's *sister-in-law*. – Your father's sister is your mother's *sister-in-law*. –The wife of your mother's brother is your mother's *sister-in-law*. – The wife of your father's brother is your father's *sister-in-law*.

sit (SIT) *v. sits, sat, sitting.* 1. Rest on the backs of the thighs or upper part of the legs. –Bob *sits* in a big chair. 2. Remain; stand; perch.–Chickens *sit* on a roost at night.

site (SYT) *n. sites.* A location; place to put a building or other structure.—A new post office will be built on this *site.*

sit·u·at·ed (SI-choo-ay-təd) *adj.* Located or placed.—An old house is *situated* on top of the hill.

sit·u·a·tion (si-choo-AY-shən) *n. situations.* Set of conditions.—When Mother returned home, she found a bad *situation:* the meat had burned, Baby was sick, and the dog had chewed up a pillow.

six (SIKS) *n. sixes* and *adj.* The number [6] coming after 5 and before 7. — Three and three make *six.*

six·pence (SIKS-pənss) *n. sixpences.* A piece of money used in England and some other countries. It is worth about seven cents of United States money.

six·teen (siks-TEEN) *n. sixteens* and *adj.* The number [16] after 15 and before 17.— Ten and six make *sixteen.*

six·teenth (siks-TEENTH) *n. sixteenths.* One of 16 equal parts.—If you divide anything into sixteen parts all the same size, each part is one *sixteenth.* It may be written 1/16.
—*adj.* Coming as number 16 in a series.—My name was *sixteenth* on the list.

sixth (SIKSTH) *n. sixths.* One of 6 equal parts.—If you divide anything into six parts all the same size, each part is one *sixth.* It may be written 1/6.
—*adj.* Coming as number 6 in a series.—Sue's name is *sixth* on the list.

six·ti·eth (SIKS-tee-ith) *n. sixtieths.* One of 60 equal parts.—If you divide anything into sixty parts all the same size, each part is one *sixtieth.* It may be written 1/60.
—*adj.* Coming as number 60 in a series.—Mike's name was *sixtieth* on the list.

six·ty (SIKS-tee) *n. sixties* and *adj.* The number [60] coming after 59 and before 61.—Thirty and thirty make *sixty.*

size (SYZ) *n. sizes.* The bigness or smallness of a thing; the amount of room or space a thing takes up.—The *size* of an elephant is large compared with the *size* of a dog.—I wear *size* 7 shoes and Mary wears *size* 6 shoes.

siz·zle (SIZ-əl) *v. sizzles, sizzled, sizzling.* Make sputtering and hissing sounds, as frying fat does.—The steaks are *sizzling* on the platter.

skate (SKAYT) *n. skates.* 1. A short runner attached to a shoe for gliding over ice.

2. A platform with four wheels attached to the shoe for rolling over any smooth surface. —*v. skates, skated, skating.* Glide on skates or roller skates.—Bob likes to *skate* on the pond in the winter.

skat·er (SKAY-ter) *n. skaters.* A person who skates.—Bob is a good *skater.*

skein (SKAYN) *n. skeins.* An amount of yarn put up in long loops. —Mary helped wind a *skein* of wool into a ball.

skel·e·ton (SKEL-ə-tn) *n. skeletons.* 1. A bony framework. — This picture shows the *skeleton* of a person's body.
2. A framework of any kind.—The *skeleton* of a house is of wood.

skel·e·ton key (SKEL-ə-tn kee) *skeleton keys.* A key which opens many different locks.

sketch (SKECH) *n. sketches.* 1. A rough drawing.—Bob showed the *sketch* of the plane to Father.
2. A short play or story.—The children gave some little *sketches* about school life as part of their show.
—*v. sketches, sketched, sketching.* Draw a rough picture or outline of.—Jack *sketched* the house.

ski (SKEE) *n. skis.* One of two long wooden runners that are fastened to the shoes for gliding over snow.

—*v. skis, skied, skiing.* Glide on skis.—It is fun to *ski* in winter.

skid (SKID) *n. skids.* 1. A runway to slide something on.–The logs were sent down a long *skid* into the river.
2. A slip; a slide.–The car took a *skid* as it went up the icy road.
–*v. skids, skidded, skidding.* Slip or slide.–Do not put on the brakes too quickly when you are driving on icy streets, or your car may *skid.*

skill (SKIL) *n. skills.* Ability to do a certain thing well as a result of practice.–Bob shows much *skill* in baseball.

skil·let (SKIL-it) *n. skillets.* A heavy, shallow, metal pan with a long handle. A *skillet* is used for frying foods.

skill·ful or **skil·ful** (SKIL-fuhl) *adj.; skillfully, adv.* Expert; having much ability.–A *skillful* workman is one who knows much about his work and does it very well.

skim (SKIM) *v. skims, skimmed, skimming.*
1. Take off from the top. – Mary helped Grandmother *skim* the cream from the milk.
2. Move lightly over. – The speedboat *skimmed* the water.
3. Read hurriedly and not thoroughly.–Bob *skimmed* through the story just to get an idea of what it was about.
–*adj.* The milk that is left after the cream is skimmed off is *skim* milk.

skimp (SKIMP) *v. skimps, skimped, skimping.* 1. Save carefully.–Mother has to *skimp* to make her money last all week.
2. Provide or use too little of. – Bob told Mother not to *skimp* the frosting on the cake.

skimp·y (SKIMP-ee) *adj. skimpier, skimpiest.* Not enough; too little.–Sally gave Ann a *skimpy* portion of green beans. She did not know how much Ann could eat.

skin (SKIN) *n. skins.* The outer covering of the body of a person, animal, vegetable, or fruit. – If you cut through the *skin* on your hand, it will bleed.–Bob cut off the *skin,* or peel, of the orange.
–*v. skins, skinned, skinning.* 1. Rub off the skin of.–Mary *skinned* her arm when she ran into the stone wall.
2. Remove the skin from. – The butcher *skinned* the rabbit so that it could be cooked.

skin·ny (SKIN-ee) *adj. skinnier, skinniest.* Thin; lean; not fat. – The hungry cat is *skinny.*

skip (SKIP) *v. skips, skipped, skipping.* 1. Jump or move with little hopping steps.–Children like to *skip* over a rope.–The girls *skipped* to the music.
2. Pass over.–Bob was so anxious to finish the book that he *skipped* some pages. He didn't read them.–Tom was in such a hurry to finish his speech that he *skipped* some of the points he had planned to make.

skip·per (SKIP-er) *n. skippers.* A commander of a boat or ship.–Bob stood in the pilot house with the *skipper.*

skirt (SKERT) *n. skirts.* The part of a dress that hangs from the waist down.–Mary wears a sweater and *skirt.*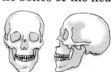
–*v. skirts, skirted, skirting.* Pass along the outer edge of.–We *skirted* the city to avoid the heavy traffic.

skull (SKUL) *n. skulls.* The bones of the head that form a case for the brain and support the face.–The man's *skull* was fractured in the accident.

skunk (SKUNGK) *n. skunks.* A small animal that has black fur with white stripes down the back, and a bushy tail. *Skunks* protect themselves by giving off a very unpleasant odor when they are frightened or hurt.

sky (SKY) *n. skies.* The air high above us.–On clear days, the *sky* looks blue.–Birds fly high in the *sky.*–The *sky* is often called heaven, or the heavens.

sky·light (SKY-lyt) *n. skylights.* A window set in a roof or ceiling.–Artists' studios usually have *skylights* to let in more daylight.

sky·rock·et (SKY-rahk-it) *n. skyrockets.* A firework on a stick that shoots high into the sky and then explodes.–On the Fourth of July, we shot off many *skyrockets.*

sky·scrap·er (SKY-skray-per) *n. skyscrapers.*
A very tall building.—
We saw the *sky-scrapers* as we came
nearer to the city.

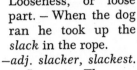

slack (SLAK) *n.*
Looseness, or loose
part. — When the dog
ran he took up the
slack in the rope.
—*adj. slacker, slackest.*
1. Loose. — The rope
walker said the rope was too *slack* to walk on.
He asked to have it pulled tighter.
2. Quiet; not active.—Spring is a *slack* season for people who sell ice skates. Not many
people buy ice skates in the spring.
3. Careless.—I was *slack* about getting my
arithmetic paper in on time. Miss Jones
asked me to try and be more prompt the next
time.

slack·en (SLAK-ən) *v. slackens, slackened,
slackening.* 1. Slow down.—Much work must
still be done, so do not *slacken* now.—When
one is tired, his energy *slackens.*
2. Become loose.—When it rains, the clothes-
line *slackens.* When it is dry, it tightens.

slacks (SLAKS) *n. pl.* Trousers; long pants.
—When Ruth goes on a hike, she wears
slacks.

slag (SLAG) *n.* The waste matter left over
after metals have been separated from their
ores.

slain (SLAYN) *v.* One form of the verb *slay.*
—The bear was *slain* by the hunter.

slam (SLAM) *n. slams.* A noise made by shutting something with a bang.—We knew Jack
had come home because we heard the *slam*
of the front door.
—*v. slams, slammed, slamming.* Shut with a
bang or with much force.—Do not *slam* the
window. You may break the glass if you do.

slang (SLANG) *n.* Made-up words and ex-
pressions that are used mostly in talk.—The
sleepy man said, "It's time to hit the hay." He
meant it was time to go to bed. — "Step on it!"
is *slang* for "Hurry!"

slant (SLANT) *n.* A leaning to one side. —
Mother writes without any *slant* to her letters. She writes straight up and down.
—*v. slants, slanted, slanting.* Slope. — Most
roofs *slant.*—The flagpole stands straight up,
but the roof *slants* downward from the top.

slap (SLAP) *n. slaps.* A blow with the open
hand.—Mother gave the dog a gentle *slap.*
—*v. slaps, slapped, slapping.* Hit with the open
hand. — When the dog got onto the chair,
Mother *slapped* him gently to teach him not
to do it.

slash (SLASH) *n. slashes.* A long cut or slit.
—The Boy Scouts' tent had a *slash* in one side,
and the rain came in.
—*v. slashes, slashed, slashing.* To cut.—Someone *slashed* the tent accidentally with a jack-
knife.

slat (SLAT) *n. slats.* A thin, narrow bar of
wood or metal. —
Grandfather nailed
some *slats* across the
chicken coop to keep
the chickens in.—Bedsprings are held up by
slats.

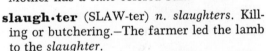

slate (SLAYT) *n. slates.* 1. A smooth blue-
gray rock that splits into thin layers.—Our
blackboard is made
of *slate.*
2. A framed square
of slate. — When
Father went to school,
the children used
slates to write on.
—*adj.* Bluish-gray. —
Mother has a *slate*-colored suit.

$$2 \times 2 = 4$$
$$2 \times 3 = 6$$
John

slaugh·ter (SLAW-ter) *n. slaughters.* Killing or butchering.—The farmer led the lamb
to the *slaughter.*
—*v. slaughters, slaughtered, slaughtering.* Kill;
butcher. — The farmer *slaughtered* a lamb
today.

slave (SLAYV) *n. slaves.* A person who is
owned by another person and can be sold by
that person. A *slave* works without pay.
There are no *slaves* in this country any more.
—*v. slaves, slaved, slaving.* Work as hard as a
slave does.—The mother *slaves* for her children.

slav·er·y (SLAY-və-ree) *n.* 1. Condition of a
slave. — The captives of the ancient army
were sold into *slavery.*
2. The owning of slaves.—*Slavery* was abol-
ished in this country during the Civil War.

slaw (SLAW) *n. slaws.* A salad made by
chopping cabbage into long, fine shreds and
then adding vinegar dressing.

slay (SLAY) *v. slays, slew, slaying.* Kill with
force.—The stained-glass window shows St.
George *slaying* the dragon.

slay·er (SLAY-er) *n. slayers.* A person who kills another.—The police are tracking down the *slayer.*

sled (SLED) *n. sleds.* A low platform on runners that slides easily over snow.—Children like to coast on a *sled.*

—*v. sleds, sledded, sledding.* Ride on a sled.—We went *sledding* after the snowfall.

sledge (SLEJ) *n. sledges.* A large, heavy hammer. — The men drove the posts into the ground with a *sledge.*

sleek (SLEEK) *adj.; sleekly, adv.; sleekness, n.* Smooth and glossy.—The kitten's fur is *sleek.*

sleep (SLEEP) *n.* Slumber or rest. — Father had only four hours' *sleep* last night because he got to bed so late.
—*v. sleeps, slept, sleeping.* Slumber; rest the mind and body; fall naturally into an unawareness of the things around one.—When we *sleep* at night we close our eyes.

sleep·er (SLEE-per) *n. sleepers.* 1. A person sleeping.—Mother was never a late *sleeper.* 2. A railroad car that has berths, or beds, for sleeping.—Father made the long railroad trip in a *sleeper.*

sleep·less (SLEEP-ləss) *adj.; sleeplessly, adv.; sleeplessness, n.* Restless; wakeful; without sleep.—It was so hot that Mother had a *sleepless* night.

sleep·y (SLEE-pee) *adj.* sleepier, sleepiest. Drowsy; ready to go to sleep.—When Baby is *sleepy,* Mother puts her to bed.

sleet (SLEET) *n.; sleety, adj.* Rain that freezes into tiny pieces of ice as it falls. — *Sleet* covered the streets and made them very slippery.—*Sleet* rattled on the windowpanes.

sleeve (SLEEV) *n. sleeves.* The part of a coat, dress, or other garment that covers the arm.

sleeve·less (SLEEV-ləss) *adj.* Without sleeves; ending at the shoulder of the garment. — Men's vests are *sleeveless.*

sleigh (SLAY) *n. sleighs.* A large sled. *Sleighs* are pulled by horses.

slen·der (SLEN-der) *adj.; slenderness, n.* Thin; slim.—Mother is *slender,* but Father is stout.

slept (SLEPT) *v.* One form of the verb *sleep.*—Baby *slept* soundly all night.

slice (SLYSS) *n. slices.* A thin, flat piece. — Mother cut the watermelon into *slices.*
—*v. slices, sliced, slicing.* Cut into thin, flat pieces.—Mary *sliced* the bread for Mother.

slick·er (SLIK-er) *n. slickers.* A raincoat; a waterproof coat.—On rainy days Jack keeps dry by wearing his *slicker.*

slide (SLYD) *n. slides.* 1. Anything on which something can move smoothly and easily.—The picture shows a *slide* for the children to go down.
2. A thin piece of glass on which there is a picture, which may be thrown on a screen by a projector.—Our teacher showed us some *slides* of animals at the zoo.
3. A small sheet of glass to put something on to look at through a microscope.
—*v. slides, slid, sliding.* Move smoothly and easily.—Children like to *slide* down a hill on their sleds.

slight (SLYT) *v. slights, slighted, slighting.* 1. Neglect, or give too little attention to. — Do not *slight* your work, or you may not pass. 2. Neglect, or treat rudely.—Bob *slighted* Sy by not asking him to play.
—*adj. slighter, slightest.* 1. Slim; slender. — Grandmother is *slight.* She's short and thin. 2. Little; small; not great.—The man at the store said there would be a *slight* charge for delivering the table.

slim (SLIM) *adj. slimmer, slimmest.* 1. Thin; slight; slender. — Mary has a *slim* waist. Her waist is not very big around. 2. Small; slight.—We have a *slim* chance of winning the game if Bob does not play.

sling (SLING) *n. slings.* 1. A device for throwing stones or other small objects. It is made of two cords joined by a piece of leather or cloth which holds the stone while the cords are whirled around in the air.—A *sling*shot has a forked stick through which the stone is shot by the force of rubber bands.

2. A piece of cloth looped about the neck.—When Jack broke his arm, he supported it with a *sling*.

3. A chain or heavy rope used to lift heavy things.—Boats are unloaded with *slings*.

—*v. slings, slung, slinging.* Hang.—When Jack goes on a hike, he *slings* his knapsack over his shoulder.

slip (SLIP) *n. slips.* 1. A mistake. — Do not make a *slip* of the tongue and tell Mother about her present.

2. A woman's undergarment.—Mother wears a *slip* under her dress.

3. A cutting; little branches cut from other plants.—These plants grew from *slips*.

—*v. slips, slipped, slipping.* 1. Slide; move quickly and smoothly.—These shoes *slip* on easily.

2. Slide accidentally and fall. — The dish *slipped* through my fingers and fell.

3. To cause to move quickly and easily.—Bob *slipped* the candy into his pocket.

4. Pass quickly.—The day at the farm *slipped* by before we knew it.

5. To move around quietly.—He *slipped* in and out without being seen.

slip·knot (SLIP-naht) *n. slipknots.* A knot made so that if you pull the cord, the knot will slide along the cord.

slip·per (SLIP-er) *n. slippers.* A light shoe that slips onto the foot easily.—Mother has silver evening *slippers*.

slip·per·y (SLIP-ə-ree) *adj. slipperier, slipperiest.* Easy to slide or slip on; too smooth to get a firm hold on.—A waxed floor and an icy street are *slippery*.—Fish are *slippery*.

slit (SLIT) *n. slits.* A straight cut, tear, or opening. — A ray of light streamed through the *slit* in the barn door.

—*v. slits, slit, slitting.* Cut a long line in.—The doctor *slit* the soldier's coat so that he could dress his wounds.

sliv·er (SLIV-er) *n. slivers.* A long, thin piece of wood or metal that has been cut off or broken off a larger piece; a splinter. — Father got a *sliver* of wood in his thumb while picking up a log.

slo·gan (SLOH-gən) *n. slogans.* A word, a group of words, or a saying used as a motto.—"We work to win" is the *slogan* of our class.

sloop (SLOOP) *n. sloops.* A sailboat with one mast and at least one mainsail and jib.

slope (SLOHP) *n. slopes.* Slanting land.—The children climbed the *slope* to the top of the hill.

—*v. slopes, sloped, sloping.* Slant. — The hill *slopes* downward to the river.—Since the roof *slopes*, water rolls off it when it rains.

sloth (SLOHTH *or* SLAWTH) *n. sloths.* A hairy animal that lives in South America. It eats leaves and fruits, lives in trees, and hangs upside down.

slouch (SLOWCH) *v. slouches, slouched, slouching.* Move, walk, or sit in a lazy, drooping way.—Do not *slouch* at your desk or you will spoil your posture.

—*slouch, n. slouches.*

slow (SLOH) *v. slows, slowed, slowing.* Go slower; go with less speed. — Always *slow* down when you come to a corner while on your bicycle.

—*adj. slower, slowest; slowly, adv.* 1. Not fast or quick.—Bob is rather *slow* in doing his work. He takes a lot of time.

2. Behind time.—Bob was late because his watch was 15 minutes *slow*. His watch said 8:15 when it was really 8:30.

3. Dull; not bright.—A *slow* person does not learn quickly or easily.

slug (SLUG) *n. slugs.* 1. A slow-moving animal something like a snail, but without a shell. — Mary found some *slugs* in the garden.

2. A metal bullet.—The hunter had a pocket full of *slugs* for his gun.

—*v. slugs, slugged, slugging.* Hit hard. — The man was *slugged* by the robber and left lying unconscious.

slum (SLUM) *n. slums.* A very dirty and crowded part of a city, where poor people live.

slum·ber (SLUM-ber) *n. slumbers.* Sleep. — Father didn't want us to disturb his *slumber.*
—*v. slumbers, slumbered, slumbering.* Sleep.— Betty *slumbers* ten hours a night.

slump (SLUMP) *n. slumps.* A falling off. — There was a *slump* in trade last month.
—*v. slumps, slumped, slumping.* Fall or sink down suddenly.—The boy *slumped* over when the ball hit him.

slush (SLUSH) *n.; slushy, adj.* Partly melted snow.—We wore rubbers because of the *slush.*

sly (SLY) *adj. slier* or *slyer, sliest* or *slyest; slyly, adv.* Able to do things secretly, or without letting others see or know.—The kitten was *sly* about trying to catch the goldfish. She waited until we had left the room and then she tried to put her paw in the goldfish bowl.

small (SMAWL) *adj. smaller, smallest.* 1. Little.—A *small* child went up to the policeman and asked him the way to the store.
2. Mean and petty.—It was *small* of the man to report the boy who accidentally broke his window.

small·pox (SMAWL-pahks) *n.* A catching disease that causes fever and a breaking out on the body.—Do not go near a person with *smallpox* or you may get it.—People are vaccinated to prevent *smallpox.*

smart (SMAHRT) *v. smarts, smarted, smarting.* Sting or pain sharply.—When the nurse put the medicine on the cut, it started to *smart.*
—*adj. smarter, smartest; smartly, adv.* 1. Stylish and in good taste.—Mother got a *smart* new spring suit.
2. Quick and clever.—Jack is a *smart* fellow.

smash (SMASH) *v. smashes, smashed, smashing.* 1. Break into many pieces.—When Mary dropped the plate, it *smashed.*
2. Break with force.—The runner *smashed* through the other team's line in the football game. He pushed everyone out of his way and rushed through.
3. Crash or fall heavily and noisily. — The airplane *smashed* into the house.

smear (SMIR) *n. smears.* A spot left by something rubbed on.—Mother had a big *smear* on her new apron.
—*v. smears, smeared, smearing.* Spread or rub over.—Mary *smeared* her hands and face with cold cream.

smell (SMEL) *n. smells.* An odor.—The *smell* of tobacco smoke came from the room.
—*v. smells, smelled, smelling.* 1. Get odors of things through the nose.—We *smell* bacon when it is cooking.
2. Give off an odor.—Roses *smell* sweet.

smelt (SMELT) *v. smelts, smelted, smelting.* Melt ore to separate the metal from the slag; remove impurities from metal by melting; refine. — Huge furnaces are used to *smelt* steel.

smile (SMYL) *n. smiles.* A look of amusement or of happiness. — The new puppy brought a *smile* to the boy's face.
—*v. smiles, smiled, smiling.* Look amused or happy by turning the mouth up at the corners.

smith (SMITH) *n. smiths.* A person who makes things out of metal. — A gold*smith* shapes things out of gold. — A black*smith* shapes horseshoes, wagon tires, and other things out of iron.

smith·y (SMITH-ee) *n. smithies.* The workshop in which a person makes things from iron or other metals.—A blacksmith shop is a *smithy.*

smock (SMAHK) *n. smocks.* A loose gown worn over one's other clothes to keep them clean.

smog (SMAHG) *n.* A mixture of smoke and fog.—*Smog* blanketed the city.

smoke (SMOHK) *n. smokes.* The cloud of tiny particles or vapor that rises from anything burning.—*Smoke* poured out of the big chimney.
—*v. smokes, smoked, smoking.* 1. Breathe in and out the smoke from burning tobacco.— Father *smokes* a pipe.
2. Give off smoke.—The stove *smokes.*
3. Cure (meat) or prepare by exposing to

smoke.–Grandfather *smokes* meat. He hangs it in a small room over a small fire that fills the room with smoke.–Meat that has been *smoked* keeps for a long time.

smoke·stack (SMOHK-stak) *n. smokestacks.* A tall chimney to let out smoke from a furnace.–Smoke poured out of the school *smokestack* when the janitor started the fire in the furnace.

smok·y (SMOH-kee) *adj. smokier, smokiest.* 1. Full of smoke. –Places where there are factories are often *smoky.* 2. Covered or darkened by smoke that has settled.–The windows are *smoky.*

smol·der or **smoul·der** (SMOHL-der) *v. smolders* or *smoulders, smoldered* or *smouldered, smoldering* or *smouldering.* Give off smoke but no flame. – The campfire *smoldered* long after we went to bed.

smooth (SMOOTH) *v. smooths, smoothed, smoothing.* 1. Remove bumps, wrinkles, etc. – Mary *smoothed* the wrinkles out of the tablecloth.–The board was rough, so Father planed and sandpapered it to *smooth* it. 2. Make peaceful and calm.–Bob and Mary quarreled this morning, but they have *smoothed* over their troubles now. –*adj. smoother, smoothest; smoothly, adv.* 1. Level; even; without bumps or roughness.– A pane of glass is *smooth.*–The lake was not *smooth* because the wind made ripples in it. 2. Free from lumps. – Mother stirred the gravy to make it *smooth.* 3. Evenly moving; in a level course. – We had a *smooth* ride in the boat. It was not jerky and bumpy.

smoth·er (SMUTH-er) *v. smothers, smothered, smothering.* 1. Die from lack of air.– Jim cut air holes in the box before he put the chick in. Otherwise the chick would *smother.* 2. Kill or extinguish by cutting off air from. –Father *smothered* the fire by covering it with dirt.

smudge (SMUJ) *n. smudges.* 1. A dirty mark or spot.–When Mary rubbed the soot on her cheek, it made a *smudge.* 2. A fire that smokes but doesn't blaze.–The campers built a *smudge* to drive away the mosquitoes. –*v. smudges, smudged, smudging.* Smear; make a dirty mark on.–Baby's face was *smudged* with jelly.

smug (SMUG) *adj.* Too sure of oneself or too pleased with one's own position, brightness, or goodness; self-satisfied.–The girl's *smug* attitude is disliked by most of her classmates. They don't think she's quite so great as she thinks she is.

smug·gle (SMUG-əl) *v. smuggles, smuggled, smuggling.* 1. Take anything in or out of a country secretly when it is against the law to do so. 2. Take in or out secretly.–The boy tried to *smuggle* his dog into school.

smug·gler (SMUG-ler) *n. smugglers.* A person who takes things into or out of a country when it is against the law to do so. – The Coast Guard arrested the *smugglers.*

snag (SNAG) *n. snags.* 1. A branch or stump of a tree under the water.–While rowing the boat, the boys struck a *snag.* 2. Unexpected trouble.–Mother couldn't finish Mary's dress on time, because she struck a *snag.* She ran out of material. –*v. snags, snagged, snagging.* Catch on something rough or sharp.–Mother *snagged* her stocking. It caught on something rough.

snail (SNAYL) *n. snails.* A slow-moving animal that lives in water and on land. *Snails* have a coiled shell into which they crawl for protection.

snake (SNAYK) *n. snakes.* A long crawling animal without legs. Some *snakes* live on the ground, some in the water. They eat insects, small animals, and the like. Some *snakes* have poisonous bites.

snap (SNAP) *n. snaps.* 1. A quick, sharp noise.–The stick broke with a *snap.* 2. A fastener which clicks when squeezed together.–Some of Mary's dresses have buttons on them and some have *snaps.* 3. A crisp, thin cookie.–Mother makes gingersnaps. –*v. snaps, snapped, snapping.* 1. Make a sudden biting motion; snatch with the teeth.– The dog will not *snap* at you if you do not tease him.–The hungry dog *snapped* up the bone and ran away. 2. Make a sharp cracking noise.–The ice on the branches of the trees made them *snap.* 3. Break suddenly.–The ice made the telephone wire *snap.*

snap·drag·on (SNAP-drag-ən) *n. snapdragons.* A garden flower with blossoms shaped like dragon heads growing along the sides of the stem.

snap·shot (SNAP-shaht) *n. snapshots.* A photograph taken quickly without much preparation.—Father took a *snapshot* of Baby.

snare (SNAIR) *n. snares.* A trap or noose designed to catch birds and small animals.—The trapper caught the rabbit with a *snare.*
—*v. snares, snared, snaring.* Catch with a trap or noose.—The trapper *snares* animals to sell their pelts.

snarl (SNAHRL) *n. snarls.* 1. A growl or curling of the lip.—The lion looked up with a *snarl.* 2. A tangle.—Father could not comb the *snarls* out of Sally's hair.
—*v. snarls, snarled, snarling.* 1. Growl or curl the lip up fiercely.—The little dog *snarled* at the big dog. 2. Tangle.—The kitten *snarled* up Grandmother's yarn by rolling in it.

snatch (SNACH) *n. snatches.* A bit or small part.—Father just read *snatches* of the book.
—*v. snatches, snatched, snatching.* Grab or catch hold of.—A thief tried to *snatch* Mother's purse in the store.—The drowning boy *snatched* at the rope thrown to him.

sneak (SNEEK) *n. sneaks.* A sly, mean person.—The *sneak* who had stolen the money let another man be accused of stealing it.
—*v. sneaks, sneaked, sneaking.* Go slyly.—After killing the chicken, the fox *sneaked* into the woods.

sneer (SNIR) *n. sneers.* A mocking or scornful look or remark.—Bob tries to pay no attention to Bill's *sneers.*
—*v. sneers, sneered, sneering.* Show by the look on one's face that one looks down on a person.—Bill *sneers* at Bob for trying so hard in school.

sneeze (SNEEZ) *v. sneezes, sneezed, sneezing.* Force air out through the nose so hard that it causes a sharp, sudden noise.—A tickling in the nose often causes one to *sneeze.*

sniff (SNIF) *n. sniffs.* Breath; smell.—Take a *sniff* of this perfume.
—*v. sniffs, sniffed, sniffing.* Take little short breaths through the nose.—When a dog smells a rabbit, he *sniffs.*

snip (SNIP) *n. snips.* Quick cut.—With one *snip* Sally cut off the extra string.
—*v. snips, snipped, snipping.* Quickly cut off.—The barber *snipped* Baby's hair.

snipe (SNYP) *n. snipes.* A long-billed bird that lives in marshes.
—*v. snipes, sniped, sniping.* To shoot from a place where one cannot be seen.

snip·er (SNYP-er) *n. snipers.* A soldier who shoots from a place where he cannot be seen by the enemy soldiers.

snoop (SNOOP) *v. snoops, snooped, snooping.* Try to find out about other people's business; pry into things.—Jack likes to *snoop* around in the refrigerator.

snore (SNOR) *v. snores, snored, snoring.* Breathe with a harsh, rough noise while sleeping.—Father *snores* when he naps.

snort (SNORT) *n. snorts.* A sudden noise made by forcing air through the nose.—Jack made a *snort* when Mary said she was going to be the greatest actress in the world.
—*v. snorts, snorted, snorting.* Force air through the nose so that it makes a sudden noise.—Horses *snort.*

snout (SNOWT) *n. snouts.* A long nose that sticks out.—A pig's *snout* is his nose. Other animals have *snouts,* too.

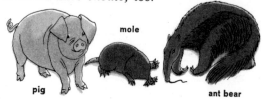

pig / mole / ant bear

snow (SNOH) *n. snows.* Small, white, star-shaped flakes of frozen water that fall from the sky in winter.—When *snow* melts, it turns into water.
—*v. snows, snowed, snowing.* Drop down snow.—Do you think it will *snow* for Christmas?

snow·ball (SNOH-bawl) *n. snowballs.* 1. A ball made of snow pressed together.—Sally likes to throw *snowballs* at Father. 2. A white flower that grows on a bush.

snow·bound (SNOH-bownd) *adj.* Surrounded by the snow so that one cannot get out. — Grandfather could not go to the city because he was *snowbound.*

snow·drift (SNOH-drift) *n. snowdrifts.* A bank or large pile of snow.—The wind blew the snow into *snowdrifts.*

snow·flake (SNOH-flayk) *n. snowflakes.* One of the small, lacy pieces in which snow falls to the earth.—Mother showed Sally how to catch *snowflakes* on a piece of black velvet.

snow·man (SNOH-man) *n. snowmen.* A figure of a man made of snow. — The children put Father's pipe in the *snowman's* mouth.

snow·plow (SNOH-plow) *n. snowplows.* A machine used to push the snow from streets, roads, railroads, and other places.

snow·shoe (SNOH-shoo) *n. snowshoes.* A frame that looks something like a tennis racket. *Snowshoes* are tied to the feet and worn when traveling by foot over deep snow to keep one from sinking into the snow.

snow·storm (SNOH-storm) *n. snowstorms.* A storm during which much snow falls; a blizzard.—We were caught in a heavy *snowstorm.*

snub (SNUB) *n. snubs.* A slight.—Mary usually tries to ignore Jack's *snubs.* When he doesn't say hello to her, she just doesn't pay any attention.
—*v. snubs, snubbed, snubbing.* Slight; treat coldly.—The boy felt *snubbed* because he wasn't invited to the party.
—*adj.* Short and turned up, as a *snub* nose.

snug (SNUG) *adj. snugger, snuggest.* 1. Close-fitting.—Bob has grown so much that his coat is too *snug.*
2. Cozy, warm, and comfortable.—The library is *snug* when there is a fire in the fireplace.

snug·gle (SNUG-əl) *v. snuggles, snuggled, snuggling.* Lie close; cuddle.—The kitten *snuggled* up close to Sally.

so (SOH) *adv.* 1. As.—Bob's story was not *so* good as Mary's.
2. To such a degree or amount.—Do not eat *so* much.—It is *so* beautiful out, that I should like to take a walk.
3. Very.—It is *so* hot today!
4. Likewise.—Jack was talking, and *so* was Bob. Bob was talking, too.
5. In order.—We eat *so* that we will grow.—Father works *so* as to earn money.
6. Referring to something said before.—If Father says *so,* it is true.
—*conj.* Therefore.—I was sick, *so* I could not go.
—*pron.* More or less.—Mary was an hour or *so* late.

soak (SOHK) *v. soaks, soaked, soaking.* 1. Wet through and through.—When Bob waded into the water, he *soaked* his shoes and socks. —Mother *soaked* the soiled clothes in soapy water.
2. Suck; absorb.—A blotter *soaks* up ink.

soap (SOHP) *n. soaps.* A material which makes suds in water. It is used to wash dishes, clothes, and other things, and to bathe with.—*Soap* is made in cake form, in liquid form, and in flakes and powders.
—*v. soaps, soaped, soaping.* Rub soap on.— Mother *soaps* the collars of Father's shirts to get them clean.

soar (SOR) *v. soars, soared, soaring.* Fly upward; fly high.—Some eagles *soar* above mountains.

sob (SAHB) *v. sobs, sobbed, sobbing.* Cry with short, jerky, loud breaths.—We heard the little child *sobbing* pitifully when he lost his tricycle.

so·ber (SOH-ber) *adj.; soberly, adv.* 1. Quiet; earnest.—Bob is a very *sober* boy. He takes things seriously.
2. Not drunk; not having had too much alcohol to drink.—The driver was *sober* when the accident happened.
—*v. sobers, sobered, sobering.* Stop laughing; become quiet.—The children *sobered* down after their mother scolded them.

soc·cer (SAHK-er) *n.* A game played with a round football that is kicked or hit with any part of the body except the hands or arms.

so·cial (SOH-shəl) *n. socials.* A friendly party.—We had an ice-cream *social* at our school.
—*adj.; socially, adv.* 1. Fond of the company of others.—Mary is a very *social* person. She likes to talk and have fun with others.
2. Having to do with people.—*Social* study is the study of people and how they live together. Geography and history are *social* studies.

so·cial·ism (SOH-shəl-iz-əm) *n.* A system of social organization based on the theory that goods and property should be owned and controlled by the community as a whole, not by private individuals. Various means proposed for reaching this goal have usually been based on different historical and local conditions.

so·ci·e·ty (sə-SY-ə-tee) *n. societies.* 1. Company.—Bob enjoys Jack's *society.* He likes being with Jack.
2. All people, living and working together; the way human beings live together.—Scientists do work of great value to *society.*
3. A club or group of people who work together for some purpose.—We have formed a *society* to help others.
4. The rich, fashionable group of people in a community.

sock (SAHK) *n. socks.* Short-legged stocking.
—Mother wears long stockings. The children wear *socks.*

sock·et (SAHK-it) *n. sockets.* A hollow part into which something fits.—Father made a *socket* to hold the flag-pole. — The light did not work because the bulb was not screwed tightly into the *socket.*

sod (SAHD) *n. sods.* Grassy topsoil that is held together by the roots of the grass.—We put new *sod* on our yard.
—*v. sods, sodded, sodding.* Put sod on.—We *sodded* the yard to make a nice lawn.

so·da (SOH-də) *n. sodas.* 1. A white powder used in cooking.—Baking *soda* is usually used in making cakes that have sour milk in them.
2. (Also called "soda water.") Flavored water that fizzes because it has been charged with carbon dioxide.—Father brought home a case of *soda* for the party.
3. A drink made with ice cream, syrup, and soda water.—Jack likes chocolate *sodas.*

so·fa (SOH-fə) *n. sofas.* An upholstered couch that usually has a back and arms.

soft (SAWFT) *adj. softer, softest; softly, adv.*
1. Not hard.—The pillow is *soft.*
2. Quiet, gentle, and mild.—A *soft* breeze blew through the trees.
3. The letter "c" in the word "cat" is hard. It has a throaty sound. The "c" in "cent" is *soft.* It is pronounced like an "s."—The letter "g" in "game" is hard. The "g" in "giraffe" is *soft.* It is pronounced like a "j."

soft·ball (SAWFT-bawl) *n.* 1. A ball game similar to baseball, but played with a softer and larger ball.—The boys chose sides for a game of *softball.*
2. The ball used in such a game.

soft wa·ter (SAWFT WAW-ter *or* WAHT-er). Water that is more or less free from the minerals that make it hard to form soapsuds. It doesn't take much soap to make suds in *soft water.*—*Soft water* feels smooth to the hands.

sog·gy (SAHG-ee) *adj. soggier, soggiest.* Soaked; wet through.—The bottom crust of the blackberry pie is *soggy.*

soil (SOIL) *n. soils.* Ground; earth; dirt.—The *soil* in our garden is black and rich.
—*v. soils, soiled, soiling.* Make or become dirty.—Baby *soiled* her clean dress making mudpies.—Her dress was *soiled.*

so·lar (SOH-ler) *adj.* 1. Measured by the sun.—A sundial is a *solar* clock.
2. Having to do with the sun.—The *solar* system is made up of the sun and all the planets and heavenly bodies that revolve around it.

sold (SOHLD) *v.* One form of the verb *sell.*—Father bought a new house, but now he has *sold* it.

sol·der (SAHD-er) *v. solders, soldered, soldering.* Join metal parts by melting a special metal or alloy and applying it as a glue. The melted metal hardens around the parts and locks them together.

sol·dier (SOHL-jer) *n. soldiers.* A man serving in an army. *Soldiers* fight the enemy in time of war.

sole (SOHL) *n. soles.* 1. Bottom of a shoe.—The *soles* of Bob's shoes were worn out.
2. Bottom of the foot.—Father walked so far that the *soles* of his feet were sore.
3. A kind of fish that is good to eat.

sol·emn (SAHL-əm) *adj.; solemnly, adv.* 1. Earnest; sober; serious.—Bob has *solemn* blue eyes; Jack has twinkling blue eyes that are full of fun and mischief.
2. Happening or done in a serious and formal way.—The inauguration of a president is a *solemn* event.

sol·id (SAHL-id) *adj.; solidly, adv.; solidness, n.* 1. The same all the way through.—A stove pipe or drain pipe is hollow. A baseball bat is *solid*.
2. The same all over.—Mary's new dress is a *solid* blue.
3. Firm and strong.—The parts of a table must be glued together to make it *solid*.—The house has a *solid* foundation.
4. Firm and hard.—Water is liquid. When it freezes, it becomes *solid*.

sol·i·tar·y (SAHL-ə-tair-ee) *adj.* 1. Alone; living or being apart from others.—A hermit leads a *solitary* life.
2. Lonely; not visited.—He lives on a *solitary* isle.

sol·i·tude (SAHL-ə-tood *or* -tyood) *n.* State of being alone; peace and quiet.—Jerry often goes into the garden to find *solitude*. He goes there to be alone in a quiet place.

so·lo (SOH-loh) *n. solos.* A piece of music to be played or sung by one person at a time.—*adj.* Without companions. — The airplane pilot made a *solo* flight. He flew all alone.

so·lo·ist (SOH-loh-ist) *n. soloists.* A person who sings or plays a piece of music alone.

sol·u·ble (SAHL-yə-bəl) *adj.* 1. Able to be dissolved.—Sugar, salt, and many other food products are *soluble* in water.
2. Capable of being solved, as a problem, or a mystery.—The riddle is *soluble*.

so·lu·tion (sə-LOO-shən) *n. solutions.* 1. Finding the answer to something, as a puzzle or mystery.—The *solution* of the crime was difficult.
2. The answer or explanation.—There seems to be no *solution* to the problem.
3. The act or process of dissolving something, as sugar in water.—*Solution* of the powder was made easy by the use of boiling water.
4. The liquid in which a substance has been dissolved.—The *solution* is too thick.

solve (SAHLV) *v. solves, solved, solving.* Find the answer to.—Mary tried to *solve* the arithmetic problem.—The police tried to *solve* the mystery.

som·bre·ro (sahm-BRAIR-oh) *n. sombreros.*  A high-crowned hat with a broad brim worn by men in Mexico, some other parts of America, and Spain.

some (SUM) *adj.* 1. A number of.—*Some* sailors came to town.
2. Any.—Tell *some* policeman about your accident.
3. Any amount of.—Put *some* sugar on Baby's oatmeal.
4. Any number of.—*Some* apples are red.

some·bod·y (SUM-bahd-ee) *pron.* 1. Some person, not named or not known.—The mother bear said, "*Somebody* has been eating my porridge."
2. A person of importance.—Father always says to Bob, "Be *somebody*, son."

some·how (SUM-how) *adv.* By some means; in one way or another.—Father will get to work *somehow* while the car is being repaired.

som·er·sault (SUM-er-sawlt) *n. somersaults.* A heels-over-head turn.—Some children can turn a *somersault* backwards.

son (SUN) *n. sons.* A boy or man as related to his father and mother. A boy is his father's *son*. Your father is your grandfather's *son*.

song (SAWNG) *n. songs.* A short piece of music with words to be sung.—"America" is the name of a *song* we sing at school.—Some poems are set to music. Then they are *songs*.

son-in-law (SUN-in-law) *n. sons-in-law.* The husband of a person's daughter.—Sister's husband is the *son-in-law* of Father and Mother.

soon (SOON) *adv. sooner, soonest.* 1. Before long; at a time not far away.—Dinner will be ready *soon*.
2. When; at the time.—As *soon* as the bell rings, the children are quiet.
3. Rather.—I would *sooner* sleep than eat.

soot (SUHT) *n.* A black dust formed when something burns.—*Soot* from the furnace fire collects on the window sill.

soothe (SOO<u>TH</u>) *v. soothes, soothed, soothing.* 1. Relieve; remove pain from.—This medicine will *soothe* the burn.
2. Calm; comfort; quiet.—Mother tried to *soothe* the lost child.

soph·o·more (SAHF-ə-mor) *n. sophomores.* A student in the second year of high school or college.

so·pran·o (sə-PRA-noh *or* sə-PRAH-noh) *n. sopranos.* 1. A woman or girl who has a high singing voice; one who can sing high notes. 2. The highest kind of voice.—Mother sings *soprano,* but Father sings bass.
—*adj.* The highest part in a piece of music written for more than one voice or instrument.—The violin often plays the *soprano* part.

sor·cer·er (SOR-ser-er) *n. sorcerers.* A person who is supposed to have magical powers obtained from evil spirits.—*Sorcerers* often are found in fairy tales.

sor·cer·ess (SOR-ser-əss) *n. sorceresses.* A female sorcerer; a witch.

sore (SOR) *n. sores.* A painful spot where the skin is broken or bruised.—The *sore* on my hand hurts.
—*adj. sorer, sorest.* Painful.—The cut on Bob's finger is *sore.*

sor·ghum (SOR-gəm) *n.* Any of several types of cereal grasses grown in the tropics of the Eastern Hemisphere. One kind of *sorghum* is used as a cereal. Other kinds are used to make syrups and fodder.

so·ror·i·ty (sə-ROR-ə-tee *or* sə-RAHR-ə-tee) *n. sororities.* A club or society for women, especially at a college or university.

sor·row (SAHR- *or* SOR-oh) *n. sorrows.* 1. Grief; sadness; unhappiness.—Much *sorrow* was caused by the accident.
2. Trouble; something which makes one feel sad.—The old king had many *sorrows.*

sor·ry (SAHR- *or* SOR-ee) *adj. sorrier, sorriest.* 1. Filled with sadness or sorrow.—I am *sorry* that you are sick.
2. Politely regretful.—I am *sorry* I was standing in your way.

sort (SORT) *n. sorts.* Kind or type.—What *sort* of ice cream would you like for dessert?
—*v. sorts, sorted, sorting.* Separate things and put like things together in groups.—Bob helped the teacher *sort* the children's papers.

soul (SOHL) *n. souls.* 1. A person.—Not a *soul* heard the bell.
2. Deep feeling; strong spirit.—Mary puts her heart and *soul* into her piano playing.

3. The part of a person concerned with his thinking and feeling.—Many people believe that the *soul* is not part of the body and that the *soul* can never die.

sound (SOWND) *n. sounds.* A noise.—The room was so quiet you could not hear a *sound.*
—*v. sounds, sounded, sounding.* 1. Make a noise.—The squeaking door *sounds* like the squeak of a mouse.
2. Cause to make a noise.—*Sound* the fire alarm!
3. Seem; appear.—The news *sounds* bad.
—*adj.* Stable; healthy.—The boy is *sound* in body and mind.

sound·proof (SOWND-proof) *adj.* Capable of keeping sound in or out.—The studio is *soundproof.* Sounds cannot pass through the walls, ceiling, or floor.

sound wave (SOWND wayv) *sound waves.* A vibration or disturbance in the air caused by any sound. *Sound waves* carry sounds to our ears.

soup (SOOP) *n. soups.* A liquid food made by boiling meat or vegetables in water or milk, with seasonings.—I like creamed tomato *soup.*

sour (SOWR) *v. sours, soured, souring.* Become acid; spoil.—Do not leave the milk out of the icebox, or it may *sour.*
—*adj.* 1. Not sweet.—Sugar is sweet. Lemons are *sour.*
2. Spoiled; gone bad.—The soup has turned *sour.* It has mold on the top.

source (SORSS) *n. sources.* The place from which anything comes; the starting place.—Farms are the *source* of most of our food.—The *source* of the river is a spring high up in the mountains.

south (SOWTH) *n.* 1. One of the four main directions. *South* is opposite north. The sun rises in the east. Turn your face to the east. Your left hand is to the north, and your right hand to the *south.*
2. (Usually spelled with a capital "S.") The southern part of a country.—Father's family lived in the *South.*
—*adj.* and *adv.* Toward the south.—We live *south* of Main Street.—The birds fly *south* in the summer.—That window is on the *south* side of the house.

South Car·o·li·na (SOWTH kar-ə-LY-nə)
n. A state on the east
coast of the United
States noted princi-
pally for the cotton
and tobacco raised
there, for its large
amount of shipping,
and for the manufacturing of thread and cot-
ton goods.

South Da·ko·ta (SOWTH də-KOH-tə) *n.* A
farming and grazing state in north central

United States. The largest gold mine in the
United States is found in the Black Hills of
South Dakota.

south·east (sowth-EEST) *n.,*
adj., and *adv.* The direction
halfway between south and
east.

south·ern (SUTH-ern) *adj.* Of the south;
toward the south.—We live in the *southern*
part of town.—Father's family was *Southern.*
They lived in the South.

south·west (sowth-WEST) *n., adj.,* and *adv.*
1. The direction halfway be-
tween south and west.
2. (Spelled with a capital "S.")
The southwestern portion of
the United States, usually con-
sidered as centering on Arizona and New
Mexico.

sou·ve·nir (soo-və-NIR *or* SOO-və-nir) *n.*
souvenirs. A keepsake; something to bring
back memories.—Uncle Ned brought Mary a
souvenir of New York. It was a scarf with
pictures of buildings on it.

sov·er·eign (SAHV-rin) *n. sovereigns.* 1.
The highest ruler of a country, such as a
king, queen, or emperor.
2. A former British coin, worth one pound.
—*adj.* 1. Independent (of a country).—The
United States is a *sovereign* nation. It runs its
own affairs without help from other nations.
2. Supreme.—The keeping of peace in the
world is of *sovereign* importance.

sow (SOW) *n. sows.* A fully grown female
pig.—Grandfather's *sow* has a litter of little
pigs.

sow (SOH) *v. sows, sowed, sowing.* Plant by
scattering seeds; scatter.—The farmer *sows*
the grain in the spring.

soy·bean (SOI-been) *n. soybeans.* A kind of
bean used for food, and for
making flour, oil, and many
other things.

space (SPAYSS) *n. spaces.* 1.
Room; place.—There is *space* in
the icebox for one more dish.
2. A blank; an empty place; a
distance.—I wrote one word
on the typewriter, then skipped a *space* and
wrote another.—The teacher asked us to leave
a *space* at the bottom of the page.—Telephone poles have short *spaces* between them.
3. Sky; nothingness.—Airplanes fly in *space.*
—The horse and rider plunged off the cliff
into *space.*
4. Time.—During the earthquake houses col-
lapsed within the *space* of a minute.
—*v. spaces, spaced, spacing.* To place with certain distances between.—Jack *spaced* the
paragraphs in his composition to make it
look neat.

space·ship (SPAYSS-ship) *n. spaceships.* A
vehicle designed to travel through space to
other planets and to the moon.

Space stations of the future may look like this.

space sta·tion (SPAYSS STAY-shən) *space
stations.* A proposed base to be "stationed" or
placed in orbit around the earth. *Space stations* would serve as stopping points or
service stations for spaceships traveling
through space.

spa·cious (SPAY-shəss) *adj.* Large; roomy.—
We have a *spacious* living room.

spade (SPAYD) *n. spades.* A gardening tool
with a shorter han-
dle and a flatter blade
than a shovel. — We
use a *spade* to dig up earth.
—*v. spades, spaded, spading.* Dig up.—Father
spaded the earth to look for angleworms.

span (SPAN) *n. spans.* 1. The distance from the tip of the little finger to the tip of the thumb on a grown person's hand when the hand is stretched out. It is about nine inches. 2. The distance or space from one support or foundation to the next on a bridge or an arch.

bridge span   span of horses

3. A pair of horses or mules driven together. —Grandfather has a *span* of sorrel horses.
4. A period of time.—Father and Mother lived in the city for the *span* of three years.—The fortuneteller told the man that his *span* on earth was far from over.
—*v. spans, spanned, spanning.* 1. Extend or stretch across.—The bridge *spans* the river. 2. Measure by one's stretched-out hand.

span·iel (SPAN-yəl) *n. spaniels.* A medium-sized dog with long, wavy hair; long ears that hang down, and short legs.

spar (SPAHR) *n. spars.* 1. A mast, or a wooden pole that holds or helps to hold a sail onto a mast.
2. Principal support of the wing of an airplane.
—*v. spars, sparred, sparring.* Box with the fists. — The boys are learning to *spar.*

spare (SPAIR) *n. spares.* An extra.—I bought two flashlight batteries and one *spare.*
—*v. spares, spared, sparing.* 1. Lend; give up; get along without.—Since Mother was sewing, she could not *spare* her thimble.—I can *spare* a glass or two of jelly; I have plenty.
2. Have mercy on; not punish or hurt.—The hunter *spared* the deer. He did not shoot the deer, even though he could have.
—*adj.* 1. Extra.—We have a *spare* tire for our car. We keep it to use only when one of the others is being repaired.
2. Free.—We read stories in our *spare* time.
3. Thin; meager. — His *spare* figure looked foolish in the fat man's clothing.

spark (SPAHRK) *n. sparks.* 1. A little piece or bit of fire. — The Boy Scouts watched the *sparks* from the campfire to see that they did not start another fire.
2. A little flash of fire.—When Mother pulled the plug out of the wall socket, we saw *sparks.*

spar·kle (SPAHR-kəl) *v. sparkles, sparkled, sparkling.* 1. Glitter, flash, or throw off little glints of light. — Mother's diamond ring *sparkles.*
2. Twinkle or dance.—Sally's eyes *sparkle* when she is planning something new.
—*sparkle, n. sparkles.*

spark plug (SPAHRK plug) *spark plugs.* A plug used in the cylinders of automobiles to make electrical sparks which will explode the gasoline. These explosions, which take place one right after the other, make the motor run.

spar·row (SPAR-oh) *n. sparrows.* A small gray or brownish bird. There are many different kinds of *sparrows.* The song sparrow has a very pleasant song.

sparse (SPAHRSS) *adj.; sparsely, adv.* Thinly spread or scattered.—*Sparse* patches of grass dot the field.

spasm (SPAZ-əm) *n. spasms.* 1. A sudden, unusual, and involuntary drawing together of a muscle or muscles.—John said he spilled the milk because a *spasm* in his arm made his hand shake.
2. Any short, sudden burst of energy, feeling, or activity.—I had to leave the church because of a *spasm* of coughing.

spat (SPAT) *n. spats.* 1. An outer covering for the ankle and instep, made of cloth and worn over the shoe.
2. A little quarrel. — The children had a *spat* over the ball game.

spat·ter (SPAT-er) *n. spatters.* 1. A spot.—Mary got a *spatter* of grease on her dress.
2. A noise made by the fall of little drops.—We heard the *spatter* of rain on the roof.
—*v. spatters, spattered, spattering.* 1. To splash or sprinkle with water, grease, mud, or other wet substance.—The rain *spattered* the car with mud.
2. Fall on in drops.—Grease from the frying pan *spattered* the stove.

spawn (SPAWN) *v. spawns, spawned, spawning.* 1. Give birth to, usually in great numbers; produce. — Countless numbers of fish are *spawned* each year in the waters of the world.
2. Produce or deposit eggs, especially into water.—The fish seem to be *spawning* earlier than usual this year.

speak (SPEEK) *v. speaks, spoke, speaking.* 1. Talk.—Bob was so surprised that he couldn't *speak.*—The teacher told us always to *speak* clearly.
2. Give a talk or speech.—The President will *speak* on the radio tonight.
3. Tell about.—The policeman *spoke* of the accident.
4. Talk to one another.—Mary and Jack are not *speaking.*
5. Say.—She *spoke* falsehoods.

spear (SPIR) *n. spears.* 1. A weapon with a sharp tip and a long, straight handle. — Guards stood outside the king's palace holding their *spears.*

2. A piece.—Mother gave each of us six *spears* of asparagus.
—v. spears, speared, spearing. Put a spear through, or pierce.—It is against the law to *spear* certain kinds of fish.—Father *speared* a piece of potato with his fork.

spe·cial (SPESH-əl) *adj.* 1. Particular. — Making model airplanes is Jack's *special* hobby.—This is a *special* soap. It is good for Baby's skin.
2. Unusual; extra nice.—Father thinks that strawberry shortcake is a very *special* dessert.—Mother wears her blue lace dress for *special* occasions.

spe·cial·ist (SPESH-əl-ist) *n. specialists.* A person who makes a study or a business of some particular subject or line of work. — When Baby had an earache, Mother took her to an ear *specialist.* She took Baby to a doctor who had studied all about, and treated things wrong with, the ear.

spe·cial·ty (SPESH-əl-tee) *n. specialties.* Something one does unusually well.—Making model airplanes is Jack's *specialty.*—Coconut cream pie is Mother's *specialty.*

spe·cies (SPEE-sheez) *n. sing.* and *pl.* A group of plants or animals that are very much alike.—Tiger lilies are one *species* of the lily family.

spe·cif·ic (spə-SIF-ik) *adj.; specifically, adv.* Particular; exact.—If you have no *specific* reason for staying at home, why not come with us?—When Mother told the doctor Baby didn't seem well, he asked her to be more *specific.* He asked Mother to tell him exactly what seemed to be the trouble.

spec·i·men (SPESS-ə-mən) *n. specimens.* A sample.—Our teacher asked each of us for a *specimen* of our drawing to hang up for visitors' week.—Bob collects moths. He took one of his *specimens* to school.

speck (SPEK) *n. specks; specked, adj.* 1. A small spot.—Father cleaned his glasses because they were covered with *specks.*
2. A small bit.—Sally took out a black *speck* that had fallen into her milk.

spec·ta·cle (SPEK-tə-kəl) *n. spectacles.* 1. Sight; show.—The Air Force put on a great *spectacle* over the parade grounds. Planes flew in formation over the area all day.
2. (In the plural) Eyeglasses.—Grandmother wears *spectacles* to help her see better.

spec·ta·tor (SPEK-tay-ter) *n. spectators.* Someone who watches or looks on.—Jack told Mother he did not take part in the rescue, but was just a *spectator.*

spec·tro·scope (SPEK-trə-skohp) *n. spectroscopes.* An instrument used to produce and examine a spectrum. The earliest known *spectroscope* was an ordinary prism. It was used by Sir Isaac Newton in the seventeenth century to examine rays of sunlight.

spec·trum (SPEK-trəm) *n. spectrums* or *spectra.* The series of colors ranging from red through orange, yellow, green, blue, and indigo to violet. White light is really composed of all these colors. You can break a beam of

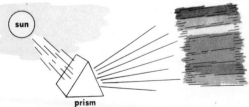

prism

white light into a *spectrum* by passing it through a spectroscope. A rainbow is the result of rain acting as a spectroscope on the sunlight that passes through it.

spec·u·late (SPEK-yə-layt) *v. speculates, speculated, speculating.* 1. Form opinions on the basis of insufficient knowledge.—When she says Mary is leaving tomorrow, she is just *speculating.* Mary hasn't made up her mind to go.
2. Try to make money by taking great business risks.—People with little money should not *speculate.* They may lose everything.
3. Meditate; reflect. — Pioneers in science *speculated* deeply about the universe before undertaking the experiments which led to great discoveries.
—*speculation, n. speculations.*

sped (SPED) *v.* One form of the verb *speed.*—The dog *sped* home when he heard Jack whistle.

speech (SPEECH) *n. speeches.* 1. The ability to speak.—People have *speech.* They are able to speak or talk. Animals do not have *speech.*
2. A talk; what one says to a group of people who have come to listen.—The mayor made a *speech* at the dinner.
3. Way of talking.—John's *speech* shows that he comes from England.

speed (SPEED) *n. speeds.* 1. Swiftness; quickness. — Mary got dressed with all possible *speed.*
2. Rate of motion or movement.—The *speed* limit is thirty-five miles an hour. That is as fast as one may drive.—The *speed* of this train is ninety miles an hour.
—*v. speeds, speeded* or *sped, speeding.* 1. Move very fast.—The train came *speeding* down the track.
2. Hurry; move faster.—The teacher asked us to try to *speed* up our work.
3. Go faster than is allowed.—The man got a ticket because he was *speeding.*

speed·om·e·ter (spee-DAHM-ə-ter) *n. speedometers.* An instrument for measuring speed and distance. You look at the *speedometer* on your car to see how fast you are going and how far you have gone.

speed·way (SPEED-way) *n. speedways.* A track or road built for fast driving.—Auto races are run on *speedways.*

spell (SPEL) *n. spells.* 1. A period; a length of time.—We went to the lake during the hot *spell.*
2. A charm; an enchantment. — The fairy cast a *spell* over the princess.
—*v. spells, spelled, spelling.* 1. Speak or write the letters of words in the right order.—C A T *spells* cat.
2. Mean.—Black clouds *spell* rain.
3. Take the place of (someone) for a short time.—If you are tired, I'll *spell* you at mowing the lawn.

spell·bound (SPEL-bownd) *adj.* Enchanted; fascinated.—The audience was *spellbound* by the magician's tricks.

spell·er (SPEL-er) *n. spellers.* 1. A person who spells.—Mary is a good *speller.*
2. A spelling book; a book with words in it to help you learn to spell.

spell·ing bee (SPEL-ing bee) *spelling bees.* A spelling contest; a contest to see who can spell the best.

spend (SPEND) *v. spends, spent, spending.* 1. Pay out.—Do not *spend* your money just because you have it.—Mother *spent* five dollars for a new hat.
2. Pass (time). — Bob *spends* his holidays making model airplanes.
3. Use up.—All his energy was *spent* after the football game. He just wanted to go home and rest.

sphere (SFIR) *n. spheres.* A ball or globe.—Every part of the outside of a *sphere* is the same distance from the center.—The earth is a *sphere.*

sphinx (SFINGKS) *n. sphinxes.* 1. An ancient Egyptian figure with the head of a man, a ram, or a hawk and the body of a lion. The most famous statue of this kind is near the pyramids of Giza, Egypt, and is known as the Great Sphinx. It is nearly two hundred feet long.
2. A figure in ancient Greek mythology with a woman's head, a lion's body, a serpent's tail, and wings.

SPHINX

spice (SPYSS) *n. spices.* A sharp-tasting seasoning made from the dried leaves, seeds, or bark of certain plants.—Cloves, allspice, cinnamon, and nutmeg are *spices.*—Mother puts many *spices* in her gingerbread.
—*v. spices, spiced, spicing.* 1. Put spice in. — Mother *spices* her apple pie with cinnamon.
2. Make lively.—The lecturer *spiced* his talk with amusing stories.

spi·der (SPY-der) *n. spiders.* 1. A small animal with eight long legs. *Spiders* are not insects, for they have eight legs and no wings; insects have six legs, and usually have wings. *Spiders* spin webs to catch bugs and insects for food.
2. A skillet; a frying pan.

spike (SPYK) *n. spikes.* 1. A long, strong, thick nail.—The men put *spikes* in the railroad ties to hold the tracks in place.
2. A sharp, pointed piece of metal.—Baseball players, runners, and other athletes wear shoes with *spikes* sticking out of the soles.
3. A pointed cluster on a plant.—This is a *spike* of grain. The picture next to it is a *spike* of flowers.

—*v. spikes, spiked, spiking.* Cut or pierce with spikes.—Bob was *spiked* in the leg by an opposing player.

spill (SPIL) *n. spills.* A fall.—We had a big *spill* when our sled hit the bump.
—*v. spills, spilled, spilling.* 1. Let a liquid run out over the edge of its container, or let loose material like sand or sugar fall or scatter about.—Baby often *spills* her milk.
2. Let fall.—The sled ran over a bump and *spilled* the children into the snow.

spin (SPIN) *n. spins.* 1. A whirling.—The falling airplane went into a *spin.*
2. A ride.—Will you go with us for a *spin* in the sports car?
—*v. spins, spun, spinning.* 1. Whirl or make whirl.—Bob likes to *spin* his top. — The top *spins.*
2. Draw out and twist wool, silk, or cotton into threads.—Long ago women *spun* their own thread and yarn on spinning wheels.

3. Make of threadlike strands.—Spiders *spin* webs to catch insects for food.
4. Feel dizzy.—My head is *spinning.* It feels as though it were going around and around.
5. Tell.—The old man loved to *spin* yarns about his youth.

spin·dle (SPIN-dl) *n. spindles.* 1. A long rod that goes round and round. It is used to wind thread when spinning.
2. A long, heavy pin for papers.—The teacher puts papers on a *spindle.*

spine (SPYN) *n. spines.* 1. The backbone. A person's *spine* is made up of many bones fitted together.
2. A thorn, pricker, or sharp point.—A porcupine's quills are *spines.*

spin·ning wheel (SPIN-ing hweel) *spinning wheels.* A machine to spin and wind thread or yarn. It has a large wheel that is turned by hand or by a foot pedal.

spin·ster (SPIN-ster) *n. spinsters.* An aging unmarried woman.

spi·ra·cle (SPY-rə-kəl *or* SPIR-ə-kəl) *n. spiracles.* An opening used for breathing by insects; a similar opening in the heads of sharks and rays.

spi·ral (SPY-rəl) *n. spirals* and *adj.* Something shaped like a coil.—A corkscrew or a coiled bedspring is a *spiral.*

spire (SPYR) *n. spires.* The pointed part of a steeple. — We saw the church *spire* from a distance.

spir·it (SPIR-it) *n. spirits.* 1. Soul or mind; the unseen part of a person concerned with thinking and feeling.
2. A ghost, elf, fairy, or other imaginary being.
3. Way of feeling; nature. — When Father went to work he was in good *spirits.* He was happy.
4. Liveliness; strength. — He defended his point of view with *spirit.*
5. Influence; feeling. — The class showed a *spirit* of cooperation in making plans for the trip.
6. (Usually plural) Liquid containing a large quantity of alcohol.

spir·it·ed (SPIR-it-id) *adj.* Lively; vigorous. —Grandfather has a *spirited* horse. It is full of energy and courage.

spit (SPIT) *n. spits.* 1. The saliva or liquid that forms in one's mouth.
2. A bar, sometimes one which turns, on which meat can be roasted.
—*v. spits, spat* or *spit, spitting.* 1. Throw out saliva or anything from the mouth.—*Spitting* may spread disease.—Baby *spits* out food she doesn't like.
2. Hiss.—Pussy *spat* at the strange dog.
3. Throw forth.—The hot pan is *spitting* fat. Be careful!

spite (SPYT) *n.* An unfriendly feeling.—The man let his dog run in the garden out of *spite* for the person who owned the garden.
—*v. spites, spited, spiting.* Show unfriendly feelings or a dislike for someone.—The boy didn't want the book but he took it to *spite* the other boys.
—*In spite of* means notwithstanding, nevertheless.—John came home *in spite of* the rain.

splash (SPLASH) *n. splashes.* 1. A throwing or scattering of liquid; the noise made by it.— When Bob dived into the water, we heard a big *splash*.
2. A spot made by spattered liquid.—When Father paints, he gets *splashes* of paint on his shirt.
—*v. splashes, splashed, splashing* Throw; dash; scatter (liquid) about.—A passing car *splashed* muddy water on Mary's clothes.

splat·ter (SPLAT-er) *v. splatters, splattered, splattering.* Splash; scatter (liquid). — Do not *splatter* ink on your paper.

splen·did (SPLEN-did) *adj.; splendidly, adv.* Brilliant; excellent; glorious.—The teacher told Dan that she was proud of him because he had done a *splendid* job on the test.

splen·dor (SPLEN-der) *n. splendors.* 1. Brilliance; radiance.—The moon rose in *splendor* over the sea.
2. Magnificence; glory.—The *splendor* of the king's court is beyond compare.

splice (SPLYSS) *n. splices.* Place where two pieces of rope or string are joined by twisting the ends together to make one long piece.
—*v. splices, spliced, splicing.* Join together in this way.—The sailor *spliced* two pieces of rope together.

splint (SPLINT) *n. splints.* A thin strip of wood or other material.—The chair seat is made of *splints*.—The doctor put a *splint* on the boy's broken finger.

splin·ter (SPLIN-ter) *n. splinters.* A sliver of material such as wood or metal. — The nurse took a *splinter* from the child's foot.
—*v. splinters, splintered, splintering.* Break, sliver, or split into long, thin pieces.—The box fell from the truck and *splintered*.

split (SPLIT) *n. splits.* 1. A crack; a long break.—There is a big *split* in the tree where it was hit by lightning.
2. A division.—There was a *split* among the members of the club over the amount of dues that should be charged.
—*v. splits, split, splitting.* 1. Break or pull apart, especially along the grain.—Bob *split* the stick from end to end to make sticks for his kite.
2. Divide.—The boys *split* the candy bar.

spoil (SPOIL) *v. spoils, spoiled, spoiling.* 1. Ruin; damage; destroy. — The hailstorm *spoiled* the lettuce.
2. Become unfit to eat.—Some foods will *spoil* if not kept cold. They may become sour or moldy, or may decay.

spoils (SPOILZ) *n. pl.* Things taken by force or won.—Great works of ancient Greek art were carried away as *spoils* by the soldiers of the Roman Empire.

spoke (SPOHK) *n. spokes.* One of the bars leading from the axle of a wheel to the rim.
—*v.* One form of the verb *speak*. — Mary *spoke* to the teacher about the lesson. — At dinner, the mayor *spoke* on the subject of beautifying the town.

spo·ken (SPOH-kən) *v.* One form of the verb *speak*.—I have *spoken* to her on the telephone, but not face to face.

spokes·man (SPOHKS-mən) *n. spokesmen.* A person chosen to speak for a group.—At the meeting, the students elected Bob as their *spokesman* to present their idea to the principal.

sponge (SPUNJ) *n. sponges.* 1. A kind of animal that lives in the sea.
2. The cleaned and dried skeleton of such an animal.—A *sponge* soaks up much water.
—We use a *sponge* to wash things.
3. A man-made imitation of a natural sponge.

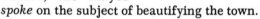

—v. sponges, sponged, sponging. 1. Rub with a sponge.—Mother *sponged* Father's suit with a damp sponge.
2. Let someone else pay one's way or do one's work.—It is better to work for yourself than to *sponge* on someone else.

spon·sor (SPAHN-ser) *v. sponsors, sponsored, sponsoring.* 1. Take responsibility for a person or thing.—John is *sponsoring* his friend for membership in the club.
2. Act as a godparent; take vows or answer for an infant at baptism.—Father *sponsored* Mary's child at the christening.
3. Pay the costs for a radio or television program. Business firms *sponsor* programs in return for the privilege of advertising their products.
—sponsor, n. sponsors.

spon·ta·ne·ous (spahn-TAY-nee-əss) *adj.; spontaneously, adv.* Arising or happening naturally, as if from some inner force; without external cause.—The audience broke into *spontaneous* applause when the President entered the auditorium.
—Spontaneous combustion takes place when something sets itself on fire by internal chemical action.—Piles of paper or rags, especially oily rags, sometimes burst into flames by *spontaneous combustion.*

spook (SPOOK) *n. spooks.* A ghost (said in fun).—On Halloween the children dress up in sheets, and pretend they are *spooks.*

spool (SPOOL) *n. spools.* A short, round piece of wood or metal with a hole through it from end to end. Thread, cord, and wire are often wound on *spools.*

spoon (SPOON) *n. spoons.* A small tool with a bowl and handle for lifting liquids or soft foods.—Baby eats with a *spoon.*

spore (SPOR) *n. spores.* A cell from which new plants grow. Ferns and other flowerless plants have *spores.*

sport (SPORT) *n. sports.* 1. Fun, play, or amusement.—It is good *sport* to go fishing.
2. Any particular kind of game, particularly an active game.—Hockey, baseball, football, skiing, and basketball are *sports.*
3. One who takes troubles well, or is a good loser.—Bob was a good *sport* about missing the game.

sports·man·ship (SPORTSS-mən-ship) *n.* Fair play; ability to follow rules or to accept conditions cheerfully.—To lose gracefully is a sign of good *sportsmanship.*

spot (SPAHT) *n. spots.* 1. A mark, stain, blot, or speck.—It is hard to get ink *spots* out of clothes.
2. One of a pattern of dots or round markings.—A giraffe has *spots.*
3. A place.—We have found a pretty *spot* to put up our tent.
—v. spots, spotted, spotting. 1. Stain; get a spot on.—Mother put a bib on Baby so that Baby would not *spot* her clean dress.
2. Locate. — John *spotted* his father in the crowd at the station.

spot·light (SPAHT-lyt) *n. spotlights.* 1. A circle of strong light thrown on something.—The singer stood in the *spotlight* so that everyone could see her easily.

2. The lamp that makes a spotlight.
3. Center of public attention.—The attendance of many world leaders put the United Nations in the *spotlight.*

spot·ted (SPAHT-id) *adj.* 1. Stained; marked with spots.—Baby's bib is *spotted.* She spilled food on it.
2. Covered with spots or marks not of the same color as the rest.—Sally's turtle has a *spotted* shell. Its shell is yellow with black spots.

spout (SPOWT) *n. spouts.* 1. A tube or pipe through which water or other liquids may run or be poured.—Teapots and coffeepots have *spouts.*—Tea pours through the spout.
2. Jet or stream.—We could see the whale's *spout* across the water.
—v. spouts, spouted, spouting. Pour; gush. — Water *spouts* from the fountain.

sprain (SPRAYN) *v. sprains, sprained, spraining.* Injure by twisting or overstretching the muscles or ligaments.—Bob *sprained* his ankle while playing ball.
—sprain, n. sprains.

sprang (SPRANG) *v.* One form of the verb *spring.*—The cat *sprang* at the mouse.

sprawl (SPRAWL) *v. sprawls, sprawled, sprawling.* Lie with the arms and legs stretched out.—The tired boys *sprawled* on the grass.

spray (SPRAY) *n. sprays.* 1. A branch of a plant with its flowers and leaves.—Mary put a *spray* of apple blossoms in the vase.

spray of flowers

spray gun

2. A kind of gun that pumps out liquid in a misty stream.

3. Fine drops of water.—The wind blew the *spray* from the sprinkler into our faces.

—*v. sprays, sprayed, spraying.* Sprinkle.—The farmer *sprays* his potato plants with a liquid to kill bugs.

spread (SPRED) *n. spreads.* A cover for a bed. — Grandmother made a patchwork *spread* with a pattern of stars.

—*v. spreads, spread, spreading.* 1. Lay smoothly.—Mother *spread* jam on the toast.—Mary *spread* her dress on the ironing board in order to press it.

2. Get further apart.—The captain told the boys on the ball team to *spread* out so that someone would catch the ball.

3. Stretch out; unfold.—The bird *spread* its wings and flew away.

4. Scatter; distribute; reach over a wide area. —News of the accident soon *spread* far and wide.—Scarlet fever *spreads* fast.

spring (SPRING) *n. springs.* 1. Ability to stretch and then go back to the usual size.—A rubber band has *spring*.

2. A coil or strip of metal that gives under pressure and then jumps back to its original shape.—These are *springs* for a chair or bed. Push them down  and then let go, and they will jump back to their usual size.

3. The season of the year which lasts from March 21 to June 21.—The four seasons of the year are *spring*, summer, autumn, and winter.—The farmer plants his seeds in the *spring*.

4. A bubbling stream of water coming out of the ground.—The Boy Scouts found a *spring* in the woods.

5. A leap.—With one *spring*, Jack was out of bed.

6. Energy; vigor.—The tired girl's step has lost its *spring*.

—*v. springs, sprang* or *sprung, springing.* 1. Jump; leap.—Have you ever seen a cat *spring* at a mouse or a bird?

2. Come up quickly; shoot up.—Mushrooms *spring* up overnight.

spring·board (SPRING-bord) *n. springboards.* A diving board; a springy board from which a swimmer dives or jumps.

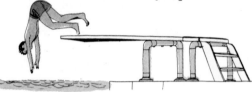

spring·time (SPRING-tym) *n.* The spring of the year.

spring·y (SPRING-ee) *adj. springier, springiest.* Able to be pressed down or together and then go back to its usual shape and size when the pressure is gone.—The mattress on Mother's bed is soft and *springy*.

sprin·kle (SPRING-kəl) *n. sprinkles.* 1. A light rainfall.—We had a *sprinkle* this morning, but the sun is shining now.

2. A very small amount.—Mother put just a *sprinkle* of pepper in the soup.

—*v. sprinkles, sprinkled, sprinkling.* 1. Scatter drops or small bits.—Mother *sprinkled* the clothes with warm water.

2. Spray; put liquid on by sprinkling.—Father *sprinkled* the garden.

3. Rain a little.—It started to *sprinkle*, so we went into the house.

sprin·kler (SPRINGK-ler) *n. sprinklers.* 1. A device fastened to a hose, for spraying. — Father uses a *sprinkler* to water the lawn.

2. A water truck or cart with tanks from which water is sprayed on the pavement.— Men sprinkle the city streets with *sprinklers* to keep down the dust.

sprint (SPRINT) *n. sprints.* A fast, short race.—The boys had quite a *sprint* across the playground.

—*v. sprints, sprinted, sprinting.* Run fast. — Jack *sprinted* up the path.

sprite (SPRYT) *n. sprites.* Fairy or elf.—The water *sprites* are supposed to have long, pale green hair.

sprout (SPROWT) *n. sprouts.* A tiny new stalk from a seed or another plant.—Mother started this plant from a *sprout.*
—*v. sprouts, sprouted, sprouting.* Start to grow. — Beans *sprout* very soon after they are planted.

spruce (SPROOSS) *n. spruces.* An evergreen tree. A *spruce* has cones.
—*v. spruces, spruced, sprucing.* Get neat and clean. — Mother told the boys to *spruce* up for dinner.
—*adj.* Neat; smart; trim. — Father looks very *spruce* in his new suit.

sprung (SPRUNG) *v.*
One form of the verb *spring.*—Jack looked behind the bush from which the little rabbit had *sprung.*

spry (SPRY) *adj. sprier, spriest; spryly, adv.* Quick; lively; full of life. — Grandfather is *spry* for his age.

spur (SPER) *n. spurs.* 1. A pointed device fastened to a horseman's heels with which to jab the horse and make it go faster.
2. Anything that forces, urges, or drives one to do a thing.—The man's hunger was a *spur* that drove him to work.
3. Any point that sticks out like a horseman's spur.—The rooster dug his *spurs* into Grandfather's hand.
—*v. spurs, spurred, spurring.* 1. Prick a horse's sides with spurs.—The cowboy *spurred* his horse.
2. Urge; drive; force. — The man's hunger *spurred* him to work hard in order to get enough food.

spurn (SPERN) *v. spurns, spurned, spurning.* Refuse scornfully.—Father *spurned* the dishonest man's offer.

spurt (SPERT) *n. spurts.* 1. A gush.—A *spurt* of flame from the stable reached the hayloft above.
2. A short burst (of energy, activity, effort, etc.).—Ann had a *spurt* of interest in stamp collecting, but she soon tired of the hobby and gave it up.

—*v. spurts, spurted, spurting.* 1. Squirt or gush. —Water *spurted* out of the hole in the hose.
2. Make a sudden, increased effort. – The black horse *spurted* ahead and won the championship race.

sput·nik (SPUHT- *or* SPUT-nik) *n. sputniks.* One of the first man-made satellites launched from Russia. *Sputnik* I was launched October 4, 1957; *Sputnik* II was launched November 3, 1957; and *Sputnik* III was launched May 15, 1958.

sput·ter (SPUT-er) *v. sputters, sputtered, sputtering.* 1. Make a spitting, hissing sound. —Hot dogs *sputter* when roasting.
2. Talk fast and in a way that cannot be understood.—Jack was so excited that he *sputtered,* and we could not understand what he was trying to tell us.
—*sputter, n. sputters.*

spy (SPY) *n. spies.* A person who secretly watches to find out something.—In time of war, a *spy* tries to get information about the enemy. He tries to find out the enemy's plans and positions.
—*v. spies, spied, spying.* 1. See; find with the eyes.—When Mary found the thimble, she cried, "I *spy* it."
2. Watch secretly; act as a spy.—The policeman *spied* on the robbers.

squad (SKWAHD) *n. squads.* A small group of as many people as are required for some activity.—A *squad* of workers cleaned up the city park. — A football *squad* includes the team of eleven players and a number of substitutes.

squad·ron (SKWAHD-rən) *n. squadrons.* A fighting unit of airplanes, warships, or cavalry.—A *squadron* of airplanes flew over the city.

squall (SKWAWL) *n. squalls.* 1. A sudden, strong, whirling rush of wind, usually with rain.
2. A loud squawk or cry.—The duck let out a *squall* when the dog chased it across the barnyard.
—*v. squalls, squalled, squalling.* Cry out loudly.—The cats on the back fence *squalled* at the sight of the dog.

squan·der (SKWAHN-der) *v. squanders, squandered, squandering.* Waste; spend unwisely.—The man did not *squander* his money. He saved it.

square (SKWAIR) *n. squares.* 1. A flat shape with four sides of the same length and four corners all alike. — A checkerboard is divided into *squares.*
2. A carpenter's tool for measuring corners to make sure that they are perfectly square, that they are like the corners of the figure in the picture.

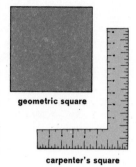

geometric square

carpenter's square

3. A city block; place or space in a city with streets on all four sides.
—*v. squares, squared, squaring.* 1. Make the four sides even, and the four corners alike.—The carpenter *squared* the board.
2. Settle; make right.—Bob *squared* his debt with Father.
3. Correspond. — His story doesn't *square* with the facts.
—*adj.* 1. Having four equal sides and four corners alike.—The table top is *square.*
2. Honest and fair.—Grandfather says that it pays to be *square* with everyone.

squash (SKWAHSH) *n. squashes.* A vegetable that grows on a vine as a pumpkin does. *Squashes* are yellow or green.
—*v. squashes, squashed, squashing.* Mash or crush. — Sally stepped on the tomato and *squashed* it.

squat (SKWAHT) *v. squats, squatted, squatting.* Sit on one's heels. — Grandfather *squatted* down to weed the garden.
—*adj.* **squatter, squattest.** Short and thick. — One pitcher is tall and slender; the other is *squat.*

squaw (SKWAW) *n. squaws.* A name for an American Indian woman or wife.

squeak (SKWEEK) *n. squeaks.* A short, shrill noise. — The *squeak* of the barn door kept Grandmother awake.
—*v. squeaks, squeaked, squeaking.* Make a sharp, shrill sound.—A door with hinges that need oiling often *squeaks.*

squeal (SKWEEL) *n. squeals.* A sharp, shrill cry.—We heard the *squeal* of the little pig.
—*v. squeals, squealed, squealing.* Make a sharp, shrill cry.

squeeze (SKWEEZ) *v. squeezes, squeezed, squeezing.* 1. Press hard.—You make orange juice by *squeezing* oranges.

2. Get (through or into a crowded or tight place). — She *squeezed* through the narrow opening.—I've *squeezed* all I can into the suitcase.

squeez·er (SKWEEZ-er) *n. squeezers.* A device for pressing the juice out of oranges, lemons, and the like.—Mother uses a *squeezer* to make lemonade.

squint (SKWINT) *v. squints, squinted, squinting.* Look with eyes partly shut.—The sun was so bright that I had to *squint* to see at all.

squirm (SKWERM) *v. squirms, squirmed, squirming.* Wriggle, twist, and turn this way and that.—Do not *squirm* at the dinner table.

squir·rel (SKWER-əl) *n. squirrels.* A small red, black, or gray animal with a long bushy tail. *Squirrels* can run fast and climb trees. *Squirrels* put away nuts to eat in winter.

squirt (SKWERT) *v. squirts, squirted, squirting.* Cause liquid to shoot out in a jet; spurt. —Harry accidentally *squirted* ink from his fountain pen onto his desk.

stab (STAB) *n. stabs.* 1. A jab or thrust.—The robber made a *stab* at the policeman with his knife.
2. A wound made by something pointed.—The child had a small *stab* in his hand from the point of the pen.
—*v. stabs, stabbed, stabbing.* Pierce with a pointed weapon.—The man *stabbed* a potato with a knife.

sta·ble (STAY-bəl) *n. stables.* A barn or building in which horses or cattle are kept.—The farmer has three *stables* for his animals.
—*adj.* Firm; steady.—Let me get you a more *stable* chair. Yours looks as though it might collapse.

stack (STAK) *n. stacks.* 1. A large pile.—Little Boy Blue was under the hay*stack* fast asleep. — Mary carried a big *stack* of plates out to the dining room.
2. A chimney (usually of a factory or other large building, or of an engine).—Smoke from the furnace goes out through the smoke*stack.*
—*v. stacks, stacked, stacking.* Arrange in a pile.—Mother *stacked* the dinner dishes in the sink.

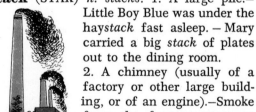

Guide to Pronunciation

After each black-type word in this dictionary there is a special spelling of the word which shows you how to say it. The special spelling has parentheses ( ) around it. Here is an example of a black-type word with its special spelling: **cat** (KAT).

On the next page is a guide to the special spellings.

This is how to use the guide. Each line tells about one sound. In the first column you will see the letters that stand for that sound. In the second column are some words in which the sound occurs. If you say those words and listen to the parts in black type, you will hear the sound. In the third column are the special spellings for those words. You can use them to practice sounding out the letters.

Some of the special spellings have both capital letters and small ones. The capital letters are the accented ones. We say them a little louder than we do the others.

In many of the special spellings there is a ə. This is a quiet little sound that is often found in the unaccented, or softly-said, parts of words. ə is just a very weak vowel. The guide will tell you more about ə.

Some of the special spellings give you a choice. They tell you that people very often say a word more than one way. These spellings look like this: (bee- *or* bə-GIN). This means that the first part of the word can be said (bee) or (bə), giving you either (bee-GIN) or (bə-GIN). Sometimes the whole word is spelled out twice, as in (kahn-KREET *or* KAHN-kreet). Then you know that it is either (kahn-KREET) or (KAHN-kreet), as you choose.